# Marketing Kit

## FOR

# DUMMIES®

### 3RD EDITION

**by Alexander Hiam**

Author of *Marketing For Dummies*

**WILEY**

Wiley Publishing, Inc.

**Marketing Kit For Dummies®, 3rd Edition**

Published by
Wiley Publishing, Inc.
111 River St.
Hoboken, NJ 07030-5774

www.wiley.com

# About the Author

**Alex Hiam** is the best-selling author of *Marketing For Dummies* and *The Portable MBA in Marketing*, as well as numerous books on management and leadership. He is the founder of INSIGHTS for Training & Development, which provides management, customer service, and sales force training to client companies throughout the world. He also designs and publishes training materials and curricula used by the in-house training departments of many companies and government agencies. You can find descriptions of his firm's marketing and sales products and services at www.insightsfor marketing.com.

Alex gives keynote addresses on topics ranging from marketing for breakthrough performance to effective leadership in business to how to negotiate with sharks. He received his BA from Harvard, his MBA from U.C. Berkeley, and was a full-time faculty member of the U Mass Amherst business school when his children were younger. Now he devotes his time to consulting, speaking, and running his own firm, where he often gets the chance to apply the principles of "streetwise" marketing himself as well as write about them for his many readers.

Alex's marketing-related consulting and training work includes leading product and branding brainstorm sessions, consulting on business and marketing planning, helping to motivate salespeople, and performing communications audits for clients. When not at work, Alex sails his ketch, the Blue Moon, throughout the waters off the East Coast of the United States.

# Dedication

To the wonderful children who enrich my life and make me proud: Noelle, Eliot, Paul, and Sadie. And to Deirdre, the wonderful woman who makes it all worthwhile.

# Author's Acknowledgments

Thanks to my able staff and associates for all their contributions to this book and the Web site that supports it, especially to Stephanie Sousbies, who runs my business on a daily basis so that I don't have to and can write books instead.

Also, I offer many thanks to the great team of editors who I have worked with on this and earlier editions over the years, including Kathy Welton. Special thanks to Kelly Ewing, who helped make this edition clear and readable. A book like this takes a surprisingly large team to produce — see the upcoming publisher's acknowledgments for additional members of the team. My thanks to you all.

Finally, a word must be said about my readers. Thanks to all of you who have gotten in touch over the years to share your enthusiasm and great stories of marketing success! There are so many of you out there, working hard to bring about good results, often on a limited budget. Your creativity, hopefulness, and professionalism are the raw ingredients of great marketing. I hope your associates, employers, and customers appreciate all you do.

## Publisher's Acknowledgments

We're proud of this book; please send us your comments through our Dummies online registration form located at `http://dummies.custhelp.com`. For other comments, please contact our Customer Care Department within the U.S. at 877-762-2974, outside the U.S. at 317-572-3993, or fax 317-572-4002.

Some of the people who helped bring this book to market include the following:

*Acquisitions, Editorial, and Media Development*

**Project Editor:** Kelly Ewing

    *(Previous Edition: Christina Guthrie)*

**Acquisitions Editor:** Stacy Kennedy

**Assistant Editor:** Erin Calligan Mooney

**Editorial Program Coordinator:** Joe Niesen

**General Reviewer:** Laurie Boyce

**Media Development Assistant Project Manager:** Jenny Swisher

**Media Development Associate Producer:** Angie Denny

**Media Development Quality Assurance:** Kit Malone

**Senior Editorial Manager:** Jennifer Ehrlich

**Editorial Supervisor and Reprint Editor:** Carmen Krikorian

**Editorial Assistant:** Jennette ElNaggar

**Cover Photos:** ©Comstock Images

**Cartoons:** Rich Tennant (`www.the5thwave.com`)

*Composition Services*

**Project Coordinator:** Katie Key

**Layout and Graphics:** Samantha Allen, Carl Byers, Melissa K. Jester, Christine Williams

**Proofreaders:** Laura L. Bowman, John Greenough, Caitie Kelly

**Indexer:** Broccoli Information Management

---

**Publishing and Editorial for Consumer Dummies**

    **Diane Graves Steele,** Vice President and Publisher, Consumer Dummies

    **Kristin Ferguson-Wagstaffe,** Product Development Director, Consumer Dummies

    **Ensley Eikenburg,** Associate Publisher, Travel

    **Kelly Regan,** Editorial Director, Travel

**Publishing for Technology Dummies**

    **Andy Cummings,** Vice President and Publisher, Dummies Technology/General User

**Composition Services**

    **Gerry Fahey,** Vice President of Production Services

    **Debbie Stailey,** Director of Composition Services

# Contents at a Glance

# Table of Contents

# Introduction

*W*hat can you do today to boost sales, attract new customers, and retain old customers? Well, for starters, you can read this book and make a commitment to work on your marketing program! In *Marketing Kit For Dummies,* 3rd Edition, I provide information, resources, and tools for the active marketer, salesperson, or manager. Furthermore, you get the benefit of an accompanying CD-ROM that's chock-full of templates for making plans, sales projections, surveys, and coupon profitability analysis, to name just a few of the goodies I put on there for you.

## About This Book

*Marketing Kit For Dummies,* 3rd Edition, covers a wide range of subjects and offers a lot of help to anyone in business, including

- ✔ Simple, powerful templates and general rules for writing a marketing plan or ad campaign and budgeting your expenses

- ✔ A collection of advertising templates, brochure templates, and even templates for letterhead and business cards

- ✔ Insights on how to successfully close the sale through improved sales or marketing techniques

- ✔ A mini-library of professional photographic images for cost-saving designs

- ✔ Plenty of ideas, examples, tips, and templates to make your sales and marketing materials look great — and function well, too

- ✔ Neat marketing software I created to help you do the chores of good marketing quickly *and* well

- ✔ Plenty of hands-on tools and activities — many of which I borrowed from high-level corporate training events and workshops — to help you boost your own performance in sales and marketing

I wrote *Marketing Kit For Dummies,* 3rd Edition, for all of you who want to take responsibility for any aspect of sales or marketing in your organization — whether that organization is a small one-person operation, a large multinational corporation, or a public sector or nonprofit organization.

*Marketing Kit For Dummies,* 3rd Edition, focuses on helping readers communicate better with customers. Whether person-to-person, through a letter, the telephone, a brochure, a Web site, or any other medium, your customer communications play a vital role in the success of your business. I've cued up an immense amount of information, resources, and templates to help you improve your customer communications and your overall business image. Have a peek at the contents of the CD to see what I mean! (But be sure to use this valuable CD — just a peek won't do — because using it correctly can make the difference between a profitable business and no business.)

# Conventions Used in This Book

When reading this book, be aware of the following conventions:

- ✔ Web sites and e-mail addresses appear in `monofont` to help them stand out.

- ✔ Any information that's helpful or interesting but not essential appears in sidebars, which are the gray-shaded boxes sprinkled throughout the book.

- ✔ Whenever I introduce a new term, I *italicize* it.

- ✔ CD files are numbered, with the first two digits designating the chapter they support and the next two digits indicating the order in which I refer to them in the chapter.

# What You're Not to Read

For those among you who just want to get down to business, you can safely skip the sidebars and still get all the info you need.

# Foolish Assumptions

I hate to make assumptions about people I don't know, but, dear reader, I did have to assume a few things about you when writing this book. Hopefully at least one of these assumptions applies to you:

- ✔ You're a marketer, salesperson, or at least someone interested in marketing.

✔ Your business isn't as successful as you'd like it to be, and you want to know how you can fix that.

✔ You know what you need to do to improve your marketing program, but you want someone to walk you through the necessary planning and actions.

✔ Or maybe you aren't sure what to do; you need to do some planning or develop a winning strategy.

# How This Book Is Organized

*Marketing Kit For Dummies,* 3rd Edition, consists of 19 chapters and a CD-ROM that has examples, templates, forms, and software organized to support and extend each chapter's coverage. Here's how I organized all this great information.

## Part I: Tools for Designing Great Marketing Programs

Things go better when you have a plan in mind. In marketing, this plan can be as simple as a back-of-the-envelope program using the Five Ps (product, pricing, placement, promotions, and people), which I cover in Chapter 1. Or it can be as complex as a detailed, systematic audit of all marketing activities, followed by a carefully written plan and a spreadsheet-based budget to go with it. I cover all these options in Part I, and I include the templates needed to take the sting out of designing a good program that boosts sales and profits. In fact, this book's planning templates are easier to use and more professional than any of the software programs I have evaluated — and those all cost a great deal more than this book.

## Part II: Advertising Management and Design

Ads are often the key element of a marketing program, and in this part, I share insights, how-to tips, and tools to help you design winning ads for your campaign. Advertising needs to start with a good plan and affordable budget, which I cover in Chapter 4. Then you have to actually design hard-hitting ads that draw attention to your message and produce leads and sales. These challenges are covered in Chapter 5.

# Part III: Power Alternatives to Advertising

Advertising is costly. In this part, I show you how to get your message across and generate leads and sales in creative ways that cost less than traditional advertising. Sometimes something as simple as a really well-designed business card is the secret to winning business and boosting sales. Newsletters, publicity, catalogs, logos and letterhead, and other marketing elements may also boost your sales. Check out this part if you want to save money on expensive advertising or just to make sure that you're doing these essentials as well as you can.

# Part IV: Honing Your Marketing Skills

Some important skills are involved in doing good marketing. For example, you need to do market research to find out what customers want and how to sell better than your competitors do. And communicating well is obviously important in marketing, so I cover writing in this part as well. The star of this section is that secret ingredient that transforms ordinary marketing into the stuff of brilliant breakthroughs: creativity. I include a chapter that shares many of the techniques and tools from my firm's corporate creativity workshops to help you make sure that you get that special leverage that only creativity can provide.

# Part V: Sales and Service Success

Sales and marketing: That's what people usually say, separating these two intertwined activities in an artificial way. I don't really know where selling stops and marketing begins. In every successful business I've seen, the two activities work hand in glove to signal new customers to the door, serve current customers, and thank past customers for their business in such a way that they feel good about coming back again. So this part on how to do great sales is an important complement to the other parts of the book. Use it to make sure that you're finding and closing as many good leads as you possibly can. Or use it to diagnose or improve any sales process, because there's often room for improved performance.

# Part VI: The Part of Tens

This part covers several topics that may give you winning ideas for your marketing program. Take a look at the collection of winning marketing strategies in Chapter 17 — maybe one of them will work for you! I also cover ways to cut costs and increase the return of your marketing investment in this part. And last but definitely not least, I've collected simple ideas for using the Web to boost sales and leverage your marketing program.

And don't overlook the Appendix, which explains how to use the CD, or the CD itself. It's attached to the inside back cover of this book.

# Icons Used in This Book

I occasionally use icons to flag certain passages. Here's what the icons mean:

This icon points out good ideas and shortcuts to make your life as a marketer easier.

Any information that's especially important and worth remembering gets this icon.

This icon points out mistakes and pitfalls to avoid. Whatever you do, don't skip these paragraphs!

This icon highlights a method or approach that has been used successfully in real life.

When you see this icon, you know that an accompanying example, form, or spreadsheet is available on the CD that comes with this book.

# Where to Go from Here

The beauty of this book is that you can skip to any section or chapter as you desire. You can certainly read the book from cover to cover, but you don't have to. Start with whatever topic is most important to you and don't forget to use the accompanying tools on the CD.

I encourage you to start using the ideas and tools from this book right away to improve your marketing and boost your sales. I also encourage you to tap into the supporting Web site, www.insightsformarketing.com, to take full advantage of all your resources as a reader of one of my books.

And if you want even more information and advice about marketing principles, check out my other book *Marketing For Dummies,* 2nd Edition (Wiley). You certainly don't *need* both books, but they do complement one another nicely, and there is virtually no overlap in their contents.

# Part I
# Tools for Designing Great Marketing Programs

## In this part . . .

**1** equip you with tools and ideas for improving your marketing and boosting your sales. I also share the secret of successful marketers — how they find their marketing zone, the formula that makes it easy to produce growth and control marketing costs. Then I help you control your marketing costs and develop your marketing plans.

Need a marketing plan? Honestly, everybody does, but most people dread the challenge of creating one. Probably the best feature in this part is the template and instructions for preparing your own marketing plan in Chapter 2. I include a really cool set of templates: a Word file that you can customize for the text portion of your plan and Excel spreadsheet templates that you use for your sales projections and marketing budget. I must be out of my mind to give these things away (my competitors charge hundreds of dollars for template software like this), so take advantage of it before I come to my senses!

# Chapter 1

# Boosting Your Business with Great Marketing

Marketing can't be reduced to formulas. Not completely. There is always a little magic in it. The magic comes from a mix of imagination, know-how, and experimentation. Gradually, as you work with these three powerful tools, you will develop your own formulas.

Did I say marketing can't be reduced to formulas? That isn't entirely true. Your marketing — the specific methods *you* develop to boost *your* sales and improve *your* profits — will eventually crystallize into a tried-and-true formula that works for you. But this formula will be unique to your business, and you can't copy it from anyone else. In this chapter, I help you work on your formula — the formula that will put you in your marketing zone with reliable results from an efficient, effective marketing program.

The goal of this chapter is to put you in your marketing zone.

## Finding Your Marketing Zone

Your *marketing zone* is the right combination of strategies and tactics to bring you all the business you need (see Figure 1-1). Finding your zone means exploring marketing options until you develop a formula that really works, a formula that you can rely on with only minor adjustments from time to time.

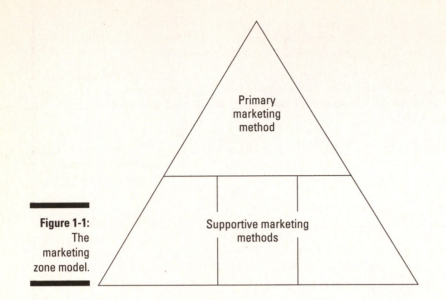

Primary
marketing
method

Supportive marketing
methods

**Figure 1-1:**
The
marketing
zone model.

Businesses that are in their marketing zone are able to count on a healthy flow of sales, which allows them to be forward thinking. These businesses are covering the basics so that they can focus on what exciting new things to do next.

For example, a dental practice has worked out, through several years of experimentation, a formula that is based on friendly service (from the person who greets you through the person who treats you), a good location, and regular customer contact via phone calls and postcards. These three elements constitute their marketing program. (The primary element of their marketing is their friendly service and great staff; the secondary elements are their location, calls, and mailings.) The practice knows how much it needs to spend to sustain this program and get consistent results. The business is profitable and successful. Now the practice can think about opening a branch office, or adding another dentist, or expanding into orthodonture, or any number of ideas that can grow the business beyond its current base. But until the dental practice had worked out its basic marketing formula and entered its marketing zone, starting any new initiatives would have been foolhardy.

How do you know you're in the zone? In your marketing zone, you should find that

  ✔ **You get reasonably consistent results every time you use a marketing tool.** For example, if you do a mailing, you should be able to predict within 10 percent how many responses you'll get.

✔ **You operate in the black.** Your marketing activities should return a profit. Successful marketing can be defined as any marketing that reliably returns more in profits than it costs to do.

✔ **You should know what your top three to five marketing activities are and how to do them well.** And you should probably be investing close to half of your marketing spending in the single most effective marketing activity.

When you have satisfied these three requirements, you'll know you've found your marketing zone. The searching is over! Now you just need to work on repeating the formula with small improvements and watch your sales and profits grow.

No formula works forever. Eventually, you'll begin to find that results are slipping or profits are shrinking. If performance deteriorates, you'll need to search again. Perhaps it's time to alter your formula and update your plans. Should a new lead marketing method replace your old one? Do you need to make a major change in one or more of your top five marketing tools? Take a close look and be prepared to spend time and effort revitalizing your zone if performance slips and you no longer can say "Yes" to the three indicators described in the preceding list.

For example, Corporate Apparel Unlimited (CAU) of Anderson, Indiana, exemplifies a contemporary approach to selling customized clothing for team use and business promotions. Traditionally, such firms always used a color catalog as their primary marketing tool, with a call service center and smaller direct mail pieces in secondary place to support it. But when CAU started in 2000, it redefined the formula with a well-designed, informative, interactive Web site as its primary marketing tool. By now, most of its competitors have had to switch to the Web as their lead marketing tool, too. (See www.cauinc.com for a great example of how these products are now marketed.)

# Pinpointing Your Top Three Sales and Marketing Tools

If your business has been operating for a year or more, then you're probably doing one or more marketing activities that work fairly well. Start by examining the methods that have been most productive for you so far and see whether you can refine them to make them work even better.

Your past experience is your most powerful source of information about what your top marketing tools should be.

Next, take a calculated look at other businesses. Start with your most successful competitors (but don't try to copy businesses that are more than three times your size, as their budget puts them in a different marketing class and you probably won't be able to afford to use their formulas right now). A good idea is to search for a successful similar company in another region and then study what they do. This approach isn't out and out copying; it's *benchmarking* (or learning from others' successful examples), which takes advantage of the fact that ideas are free and anyone can try them.

Don't copy the text or art of their marketing materials directly — those are copyrighted. Only benchmark general ideas — for example, if they use a large display ad in the Yellow Pages, try the same strategy with an ad of your own.

After you've examined similar businesses for marketing ideas, take a look at dissimilar ones. Sometimes the best ideas come from outside your industry.

For example, the owner of a small company that makes fishing lures was inspired by a friend who wrote a blog about business insurance and how to buy and use it. Nobody in the fishing equipment field was writing blogs, but obviously they were an up-and-coming marketing medium, so he started blogging and soon had more orders than he could fill. His blog became his lead marketing tool, and he supported it with a Web site, a traditional printed catalog, and a toll-free number for people who wanted to order by phone. This marketing zone formula worked well, and the business grew without high-cost, traditional marketing. His more traditional competitors advertised in magazines, but his unique formula worked just as well and cost much less. (See Chapter 9 for advice on using newsletters and blogs to grow your business.)

Change your mix until you get a formula that is predictable and highly profitable. Often, when I look at marketing plans, I find myself suggesting that the current lead marketing tool be demoted to secondary status, and a new tool put in top place. Be willing to experiment until you find a lead marketing method that really pulls its weight.

Here's a great example of the search for a successful marketing formula: A friend of mine who owned a landscape firm was doing a mix of residential and commercial work for office buildings and stores. Her business struggled with marginal profits until a large, stable, profitable contract with a big office building pointed the way toward a lucrative marketing zone. Now she avoids residential customers and instead focuses on making sales calls to commercial property owners and managers who can commit to large annual contracts. She sells using a professional-looking sales binder with testimonial letters from customers and a detailed listing of service and price options. Gone are the small, low-profit accounts. Now she has a dozen annual contracts that support a staff of ten and provide a healthy profit. She pays her staff well and hires reliable, stable people who deliver professional, consistent service. Trucks with her signs on them are often parked in front of upscale professional buildings, helping build her brand. She follows up all leads personally with a well-rehearsed office visit that often produces a new contract. Her goal is to add one to three new accounts each year — and so far, her simple marketing formula has met or exceeded that goal. (See Part V for how to make a professional sales call and close big accounts like she does.)

# Adjusting for the Economic Cycle

It would be nice if the marketing formula that worked last year would work perfectly this year, too. However, even a great marketing formula needs to be improved. New competitors, new tastes, and new technologies can outdate your products or antiquate your marketing message, pushing you out of your zone. Marketing is inherently creative for this reason (and that is what I love about it!). So you should anticipate and welcome changes.

And if the economic cycle is shifting, then you *really* have to be on your guard because your marketing formula probably will need to change dramatically in order to keep ahead of the economy. Think of the economic cycle as the key to whether you should be playing defense or offense as you formulate your marketing game plan.

 Economic cycles are inevitable. If you adjust your marketing-zone formula accordingly, you'll survive the tough times and grow in the good times, for an overall effect of faster growth and higher profits than the typical marketer who fails to adjust rapidly to changing economic weather.

## Tightening up for tough times

The 2008 rise in energy and food prices created a lot of cost and price pressures on businesses. Restaurants found the cost of ingredients going up by 30 percent at the same time that customers were trying to cut their fuel use by avoiding drives to distant restaurants. Hotels and other travel businesses also suffered from the rising cost of travel by car or plane. Book sales, casino revenues, movie ticket sales, and many other categories declined. And because banks had way over-extended their credit-card and home mortgage lending in the earlier boom period, loans became extremely tight that year, too — which meant that consumers were cutting back on spending across the board, not just in areas effected by energy and food prices.

What to do? These three steps help smart marketers get through that tough period and emerge stronger:

1. **Control your own costs.**

   Sales fall because *your customers* are trying to control their spending. If *you* don't cut your costs more aggressively than they do, your profits will be squeezed. Renegotiate contracts whenever possible. Switch to lower-cost suppliers or ingredients. Lay off idle workers. Find ways to reduce your use of energy, even if it means doing your baking at night when electricity is cheapest or closing off part of your space and not heating it. Be a miser. Don't make the mistake of waiting to see what happens. Take the lead in changing the rules of your business.

2. **Change your offerings.**

   The things people buy in good economic times are different from the things they buy in bad times, but people still buy. Figure out what you should be selling in a down economy by imagining that you're starting a new business for this economy, using the assets of your old business as building blocks. For example, if you own a luxury restaurant, think about what kind of food establishment you can convert it to that will be profitable with a menu based on lower-priced ingredients, a smaller, less-highly-trained kitchen staff, and fewer wait-staff. As soon as you've worked out the details, print a new menu and make the changes.

   To hesitate is to lose money, so make those changes right away. You can always go back to the old formula next year or whenever the economy turns around. Ideas for adjusting your offering (if you're a restaurant adjusting for a down economy) include smaller portions, less expensive ingredients or components, shorter-term contracts and options, and anything that reduces the price, risk, or upfront investment for your customers. Scaled-back offerings are considerate and appropriate in harder times.

3. **Keep marketing!**

   Don't disappear from customer radar screens. Once you've controlled your costs and adjusted your offerings for the current situation, get back out there with modest, short-term investments in new signs and local newspaper ads, listings in Web directories, radio ads, a mailer, or whatever you think might work to reach gun-shy consumers. (See Part III for ways to promote your business without a big ad budget.)

   Increase your use of search-term ads (pay-per-click advertising) on Google and Yahoo! because these search engines target only those customers who are still shopping in spite of the bad economy. Even though sales are down, some people will buy. Be the visible, realistic choice for them, and you may even grow your business in the bad times — and emerge a stronger leader come the next economic boom. (See Chapter 19 for more ways to market on the Web.)

These three simple steps work pretty well for any business, so long as you're capable of controlling costs and avoiding large losses. However, if you find your costs are out of control, and you're bleeding money, consider a more radical response: Shut down, sell, or convert your business into something that can make money. Never go down with the ship! In every economic downturn, many businesses are too poorly prepared or too weak to survive. You can tell whether yours is one of them if it proves impossible to control your costs in spite of a month or two of hard effort. If so, stop bailing and bail out. However, most businesses can be adjusted to survive the downturn and emerge stronger (although perhaps smaller) when the economy recovers.

Another word of warning: You have to use these three steps *in order.* If you try to fix all your problems with a new advertising campaign or other marketing gimmick (Step 3) before you've controlled costs (Step 1) and adjusted your offering for the current economy (Step 2), your marketing initiative will lose money and put you further behind. Don't say I didn't warn you!

## Taking advantage of a growth economy

What about when the pendulum swings the other way, and the economy starts to grow at an accelerated rate? This situation also requires adjustment. Marketers who continue to be conservative get passed by flashy new competitors.

Here's how to adjust to a growth economy after you've survived the downturn:

1. **Pick your fastest-growing product or service and invest in it.**

   Whatever seems to be sharing in the economic momentum should be promoted aggressively. Find new customers. Do more sales and marketing. Run more ads. Expand your territory. You need to grow sales in the easiest way possible, in order to start bringing in extra profits right away. Otherwise, you won't accumulate the cash needed to invest in growing your business rapidly during the upturn.

2. **Redesign your product line and pricing with the single-minded goal of raising the size of the average purchase.**

   Add options and extras. Cross-sell with a special two-for-one or trial offer. Increase the size of your packages and offer a quantity incentive. Ideally, you should at least double the average sale during an economic boom.

3. **Look for new products and/or customers.**

   Expanding into new categories and territories is your next source of growth, after you've successfully leveraged your most promising product and doubled the size of the average purchase. Now is the time to innovate. Pick up a new line of products that seem exciting and different.

Go after an emerging group of customers with new tastes or needs. But don't forget to keep your core business healthy and profitable (see Steps 1 and 2) because a profitable core business gives you the capacity to try exciting new growth ideas.

# Marketing Smart to Avoid Costs and Risks

Marketing can be a dangerous game. I've seen many businesses commit to a marketing plan, only to find that the expected sales didn't materialize and they ran out of cash. What happens if you use most of your marketing budget to buy a mailing list and print and mail a new catalog, but hardly any orders come in? This event happens all too often. As the author of books on marketing, I get requests for help from people who have made this kind of mistake every month.

Here are some rules to keep you from blowing your marketing budget on things that don't bring in a good return:

- ✔ **Spend no more than 10 percent of your marketing budget on unproven ideas.** If it hasn't worked several times for you already, it's unproven for you, no matter what others may say. You have to test it for your business before you admit it into your marketing zone.

- ✔ **Test each marketing idea several times on a small scale before committing to a big buy or large run.** You don't know enough to draw firm conclusions until you've seen what happens with repetition. (A small Web site needs to bring orders before you invest in a big, expensive one.)

- ✔ **Make sure the ad, mailing, Web directory, or other marketing tool reaches _your_ customers.** Many media buys sound great because they promise a big reach — large audience — but who cares? What matters is whether your good customers and prospects are in that audience. For example, if your customers don't listen to public radio, avoid the temptation of sponsoring your local public radio station, even though it's cheaper than buying ad time on commercial radio stations.

- ✔ **Don't try to imitate the big spenders.** The Coca Cola brand is maintained in the public minds through millions of dollars of TV and outdoor advertising every day. Obviously, most businesses can't afford to flood the world with their brand identity. Nor can they print glossy catalogs every month that look as fancy as the latest Victoria's Secret mailing. These highly visible marketing role models are completely useless for 99.9 percent of my readers! Look for successful _local_ marketing and advertising because successful small and mid-sized businesses offer the most practical and affordable benchmarks.

✔ **Collect junk mail.** One person's trash is another's treasure. Many of the best marketing talents are busy writing postcards and pitch letters, designing coupons and special offers, or brainstorming new ways of making the outside of a mailing so intriguing that it actually gets read before it's recycled. Learn from their work. Also, a lot of your junk mail is from local and small-scale marketers, and they're your best sources of good ideas if you're a small to mid-sized marketer, too. I keep a file drawer of hanging folders just for the latest junk mail, and I often browse through it for fresh ideas. I also keep a bookmark folder on my computer where I have links to interesting Web pages and blogs. When I need a new idea, I look for *low-cost* examples to fuel my marketing imagination. The bigger my file of examples, the more likely I am to come up with something that will do the trick at a modest cost.

In addition to these risk-reducing marketing tips, I strongly recommend that you keep a close eye on cash flow. Sometimes marketers get new-idea fever: They get so excited about a new marketing concept that they gamble too much on its success. Don't overspend on marketing! The best marketing budget is the one you can afford to lose if nothing goes the way you hoped and planned. Yes, that is a pessimistic statement, but it's born of reality.

For example, an expensive ad campaign may or may not work. If it produces few or no sales, you better make sure that you can survive to try another idea. My recommendation is that you spend your *extra* cash on your marketing. Don't spend money that you have to earn back by the end of the month to pay the rent and electric bill. Nothing in marketing is guaranteed. Everything is a gamble. As you refine your formula and find your marketing zone, the risk goes down — but it never goes away completely.

# Strengthening Your Marketing Skill-Set

Some people are much better at marketing than others. You can continue to feel challenged in this arena, or you can commit to strengthening your skill-set and becoming one of those all-too-rare expert marketers.

Skilled marketers are rare because marketing requires a wide range of skills: creativity, problem-solving, communications, forecasting, research, budgeting, and pricing, plus technical knowledge of printing, the Web, database management, and more. Not to mention presentation and sales skills, customer service and service recovery skills, and the ability to shift rapidly from one of these skills to another . . . and another . . . and another. I think marketing is incredibly challenging and difficult, and I rarely meet anyone who is truly great at it.

I do meet a lot of successful businesspeople who have one thing in common: an enthusiasm for strengthening their marketing skills. They've gradually gotten pretty good at the majority of these skills. To follow in their footsteps, you need to be willing to be an adult learner. Pick up a good book, learn a new software program, talk to someone who knows all about something you know nothing about — be open and interested, and you'll expand your skill-set, too. (I include a workshop-style section on marketing skills in Part IV of this book.)

## Design, copywriting, creativity, and more

In this book, I help you work on a variety of marketing skills. Graphic design comes to the forefront in ad and business card design (see Chapter 6). Copywriting surfaces in Chapter 9 when I address blogging and newsletters and in Chapter 10 when I address publicity. Communication is so essential to good marketing that I also cover the basics of persuasive writing in Chapter 13.

Research skills are invaluable to the marketer, and I share some of them (along with tools for your customer research) in Chapter 11. Creative thinking is perhaps the most important marketing skill of all, and I hope that the creative examples and ideas in every chapter of this book will help you power up your marketing imagination — but to be doubly sure, I include skill-building information in a miniworkshop on creativity in Chapter 12.

## Artful persuasion: Sales skills to the fore

What is the most important marketing skill? Is it communicating? Thinking creatively? Researching new opportunities? Planning? Pricing? Wow, it sure is hard to decide, because so many skills are important. Some people would say that the single most important skill is salesmanship.

I know a lot of excellent salespeople, and I know a lot of business owners and managers, but honestly, the two lists don't really overlap. Most of the people who read my marketing books don't feel very confident when they have to do sales. That is why I recommend studying Part V carefully. You have so many opportunities to use a little salesmanship — make sure that you have the skill-set needed to take advantage of every opportunity!

## *Quick skill-building tricks and tips*

You have plenty of time to refine your skills, so I don't go into depth on the topic now (Part IV goes into skill-development in depth). However, I want to pass on several skill-building tips that you can begin to practice right away, and that ought to improve your marketing performance even before you get to any of the later chapters:

- **Say it in half the words.** That advice means cutting the other half. Almost every letter, slogan, e-mail, ad headline, blog, product description, sales pitch, or Web page is too long. Discipline yourself to communicate succinctly. You'll be amazed at the impact.

- **Be concrete.** Give examples. Quote satisfied customers. Give specific information (statistics, specifications). Let the facts do the selling for you.

- **Know your customer.** If you can describe your target customer very clearly, you're probably ready to grow your sales. Too often, marketers have only a vague concept of who they need to reach and make a sale to. A lack of clarity about your target customer makes your entire marketing program poorly focused, which dooms it to low response rates and low profitability.

- **Give your brand a winning personality and make everything consistent with it.** Customers need to *like* your brand, so please try to imagine it as a person, and make sure that it goes to work each day with a cheerful demeanor and appropriate attire. Inconsistent, unappealing presentations are the bane of good marketing. Make sure that everything the customer sees (from a billing statement to a storefront) is appealing and consistent with the image you want to project.

If you're not already doing these four things well (and most marketers aren't), then get to work on them right now. There is no time like the present for boosting your marketing skills — and your marketing results!

# Designing Your Marketing Program

Your *marketing program* is the coordinated, thoughtfully designed set of activities that put you in your marketing zone. (For more on this topic, see the section "Finding Your Marketing Zone," earlier in this chapter.) As you may recognize from Figure 1-1, earlier in this chapter, good marketing programs usually have a primary marketing method, supported by several strong secondary methods.

In addition, good programs usually include a range of small activities that make up a learning foundation at the bottom of the pyramid. All together, these small foundation blocks should not add up to more than a fifth of your budget. They include basics like your business cards and telephones, as well as experiments with new marketing methods that may some day rise up to replace older methods in the base or top of your marketing pyramid.

Your marketing program may consist of any one of the hundreds of things marketers do to spread the word about a brand or ask customers for a sale. It's almost impossible to make a master list of all the possibilities. For example, think of how many options you have just for displaying an advertisement. You can place it in a consumer or trade magazine, a newspaper or newspaper insert, the phone book or other printed directories, Web pages with high traffic, bus and bus stop signs, highway billboards, airport posters and backlit displays, subway car posters, automobile signs and bumper stickers, sponsorship signs at sporting events, and so on. Which of the many of advertising options should be in your program?

To make program design even tougher, many alternatives compete with advertising. You can mail postcards, free samples, catalogs, direct response sales letters, e-mails, or other communications directly to prospective customers. Hundreds of list brokers and printers are eager to design and deliver a direct response marketing piece for you, if you think this approach is a better use of your marketing buck than print advertising. Or what about the old saw that the three secrets of success in marketing are location, location, location? Maybe you need to emphasize having a storefront or accessible office or showroom in a good location, with plenty of appealing signage or window displays to draw customers in. Then again, perhaps all these marketing ideas are too costly, and customers would rather you keep it bare-bones and offer them a rock-bottom price instead. Speaking of price, what about coupons, discounts, and other special offers? You have lots of options in this area, too.

It's no wonder that most marketers throw up their hands and just do the same thing they did last year. Changing their marketing mix and planning a new program seems daunting. However, I promise you one thing is for certain: If you use the same program you did last year, you'll get worse results. Marketing programs need to be studied and improved from year to year.

The variety and complexity of choices makes getting organized and focused difficult. Fortunately, you can use the Five Ps to organize your thinking, decide what to do, and document and budget your program.

The *Five Ps* stand for the five broad areas (product, price, placement, promotion, and people) you can look to for ways to boost sales or accomplish other marketing goals as you build customer commitment to your brilliant products, services, or brands. As you design your marketing program, decide which of the five Ps is most important for you right now. Rank them by importance so that you'll know where to focus your efforts and spending.

For example, if you're the inventor of a hot new product, then product is probably your No. 1 priority. You need to put the most resources into refining and producing the product because it's the star of your program. To sell it, you probably should focus on giving away samples and getting people to test it. Then your product can sell itself.

The following sections explore each of the Five Ps.

## Product

To marketers, *product* is what you sell, whether it's a physical product or a service, idea, or even another person (like in politics) or yourself (like when you search for a new job). When you think about ways of changing your product offering to boost sales, you can look at anything from new or upgraded products to different packaging to added extras like services or warranties. And you can also think about ways to improve the quality of your product. After all, people want the best quality they can get, so any improvements in quality usually translate into gains in sales as well.

## Price

To marketers, *price* is not only the list price or sticker price of a product, but it's also any adjustments to that price, such as discounts and other price-oriented inducements to buy, including coupons, frequency rewards, quantity discounts, and free samples. Any such offers adjust the price the customer pays, with the goal of boosting sales.

Price-based inducements to buy are generally termed *sales promotions* by marketers, just to confuse the issue hopelessly. As I delve further into this subject in Chapter 8, you'll also find out how to use price-based promotions to boost your sales and attract new customers. (I also cover pricing in depth in the companion book, *Marketing For Dummies*.)

## Placement

*Placement* is where and when you present your product to customers. You have many options as to how you place the product in both time and space. Whether you're dealing with retail stores, catalogs, sales calls, Web pages, or 24-hour-a-day telephone services that can process customer orders, you're dealing with that placement P.

If you want a feel as to how valuable this P is to the marketing mix, just think about how valuable shelf placement at your local grocery store is to, say, Coke or Pepsi. Imagine what that placement is worth to the marketing of those products!

Oh, by the way, marketers stretch a point by calling this third P "placement" because it's more conventional to call it "distribution." But that starts with a *d*, so it doesn't sound as good. However, just remember that when people talk about distribution, they're talking about placement, and vice versa.

You'll hear one more term that relates to placement: logistics. *Logistics* is the physical distribution of products — shipping and taking inventory, and all the fancy transportation and information technologies that you can harness to improve the efficiency and effectiveness of your distribution processes. Logistics is another useful path to go down when you want to think about where products should be placed for easy purchase.

Distribution concerns where and when products are offered for sale, whereas logistics addresses how they get there. These are related concerns, of course, so they both fall under the list of options when you want to think hard about placement. You can play around with either or both in your efforts to build a strong marketing program. For example, if you add distributors and enhance your Web site to offer online ordering, you're boosting placement by enhancing both distribution and logistics to create more ways to get the product to customers. Some marketing programs place distributors in the primary spot at the top of their marketing zone pyramid.

If you have something unique and can afford to sell at *wholesale* (at least 50 percent off the list price), then seriously consider finding distributors and letting them do the heavy lifting when it comes to finding customers and making sales. The more marketers, the better!

## Promotion

*Promotion* is all the sales activities, advertising, publicity, special events, displays, signs, Web pages, and other communications designed to inform and persuade people about your product. I like to think of promotion as the face of marketing because it's the part that reaches out to ask customers for their business. It ought to be a visible and friendly face because you can't just tell people what to do and expect them to obey. Instead, promotion must find ways to attract prospective customers' attention long enough to communicate something appealing about the product.

The goal of all promotions is to stimulate people to want to buy. Promotions need to be motivational. They also need to move people closer to a purchase. Sometimes a promotion's goal is to move people all the way to a purchase. That's what a so-called direct-response ad is supposed to do. *A direct-response ad* invites people to call, e-mail, fax, or mail in their orders right away. Many catalogs use this strategy. Readers are supposed to select some items, fill in their order forms, and mail them in with their credit-card numbers, for example.

Other promotions do less. For example, a 30-second television spot may be designed only to make people remember and like a brand so that they'll be a little more likely to buy it the next time they're in a store where it's sold. But all promotions work toward that ultimate sale in some way, and when you think about all the creative options for communicating with prospective customers, you should always be clear about what part of the customer's movement toward purchase your promotion is supposed to accomplish.

## *People*

In most businesses, people are responsible for many aspects of product or service quality. The personal connection between your people and your customers and clients may be a powerful influence on *referral marketing* —where your customers serve as a sort of mini sales force for you. They refer others to you because they've had a positive relationship with your people. In many businesses, people are directly responsible for the customer contacts through personal sales and service. If your employees work directly with customers, then add training, recognition, and reward to your marketing program, because it will help to make those people positive and enthusiastic.

You can find many connections between how employees feel and how customers feel. For example, I often work with companies where the salespeople or service people say that they're frustrated because they have to deal with angry, uninformed, or otherwise difficult customers. If the employees feel this way about the customers, then, of course, they tend to be negative (impatient, curt) with customers, which makes the customers even more difficult. In my training and consulting work, I explore a variety of interesting techniques based on building the motivation of salespeople and other employees, improving communications with customers, and handling service problems and customer frustrations. (See Chapter 16 for some of the most important ways of improving customer service.)

The people side of marketing is often the least visible — that's why people aren't traditionally included in the list of marketing Ps. But adding people to the list offers you another powerful lever for achieving your sales and marketing goals.

## *Profiting from the Five Ps*

I should tell you that the Four Ps is the first thing taught to students in a formal marketing class. It's just like my list, except it leaves out the people (a big mistake in real-world marketing, if not at business schools). To profit from the Five Ps, use the list as a mental tool to think about these five broad ways of growing your business and boosting your sales. The Five Ps are just a starting point — the street signs along the road to a great marketing program — and to benefit from them, you have to explore the blocks they mark.

One way you can profit from the Five Ps is to systematically look for weaknesses and strengths in each of the five areas: your product, pricing, placement, promotions, and personal connections with customers. CD0101 is a form you can use to do a quick planning exercise based on the Five Ps. Print a copy of it and sharpen your pencil, and your wits, to see whether you can brainstorm some ideas for improving your marketing program in one or more of the Five Ps' areas.

A good way to profit from your knowledge of the Five Ps is to do some creative thinking about each of the Five Ps every day. Stop and ask yourself these five simple, powerful questions and see whether you can find ways to build your sales by doing something new and creative in at least one of these vital marketing areas:

- What can you do to make your product more appealing?
- What can you do to make your product more accessible?
- What can you do to make your prices more appealing?
- What can you do to make your promotions more visible and persuasive?
- What can you do to make your human interactions with customers more friendly and helpful?

Notice that these questions are open-ended. They don't have right answers. Instead, they invite exploration and experimentation. They're the kind of questions you can even ask your employees — and offer incentives for new ideas. These questions tease the imagination. That's because a considerable amount of imagination is necessary to grow any business or boost the sales of any product. You won't find any pat formulas that are guaranteed to work.

Marketing isn't like chemistry or algebra or bookkeeping: Marketing has no right answers — only the answers you invent, test, and develop. After much thinking and trying, you develop new and better formulas for yourself and your business; formulas that'll give you pretty good results, at least for a time, and then you'll have to update or replace them in order to keep sales flowing and growing.

# Exercising Your Marketing Imagination

What's marketing imagination? It's the one term I wish everyone would associate with marketing if they remembered only one thing, because it's even more important than the Five Ps. (See the section "Designing Your Marketing Program" for more on the Five Ps.) In fact, marketing imagination is the most important factor in marketing. *Marketing imagination* is creative questioning about everything and anything that may help boost sales and make for more satisfied customers. And marketing imagination is what drives growth and development in your business.

Look at any successful business, and you find that it's done innovative things and tried many new ideas. Business leaders are imaginative and willing, even eager, to try out new ideas and approaches. They have active marketing imaginations. Good marketing is creative marketing. Having marketing imagination is always seeking new and better ways, always looking to perfect all five Ps.

Oddly, creativity is often left out of books and courses on marketing. People tend to think of advertising as creative, but they overlook the importance of creativity in all aspects of marketing. Yet a creative approach to your basic marketing strategy can also be very powerful. Think about the success of Ebay.com, the first company to offer virtual auctions that you can participate in from any computer in the world. I guarantee that you can innovate in your distribution and logistics in order to win more sales through placement, if you're willing to be open-minded and inquisitive about your options. (For more on marketing strategies, see Chapter 3. For more on using the Web in your marketing, see Chapter 19.)

Similarly, plenty of examples of creativity exist in pricing and product offerings. How many times does a business succeed by offering a new or different product selection?

Here's a simple example from the town where my offices are located. Quite a few gyms in the area compete for customers, and one of them recently made two simple changes:

  ✔ **Product innovation:** They introduced a new class on *capoeira* — a blend of martial arts and dance to Brazilian drums — featuring a high-energy workout that appeals to younger people who are looking for something new and exciting to do.

  ✔ **Pricing:** They advertised a first-class-free policy for the new capoeira class because they felt that people would really like it if they just tried it. The price promotion worked. It attracted a whole bunch of curious people, many who liked the free course so much that they signed up for ten more courses at full price. And some of them went on to become full members of the athletic club, using the weight machines and other services, too.

This example illustrates two important points about the exercise of marketing imagination. The first point is that you don't have to come up with something dramatically new. Sure, a patentable new invention might be a great product innovation. But in general, you can make plenty of progress simply by coming up with many small ideas. I'm not talking rocket science here. Anyone in business has enough intelligence, imagination, and funding to be a great marketer. And the second point is that you have to go out and try your ideas; try them in simple, easy ways that don't expose you to excessive risks of failure. (For more on risks, see the section "Marketing Smart to Avoid Costs and Risks," earlier in this chapter.)

Great marketing arises from frequent cycles of thinking (or intuiting) and trying. You have an insight or idea. You think of ways to try it out. You test it in the real world and see what happens. You learn from how customers respond. Their responses fuel more imagining and planning, which then leads to more testing and trying. And so the process goes on in an endless loop driven by your marketing imagination but firmly rooted in the real world of customer opinion and action.

What you want to remember about marketing imagination is that it's not only creative, but it's also experimental. Great marketers wear two hats — the hat of the artist and the hat of the scientist. A great marketer may have an "Ah ha!" experience in the shower one morning and show up at work thinking, "Wouldn't it be cool to do such and such?" By lunchtime, she's changed hats and is carefully reviewing her options for trying out the idea. By the time she goes home, she's already said to herself, "I think I've figured out how to safely test my cool new idea."

# Reframing Your Presentation

Every marketing program has a common theme — communications that present the product offering in a persuasive manner. Whether you rely on advertising, packaging, a brochure, catalogs, Web sites, signs, or even public relations (news coverage), you're relying on the persuasive power of information.

A great use for your creativity is to rewrite your marketing communications. Bump them up. Make them more persuasive.

And before you start working on clever or humorous ad concepts like the expensive ads you see on national TV, I want to ask you to focus your creative communications more simply than that. Just try to get across a few compelling facts. Figure out what information you can share with prospects that will help convert them to purchasers. The better you support your information, the easier it is for people to take a chance and make a purchase.

## The persuasive power of information

I want to illustrate how to use information to pump up your marketing by introducing you to the sport of squash. This very fast-paced indoor racket sport is popular internationally, but not well known in the United States. However, my daughter and I happen to play it, and we both broke our rackets recently. You can't walk into a typical U.S. sporting goods store and buy a good racket, so I went online to www.just-squash.com to shop and was interested in the new Feather Heavy Hitter racket. Why? Because, according to this Web site, the racket was recently used by three British Open winners. That fact gets a shopper's attention.

I should also add that the Feather (which is made by an entrepreneurial Los Angeles company founded by top squash players) costs $160, which is about 50 percent more than the last racket I bought. So before buying, I needed to feel confident that it was worth the higher price. I Googled the maker (www.feather sports.com) and followed the link to its news page (www.feathersports.com/news) where I quickly read stories about young winners who use the racket. For example, Karim Ali Fathi of Cairo, Egypt, won the British Open in the Under 15 category while playing with a Feather. A photograph on the Web page showed a handsome young man setting up for a mighty shot, his red and yellow Feather racket firmly in hand. I decided my 15-year-old daughter would be okay with the idea of playing with the same racket that he plays with.

The manufacturing data on the Feather was also impressive: Reinforcement meshes of titanium and nickel and a frame of 100 percent carbon with a strung weight of 148 grams, which may mean little to you if you don't play, but to a squash player it suggests high performance. I decided to run up the credit card and buy Feathers for both of us.

I recommend the Feather if you want to win the game of squash. And I highly recommend harnessing the power of information if you want to win the game of marketing. What information can you assemble to make as strong a case for your product as Feather Sports does for its racket? Make your case clearly and well with a short list of impressive facts, and you're sure to increase sales. You may even be able to raise your price.

# The Five-Minute Marketing Zone Plan

This plan is a quick exercise that will help you design a winning marketing program. Do it now or wait and use it as the foundation for a more detailed planning process based on Chapter 2. It's the perfect transition into that topic and chapter. Oh, but what, exactly, is "it"?

Print the files labeled CD0102 and CD0103. The first is a worksheet for listing and analyzing all the marketing activities that are candidates for your marketing program. Use it to focus your search on the most appropriate and powerful marketing activities for your particular business. The second file is another worksheet, this one in the form of the marketing zone pyramid. Use it to create a sketch of your marketing program by filling in the blanks. This sketch will help you structure the plan by defining your primary marketing method or tool (which should receive roughly 40 percent of your marketing budget), your several secondary tools (which together should receive no more than 50 percent of your budget), and your tertiary options (which receive no more than 15 percent of your budget).

It's possible — and sometimes desirable — to do more detailed and laborious planning. However, the results from these quick worksheet exercises are often fairly good and can improve your focus and clarity about how to market your product. If you think these exercises have done the trick and you know enough now to forge ahead without more formal planning, be my guest. You can skip to later chapters that apply to your primary, secondary, and tertiary marketing tools. (Also keep in mind that you can find additional information in my companion book, *Marketing For Dummies,* and on the Web site I maintain for my readers at www.insightsformarketing.com.) Or if you want to be more thoughtful and careful about your planning, take your worksheet results and flip to Chapter 2.

# On the CD

Check out the following items on the CD-ROM:

- ✔ Five Minute Marketing Plan (CD0101)
- ✔ Your Marketing Zone Program Worksheet (CD0102)
- ✔ Your Marketing Zone Planning Diagram (CD0103)

# Chapter 2

# Crafting a Breakthrough Marketing Plan

You're not going to believe all the great tools on the CD for this chapter. I can hardly believe them myself. The CD contains dozens of pages of templates, audit forms, and interactive forecasting, planning, and budgeting tools for you to use. The reason I put so many cool tools on the CD for marketing audits, plans, and budgets is that I get more questions about these topics than any others. Many readers wrestle with how to audit and improve a marketing program, and how to write a marketing plan and prepare a good budget. These tasks are difficult. The only way to make it relatively easy is to have someone walk you through the process, which is what I do in this chapter.

## Auditing Your Marketing Activities

A *marketing audit* often identifies problems that are holding you back. It reviews everything that influences customer behavior and helps you identify hidden problems and opportunities. A *marketing plan* lays out your analysis of the situation in your market along with your strategies and how you'll use the various elements of your marketing mix (such as advertising, your Web site, and pricing) to execute the strategy. It also has sales projections and a budget for your marketing spending.

An audit is a great way to quickly find and work on weak areas in your marketing process. A marketing audit can also form the basis of your marketing plan. How? Well, if you take the audit, which you can find on the CD, and then make a list of the items that you scored a "No" on, this information can become a starting agenda for what to do in your next plan to improve your marketing performance and results.

The editable Microsoft Word format marketing audit on your CD (filename CD0201) is divided into nine areas, each with a list of a dozen or more specific questions. The questions have Yes/No answers, which makes the audit quick and easy to complete. In case you find it difficult to open this file or you want a simpler, non-editable file format, you can print CD0202, which is the same audit saved as a PDF file. Use the printout of CD0202 to complete your audit in pencil.

When you complete the audit (using either CD0201 or CD0202 depending on your preference for file formats), simply count the number of Yes answers in each section and divide by the number of questions to get your section scores. You may find it easier to calculate your scores manually by using Table 2-1. Alternatively, if you have access to Microsoft Excel, don't score the audit manually. Instead, open file CD0203 and use the calculator it provides.

| **Table 2-1** | **Marketing Audit Worksheet** | |
|---|---|---|
| *Activity Area* | *Formula* | *Profile Score* |
| A. Marketing focus | # of yeses_____ ÷ 12 = | _____ % |
| B. Marketing scope | # of yeses_____ ÷ 10 = | _____ % |
| C. Customer acquisition activities | # of yeses_____ ÷ 17 = | _____ % |
| D. Information-gathering activities | # of yeses_____ ÷ 16 = | _____ % |
| E. Marketing planning activities | # of yeses_____ ÷ 18 = | _____ % |
| F. Communications activities | # of yeses_____ ÷ 37 = | _____ % |
| G. Customer service activities | # of yeses_____ ÷ 15 = | _____ % |
| H. Management and control | # of yeses_____ ÷ 12 = | _____ % |
| I. Creativity | # of yeses_____ ÷ 13 = | _____ % |
| Overall Score Calculation | Total # of yeses_____ ÷ 150 = | _____ % |

Obviously, a 100 percent score is the best. Any score less than 85 percent for a section indicates a weakness in an area that probably deserves close attention. After you convert all your section scores into percents, you can compare them and see which areas are lacking and deserve attention. Working on the one or two areas where your scores are lowest is a good idea because it gives you a helpful focus in your efforts and plans.

After you take the marketing audit, you can analyze your results in each of the nine areas.

You should make marketing decisions according to the Five Ps (by deciding what your product, pricing, placement, promotions, and people should be), as I show you in Chapter 1. But you should also monitor ongoing actions across the Five Ps by looking at activities in the nine areas of the marketing audit.

You'll probably notice that most of the sections of the marketing audit have questions about the Five Ps. That's because you really need to take actions to help implement your marketing program across all the Ps. For example, your workers in information gathering need to keep you informed about competitor product development, customer reactions to your pricing and promotions, and so on. If you like having everything integrated into one big model, you can think of the audit as cutting across the Five Ps, and you can even build a big grid out of the two lists, if you want to.

## Evaluating your marketing focus

Part A of the marketing audit helps you evaluate your *focus,* which means how clearly and how well your marketing takes aim based on your strengths and opportunities.

The following questions are just about the most important questions you can ask, and they need to have good, clear answers before you worry about any of the hundreds of details of your marketing program:

- ✔ Do you have specific growth goals to motivate and focus your marketing efforts?
- ✔ Do you have a clear strategy to help you achieve those growth goals?

Don't take action until you have a clear strategic focus to give your actions purpose and direction. You want your marketing program to be a wolf leaping forward, not a hundred scared rabbits hopping in all directions at once.

Although 85 percent is a minimum score for passing the audit, you really want to get as close to 100 percent as possible on the focus section. Consider referring to the exercises and customer commitment worksheets in Chapter 1 to explore your strengths and weaknesses and to see how you can best build greater customer commitment in general and, more specifically, in each of the Five Ps (product, price, placement, promotion, and people).

## Evaluating your marketing scope

Think of the *scope* of marketing as how broadly and aggressively you pursue customers and try to make sales. To win the great game of marketing, you have to first show up. Auditing your scope helps you figure out whether you're showing up and pursuing sales in the markets and with the customers who matter to your success and on a large enough scale to achieve your goals and realize your potential.

Don't even think of skipping this section of the marketing audit. Saying that your marketing has to have enough scope to achieve the impact you want may sound simplistic or obvious, but in almost every company I visit that's having problems with sales or marketing, I can trace at least some of the problems to the issue of scope. Thinking big isn't enough — you have to act big, too.

For example, many companies provide just one or a few products or services to their customers when offering a broader range would be easy — and helpful to the customers. Don't limit your potential by offering just one product or service or in any of the other ways covered in Part B of the marketing audit.

Take a look at the questions in this section of CD0201 and, if you answer No more than once or twice, rethink the way you're approaching marketing. Ask yourself what you can do to think bigger and expand the scope of your marketing efforts. Maybe the solution is as simple as advertising to a larger geographic area or seeking new, larger, and more professional sales representatives or distributors. Aiming for the best customers in your market — the biggest purchasers or the ones who set the lead in buying trends and fashions — is important, too.

Thinking big is an important part of marketing success.

## Auditing your marketing activities

Parts C through G of the marketing audit look at many of the specific activities that you ought to be doing or having competent people do in order to have a really good marketing program. Depending on your business's size and type, some activities may not be relevant to you, but most, if not all, of them are important. Take a good hard look at any No answers in these parts and try to introduce activities to fill in the gaps. (You can find lots of specifics about your marketing activities in this book.)

I divided the audit of marketing activities into multiple sections to reflect the reality that, in effective marketing programs, you need to be active in each of the following areas:

- ✔ **Customer acquisition:** Actively reaching out to attract and retain good customers
- ✔ **Information gathering:** Studying and tracking trends, listening to customer input, and conducting other activities that help you learn about your customers and market
- ✔ **Planning:** Organizing and coordinating the activities to give them focus
- ✔ **Communications:** Sending clear, well-targeted messages through multiple channels and media
- ✔ **Customer service:** Interacting with customers to make sure that their experience is rewarding and to encourage them to become ambassadors for your company, product, or service

I'm a big believer in taking an activity-based approach to planning and managing your marketing. You can't just talk and write about marketing, you have to *do* specific things to get any desirable results. All a marketing program or plan really comes down to is a set of actions that (hopefully) has a positive influence on sales and profits. So the section of the audit where you evaluate your marketing activities strikes at the very heart of your marketing and can quickly tell you whether your program is coming up short.

## Analyzing your management and control

Control is sometimes hard to achieve in marketing. Some businesses don't really know what's going on in their marketing because so many marketing activities can occur and customers can be so widespread and difficult to track. For these reasons, many companies waste time and money on their marketing and don't even realize it.

### Writing everything down

One of the first things you should do to control your marketing is document and record every action and expense. Keep good records and make careful lists.

This concept may sound obvious, but keeping track of your marketing can be difficult to do. For example, my firm sells training materials and publications to companies directly for use in their training programs. We track our direct contacts with clients and know who buys and uses what. Or do we? We also work with multiple distributors and publishers who may sell our publications to companies, sometimes without our knowledge. And to make the situation more complicated, we also sell publications to consultants who then sell trainings based on our publications to companies. So a company can purchase one of our products in many ways.

What all this means is that we don't always know who's using our products or which products they've tried and which they haven't. That lack of control gets to be a problem when we want to send a letter promoting a specific product. We may send the letter to some companies that already use that product without our knowledge, which is a waste and makes us look disorganized. Even worse, we don't have the names of all the companies that have used one of our products and thus would be especially receptive to a promotional letter. I'm gradually working on my firm's business partners to get them to trade customer lists with me, but not all of them are willing to do so. Controlling something as simple as our own customer lists isn't as easy as it sounds.

If you have a big enough budget, you may want to explore customer relationship management (CRM) software. Most marketers may do better to build their own systems using available tools. If you have under a hundred customers, a file cabinet with a folder for each customer works pretty well. Alternatively, you can use an Excel spreadsheet with a row for each customer and add notes in the columns for each update on what they ask about or buy. Some marketers use their accounting software as the core of their customer database because they're already capturing customer names, addresses, and orders in it. Even if you don't have a fancy (and expensive) CRM system, you can and should track customer activity and compile notes about each customer.

### Keeping the communication lines open

Another foundation of marketing control is what I think of as the human element, which encompasses how people are organized and how they divide the work and communicate about it. Make sure that you've clearly defined roles and goals — this element is fundamental to good marketing management.

And ask lots of questions and share lots of information to keep the communications flowing. I bet you haven't heard about all customer complaints or concerns — most marketing teams don't. I also bet your company offers products that some of your customers don't yet know about; this issue is also a common communication problem in marketing. Management and control are all about making sure that your company has an efficient, effective connection to your market.

# Checking your creativity

The very idea of auditing your creativity may seem strange because audits and creativity sound like opposites. But because creativity is an essential component of your marketing success, you do need to manage it, just like any other important business activity or asset.

How do you know whether you're being creative? Consider the following:

- ✔ **Creativity means doing things differently and doing new things.** If your marketing seems routine, tame, and overly familiar, it doesn't pass the first creativity test: freshness. You really ought to try something new.

- ✔ **Creativity equals originality.** If you're not leading the way with a new idea, method, or approach this year in your industry or market, then you're not being very original. Yet you *are* a unique individual: Your company is like no other, your products have many minor differences, your employees have unique cultural and geographic roots, and so on. Tap into these differences to come up with original ideas and approaches. Try to make your marketing distinctive and special, not me-too and imitative. Why? Because the first person or company to try something new usually gets more money and success out of it than any imitators.

When you weave creativity into your marketing, it gives your marketing activities more impact and helps your business grow. A dollar spent on a dull, typical ad, mailing, brochure, or Web site doesn't have much impact. Any company, big or small, in today's competitive market and unsure economy has to figure out how to maximize every dollar. However, if you have limited funds, then you really do care how much impact your marketing has. A creative approach can increase your marketing's impact by 10 percent or more. That's how powerful creativity is, so please give this last section of the audit (on CD0201) careful attention.

If you need help making your marketing more creative, take a look at Chapter 12. I also offer additional creative tools and techniques at www.insights-formarketing.com in Portable Document Format (PDF) files that you can download and use for free.

# Using Audit Results to Focus Your Plan

When you look at your scores on all nine sections of the marketing audit, you're able to see your *audit profile,* defined as the overall strengths and weaknesses from your audit. This profile is a useful planning tool. Use it to identify areas where you need to improve and areas where you have strengths you want to maintain and take advantage of. (If you haven't completed the marketing audit, see the section "Auditing Your Marketing Activities," earlier in this chapter, and the CD file CD0201.)

One of my associates, Professor Charles Schewe of University of Massachusetts Amherst, used a version of this marketing audit to help executives from electric utilities look at their marketing functions. They all faced the challenge that their markets were opening up to competition for the first time due to deregulation. This challenge meant that these utilities could no longer take their customer base for granted.

Of course, you probably haven't been able to take your customers for granted. But wouldn't having regulatory protection of your market area be nice? Ah, well, the days of regulated monopolies are ending, and even utility companies have to find out how to recruit and retain customers.

The loss of regulatory protection of their customer base made the marketing audit a very powerful marketing tool for these electric utilities. The marketing audit was a real eye opener, to say the least: It revealed large areas of marketing in which the businesses simply weren't active. In some of these organizations, the audit led to an agenda that required several years or more to complete.

In your business, the results may be less radical than in the case of the electric companies, but I'm sure that your marketing audit can lead to an agenda of some sort. Marketing audits always seem to reveal some needs and generate a few good ideas for positive action. Being fully customer-oriented is hard, and creating and integrating effective marketing actions in all areas of your business is very hard to accomplish, too. So a great next step is to review the findings — especially in areas of particular weakness or strength — and develop agenda items that'll help you better attract and retain customers.

Immediately after completing your marketing audit, I recommend that you work up an action agenda based on your results. If you can't come up with at least five high-priority actions for your agenda as a result of the audit, I'll eat my marketing hat. But do put a good effort into it, because I'm rather attached to my marketing hat. I wear that hat quite often when running my own business!

You can find a template on your CD (filename CD0204) for developing your marketing agenda based on the marketing audit you performed. Print it out and fill it in to help you turn your audit into action. Figure 2-1 shows you what a sample planning form looks like (although four more sample forms are on the CD, so you can develop a five-item agenda if you want).

Agenda item #1 is to: _____

Mini-plan for agenda item #1:

**Who** should spearhead this action? _____

By **when** should it be completed? _____/_____/_____

What special **resources** might be needed?

      Other people?

      _____

      _____

      _____

      _____

      Money?  $_____

      Special expertise? _____

      Special supplies/equipment? _____

What should this action **accomplish**?

      Key objective: _____

**Figure 2-1:**
A sample
planning
form.

# *Formatting Your Marketing Plan*

This section offers two alternative outlines for marketing plans. You can design a marketing plan in many ways. No two plans are identical in their formats and structures because no two organizations are identical in their needs. Don't be afraid to adapt planning outlines and templates to your own needs.

In the next section, "Writing Your Marketing Plan the Easy Way," I show you how to use the planning template on the CD. If you want to use my template, then you don't need to worry about the format. I've already built a format into the template, so you can skip that section. However, if you're writing a plan from scratch, you may find it helpful to look at the two outlines that follow. One of them may fit your planning needs.

Here's an example of a plan outline used by a divisional manager at a large industrial chemicals company. It includes a good situation analysis, which makes it a strategic marketing plan. If you think you might need to change your strategy or basic approach, then choose this outline:

**A Sample Marketing Plan**

Situation Analysis

    Sales history

    Market profile

    Sales versus objective

    Factors influencing sales

    Profitability

    Factors affecting profitability

Market Environment

    Growth rate

    Trends

    Changes in customer attitude

    Recent or anticipated competitor actions

    Government activity

Problems and Opportunities

    Problem areas

    Opportunities

Marketing and Profitability Objectives

    Sales

    Market profile

    Gross margin

Marketing Strategy

Marketing Programs

Product Assumptions

You may not need a detailed situation analysis and a strategic examination of problems and opportunities. Sometimes a simpler outline is fine. A different and simpler way to outline your plan is to base it on the Five Ps. A Five Ps' plan is the format I have people use when I run a workshop or class on marketing plans:

**A Five Ps Marketing Plan**

Situation Analysis (reporting on your customers, competitors, products, and results from the past period)

Strategies and Actions (with Budgets and Timelines) for the Five Ps

Products

Placement

Pricing

Promotion

People

Budget Analysis

Responsibilities (who will do what)

After you choose an outline, then, of course, you have to start writing. This is when writer's block (and panic) may set in. A good way to simplify the writing challenge is to convert one question into many. The starting question you have is probably, "What is my marketing plan for next year?" That's too big a question to answer in one sitting. Try breaking it down into a bunch of easy questions, such as "Would a newsletter would be useful and interesting to our customers?" That question is very specific, and it's one you can probably answer on your own with a little thought.

If you decide that, yes, a newsletter may be appealing to your customers, then you can think about a bunch of even more specific questions, such as "How many people are on my mailing and e-mail lists?" and "Will I write the articles myself, or do I need to hire a writer or perhaps purchase the rights to reprint content?" By drilling down to specifics, you can turn a big, hard-to-answer question into a series of fairly easy, detail-oriented questions. Each specific question and answer fits into one of the sections of your outline and fills it out into a useful document.

# *Writing Your Marketing Plan the Easy Way*

What if you try to write your plan but end up with a lot of scribbled notes and no clear idea of how to complete it? Time for a template! This section walks you through the planning process using the planning template in CD0205. The advantage of a template like this one is that your plan is already half written — you just have to supply the details. The corresponding disadvantage, however, is that the outline and general approach are already decided for you, so you have less scope for individualizing the plan than if you write it yourself.

Lucky for you, the planning template in CD0205 helps you produce a detailed, well-written plan. If you pull up the template and take a look at it, you'll probably notice right away how detailed and lengthy the table of contents is. That's because the table of contents reflects the specificity of the questions that the template raises for you to think about. I divided the plan into lots of very specific, small sections, so you never have to wing it and make up a lot of structure on your own. Instead, you always have specific, small chunks of thinking and writing to do — which is much more manageable.

A marketing plan is really a collection of multiple smaller plans that have synergy between them. Each small plan is easier to write compared to a big plan, so I want you to take this one building block at a time.

For example, if you look at the table of contents of the plan template in CD0205, you'll see that the following subsection covers a plan for publishing a newsletter:

**Harnessing the Power of Newsletters**

> Plans for Writing Our Newsletter
>
> Plans for Designing Our Newsletter
>
> Plans for Distributing Our Newsletter
>
> Schedule and Budget for Our Newsletter
>
> Expected Benefits

This template is, obviously, a plan for a newsletter, with places to describe how you'll produce and distribute it, a place to summarize the costs and timing of the project, and an end section to describe the benefits or returns from this newsletter plan (in terms of additional customer loyalty and orders, referrals from pass-along of the newsletter to new customers, and so on; the template guides you on how to fill in each section). Filling in a paragraph or two under each of these headings and working up some estimates for costs and benefits isn't that difficult because a newsletter is a specific, discrete thing to think about and plan.

At the end of the section on newsletters in CD0205, you'll have bottom-line costs, the timing of those costs, and also a sense of when you may get what kinds of returns from your investment in a newsletter. You can use these figures as a basis for entering some numbers in the summary row in your overall marketing budget for your plan (using the Excel spreadsheet template on CD0206). And with the detail section of the plan to support that row of your budget, you can feel pretty good about the numbers you enter there. Build up your budget in CD0206 this way one line at a time as you do each of the smaller, easier-to-think-about mini-plans in each subsection of CD0205. From the details, the big picture emerges, and you'll be pleasantly surprised to find that the budget almost writes itself as you work through the plan. Similarly, the returns you predict from the newsletter can support a row in the Sales Projection Worksheet on CD0207.

# Using the marketing plan template

The best idea I've had in a long while was to make the marketing plan template (CD0205) rely on this book so that you can draw on each chapter as you write a corresponding section of your plan. In other words, this book becomes your master reference guide as you write your marketing plan.

A marketing plan template based on this book is quite helpful and practical. If you need to add more topics to the template, I suggest getting a copy of the companion book to this one, *Marketing For Dummies* (Wiley), written by yours truly, to provide you with the support you need to cover subjects beyond the ones that I cover here. (I mention some sections of *Marketing For Dummies* as optional reference aids in parts of the marketing plan template.) But if your plan is like most of the ones that I've worked on over the years, you'll probably find more than enough information in this book and the template to get you through a planning process and produce a serviceable draft of your plan.

By the way, I walk you through the Excel spreadsheets that are also on your CD for doing sales projections and marketing budgets later in this chapter. Combining the spreadsheets (CD0206, CD0207) with the Word file of CD0205 gives you a complete and very detailed marketing plan.

# Gathering information before you start

Before you even start customizing the template in CD0205, I recommend taking a little time to assemble your marketing information. Make sure that you have records of last year's marketing activities, including expenses, and dig out all the sales records you can find. Also, if you have a little more time, use the audit and survey forms in the section "Auditing Your Marketing Activities," earlier in this chapter, which provide good ideas and information that you can use as you work on your plan.

In addition, you may want to do a little extra research to gather more information about your market. For example, you may want to do one or more of the following:

✔ Ask salespeople or distributors about their views of quality, trends, competition, and so on.

✔ Gather details of sales for the last year or more.

✔ Get breakdowns of sales by product, region, or other category.

✔ Get some general statistics on sales in your market or product category so that you can see what your market share is and whether you're gaining or losing shares.

✔ Collect any information on where sales came from and which sales and marketing practices worked best in the last year or two.

✔ Get prices on printing, ad purchases, design services, or other costs you know you'll need to include in your budget.

✔ Quiz some customers about the quality of your service or product and get their ideas and suggestions on how to improve it.

✔ Plan some sales promotions and work out projected costs and returns. Special offers are a great way to get customer attention and stimulate new customers to try your service or product.

✔ Collect cost and price information to use in budgets and projections. For example, what is the total cost for your company to deliver one unit of your product to a customer? What net price does the average customer pay after any discounts or special offers? And how do your prices and discounts compare to your competitors?

✔ Get information on any new products that you'll be introducing during the plan's period.

✔ Decide whether you want (and can afford) to hire a marketing consultant to coach you through the planning process. Or, if hiring a consultant is out of your reach, you can hire one to spend a day with you clarifying your strategy before you start writing. (Some ad agencies are also happy to help with general marketing planning, so you could ask local agencies for proposals, too.)

Researching this shopping list of questions may occupy you for several days or more. Simply gathering the information needed to do a good plan is a serious undertaking. Fortunately, all this upfront work helps make the writing part much easier.

Eventually, you have to roll up your sleeves and start writing. But don't just stare at a blank page or screen. (I'm reminded of a quote from author Gene Fowler: "Writing is easy. All you do is sit staring at a blank sheet of paper until the drops of blood form on your forehead.") I want you to avoid writer's block, anxiety, and the lack of structure that the blank-sheet-of-paper method provides! And I also want you to avoid the common mistake of making minor edits to last year's plan (if you have one). That method doesn't force you to rethink your marketing; it just creates something that fools you and others into believing that you've done real planning.

Instead, I want you to really write a plan because the writing process is also a thinking process, and coming up with good strategies and tactics takes a lot of thinking. But to make the writing process easier, I recommend following my template in CD0205. It includes detailed instructions for each section of your plan.

# The outline used in the planning template

ON THE CD

CD0205 contains a Word file that I wrote as if I were laying out a professional marketing plan, with a title page, table of contents, headings for each section, and body copy. But instead of writing a specific plan for a client, I used the body copy to give you suggestions, examples, and tips for how to fill in your own details. The outline of this planning template is as follows:

**Introduction**

**Part 1: Program Overview and Marketing Strategies**

Overview of Last Year's Marketing Program

Long-term Investments and Administrative and Overhead Costs

Audit Results and Agenda Items

Marketing Strategies

**Part 2: Information and Skills Required for the Plan**

Market Research

Creative Concepts and Plans

Guidelines for Written Marketing Communications

Testimonials and Customer Stories

**Part 3: Advertising Management and Design**

Planning and Budgeting Our Ad Campaign

Advertising Designs and Programs

**Part 4: Other Elements of Our Marketing Program**

Branding through Business Cards, Letterhead, and So On

Brochures, Catalogs, and Spec Sheets

Pricing, Coupons, and Other Promotions

Harnessing the Power of Newsletters

Media Coverage through Publicity

Web Site Development and Promotion

Trade Shows and Special Events

**Part 5: Sales and Service Success**

Plans and Improvements for Our Sales Process

Improving the Way We Close Our Sales

Strategies for Dealing with Difficult Customers

Sales Projections

**Part 6: Marketing Budget**

Overview of the Marketing Budget

Marketing Budget and Spreadsheet Printouts

The outline is detailed to give you a lot of structure, which is helpful when writing a plan. The most you have to create on your own is a paragraph or two per header.

Also, you can incorporate many other forms on the CD (mostly Word and Excel files), described in other chapters of this book, directly into this planning template. Each time you use one of the other CD files, you're taking a shortcut to completing your plan. I want you to use all the resources in this book as fully as you can during your planning process so that it's as painless as possible! My philosophy is if you wanted to do it the hard way, you wouldn't have bought this book, so I want to make your planning as easy as I can.

# Developing Your Marketing Strategy

I don't need to guide you through every section of the planning template on CD0205 because most of the sections have a chapter devoted to them elsewhere in this book. But the section on your marketing strategies doesn't have its own chapter, so I discuss it here.

In the strategy section of your marketing plan, you describe the big-picture thinking behind your plan. The latter parts of your plan get into all the specifics — the whats, whens, and hows. The strategy section is about the whys. Good thinking on the strategic level will make the rest of your plan much easier to write — and also much more profitable and effective!

I have to tell you before you write the strategy section of your marketing plan that strategic planning is difficult. It's the most difficult thing any marketer, manager, or executive ever has to do. If you hire an expert consultant to do strategic planning with you, expect to spend many long meetings discussing it over a period of months. You probably don't have that kind of time today, however, so I will show you all the shortcuts I know. I can help you craft a rough-and-ready set of marketing strategies in as little as a couple of hours, if you're willing to focus hard on it for that long. If you have the time and funding to do a more formal planning process, by all means do, and use this section of your plan to summarize the results. But if you're in a hurry, don't skip the strategy section. Just follow my pointers and choose one strategy from my list, or perhaps (at the most) several strategies that seem to complement each other and fit your situation and opportunities well.

## Basing your strategies on your core brilliance

Strategies have to be based on your product's genuine strengths: what I call *strategic assets*. The idea is simple and powerful: Get in touch with your best strengths — the thing(s) you can contribute to your market and to the world — and make sure that you base your strategies and plans on them.

Think of your greatest strengths as the foundation of a lighthouse. Your strategies are the ground-level section of the structure. Later parts of your plan build higher, until your promotions at the top provide a beacon to draw customers into your anchorage. Your marketing plan has to be an integral structure, based on a solid foundation of strategic assets. One person's or business's winning strategy is another's failure; the success of your strategy all depends on whether you have the right foundation for it!

## Deciding whether to adopt a new strategy or improve an old one

If you simply need to improve upon and continue using an already-successful strategy, say that clearly in this section of your plan and shape the plan to improve the efficiency of the marketing program you used last year. If, however, you really need to shop for a new and better strategic approach, then say so now and realize that you first need to figure out what your effective strategic plan is before you can expect to optimize any program based on it. In other words, pick one of these basic orientations for your plan:

- ✔ **Efficiency-oriented:** Your plan should introduce a number of specific improvements on how you market your product but should not alter your basic strategy from last year.
- ✔ **Effectiveness-oriented:** Your plan needs to identify a major opportunity or problem (of the customers') and describe a strategy to respond to it.

Take a minute to think about the distinction between perfecting the implementation of last year's strategy and trying a new one. Which strategy you choose makes a big difference that will affect everything else about your plan! If you use last year's strategy and just try to do it more efficiently, then you can plan to do things on a fairly big scale. For example, you can plan to do one big mailing a quarter (assuming that you do mailings — if not, imagine I'm talking about advertising, trade show booths, or whatever you do a lot of). But if you try some new strategy, don't plan to do a few big marketing activities because you may fail at one or more of them and blow your marketing budget in a hurry. Instead, plan to test a lot of smaller mailings and other kinds of marketing. Do a lot of marketing activities on a small scale and build in enough repetition to give yourself opportunities to learn as you go.

### Improving your current marketing strategy

When designing your plan's strategy, the first choice you have to make is whether you have a pretty good overall strategy right now or not. If it *is* good and should continue to work for the next few years, then all you need to do in your plan is show how you'll pursue that strategy efficiently. The main point of your plan is to do marketing like you did last year, but better. In that case, your strategy section can be short and sweet. Just describe the strategy and why you think it's going to continue to work and then say that the main contribution of your plan is to improve the efficiency of marketing by making certain improvements to last year's program.

A marketing audit (see the section "Auditing Your Marketing Activities") or your independent research can guide you to specific areas where improvements are likely to pay off. Mention those general areas briefly here, but save the details for later in the plan.

### Scrapping the old strategy and creating a new one

If you feel that a new strategic direction or approach is needed or you want to try one because you see good opportunities, then your plan should be more effectiveness-oriented. You're going to define a new strategy that, if it works, will bring you exciting new opportunities for sales, profits, and overall business growth. So the critical issue for your plan and your next year's marketing program is whether you can you effectively achieve some new strategic vision and accomplish the new objectives that you set for that strategy. If you even achieve this new strategic vision halfway, you'll probably be happy because doing something new isn't easy. Your plan should be about making your overall marketing approach more effective through a change of strategies.

Don't worry about sweating every detail of your new strategy. Just try to prove that it works without losing money doing it. Next year, you can switch gears and design an efficiency-oriented plan that perfects this year's more experimental one.

If you're trying a new strategy and don't have proven marketing formulas, you can't write an efficiency-oriented plan. For example, if you don't do mailings to purchased lists right now, then don't say that you're going to increase the response rate on mailings from 2.5 percent to 5.5 percent next year. Instead, plan on testing a variety of mailings and plan to have some of them fail (a less than 1 percent response rate) and hope to have one or two of them do pretty well (a 3 percent plus response rate). But you can't guess which ones will fail and which ones will succeed.

# Choosing your strategy

If you're sticking with your existing strategy, you still need to clearly articulate it in this section of your plan and explain why it's so good that it can power your marketing for another year. If you're pretty sure you need a new strategy, then use this section of the plan to say why and to elaborate on your decision. For example:

"Our strategy is a _____strategy. Specifically, we are planning to _____."

Can you easily fill in the blanks, or are you scratching your head?

Most people find completing those two simple sentences difficult, but I can make it easier. In the following sections, I give you a master list of marketing strategies to choose from. You need to be using one (or possibly two or three, at the most) of these strategies in your marketing for the next year. Pick one strategy, and you're ready to fill in the blank in the first sentence.

The second sentence requires a bit more thinking on your part because it says how that strategy applies to your own situation and market. My notes about each strategy (described in the following sections) offer clues on how to customize that strategy to your own plan.

By the way, I put the strategies in the order I want you to think about them; the easier ones are first. The farther you get into this list, the more difficult the implementation usually becomes. So all else being equal, I generally recommend using the easier ones.

### Reminder strategy

The *reminder strategy* is a very simple communications-oriented strategy that reaches out to loyal, regular customers to remind them to make a replacement purchase. If you have a solid base of loyal customers who ought to continue purchasing regularly, this strategy is for you.

You can implement this strategy fairly easily: Just make sure that you give your customers periodic reminders and perhaps small incentives or rewards so that they don't forget your product and wander off to some competitor.

Don't forget: It costs ten times more money to acquire a new customer than it does to keep an existing one.

### Simplicity strategy

The *simplicity strategy* emphasizes ease and convenience for customers. Can you simplify the purchase and use of your product or service to such an extent that simplicity alone can be a major selling point? If so, seriously consider this strategy, but be committed to keeping things simple — simpler than the competition. Otherwise, you won't have a durable advantage.

If you use the simplicity strategy, follow through with simplifying steps in all Five Ps, not just in your promotional messages. Just saying that your company is easier and simpler to do business with isn't much good — it really has to be!

### Quality strategy

If you can figure out how to make a better-quality product or offer better service, by all means do it! The most durable and profitable strategy in marketing is to be better than the competition — in your customers' eyes, not just your own.

You can implement this *quality strategy* in many ways, such as by

- ✔ Making fewer errors
- ✔ Having better designs
- ✔ Offering more reliable or rapid delivery

Pick one or two dimensions that your customers associate strongly with quality when they talk about your product category. Focus on these aspects and be prepared to redesign your business processes and your products to achieve noticeably better quality.

The fields of Total Quality Management and Process Re-engineering are dedicated to the technical challenges of redesigning businesses so that businesses can truly offer better-quality products and services without incurring high costs or raising prices above what customers can afford. I've written about the art and science of Total Quality Management and filled whole books on the topic, so I won't even try to cover it here. I just want you to recognize that you have to pursue this strategy seriously in every aspect of your business, not just in flashy advertisements or promotional claims!

## Market share strategy

The *market share strategy* is a straightforward effort to get a bigger piece of the market than your competitors. Size often matters in competition, so gaining on your competitors by using aggressive sales and marketing to get more customers or more sales dollars than they do in the next year can be a good strategy.

You can be fairly careful and conservative when you use this strategy if you don't need to gain a lot of market share quickly. If that's the case, you may think of this strategy as being based on the basic efficiency orientation I describe in the section "Deciding whether to adopt a new strategy or improve an old one," earlier in this chapter.

Other times, your goal is to make significant progress in capturing market shares compared to competitors, even if you have to overspend on marketing and reduce your profit margin for a year or two. You can use this new strategic effort to achieve greater effectiveness by changing your position in the market. The prize is that, if you succeed in becoming one of the leaders in your market, you can hope for high profits in subsequent years as your payoff for investing in competitive growth now.

## Positioning strategy

The *positioning strategy* is designed to create or maintain a specific image (or position) in the customer's and potential customer's minds. This strategy is psychological, and it's all about how people think and feel. It uses words, stories, and imagery to reach out to customers so that they form strong feelings or beliefs about your product. Often, this strategy looks at how customers perceive the competition because communicating your own unique position in the marketplace — and not a confusingly similar position — is best.

To design a positioning strategy, you really need to find out what people think and what they care about. You can use the exercises (and surveys) in Chapter 1 to get a handle on how customers see the product category in general and what they specifically like most about your product, which is what you should build on when deciding how to position your product in their minds.

In Chapter 1, I talk about the importance of being brilliant at what you do. In a positioning strategy, your goal is to communicate this brilliance in such a powerful way that you "own" that claim to brilliance and are strongly associated with it in customers' minds. Clearly, this strategy is going to need a lot of brand-building and marketing communications in the implementation parts of your plan. (See Parts II and III for extensive how-to advice on branding and promotional communications.)

### Product life cycle strategy

The *product life cycle strategy* adjusts your marketing to the growth stage of an overall product category. Any product category goes through a broad life cycle, from early introduction through growth, to a slower-growing maturity and, eventually, to declining sales and death.

Innovation drives this cycle: New products are invented and introduced, and then they catch on, eventually getting replaced by even newer products. As the cycle goes on, competition grows because the once-new product gradually becomes commonplace and easy for many competitors to make and sell.

The most fun period in this life cycle is the growth phase. During this phase, the market is beginning to embrace the new product and its sales take off. And during that phase, becoming a star by achieving high sales and profit growth is easiest.

You can use the life cycle strategy to refocus your efforts behind a rising star — a product or product line that you expect to experience fast growth in the next few years. Or you can use this strategy to adjust your expectations and refocus your efforts on competitive jockeying if you realize that your once-growing star is now fading and you don't have a replacement. Either way, knowing where you are in the life cycle of your product category is helpful so that you can adjust your efforts and expectations accordingly — and seek a new product with growth potential if your main product is getting too old.

### Market segmentation strategy

A *segment* of a market is simply a subgroup of customers with needs that make them special in some way. For example, if you sell breakfast cereals for adults instead of children, you're targeting (that's what marketers say) the adult cereal market. When you specialize in just one segment of a broader market, you can be more specific and helpful to your customers.

A *market segmentation strategy* often requires a broader geographic area — perhaps even national or international — because your segment of people or businesses with special needs may be relatively rare.

You may be using this strategy already, or you may decide to adopt it now as a way to compete more effectively in the market. Segmentation and specialization can be a great way to make yourself more valuable to certain customers, which allows you to outsell more generalized competitors within the target group or segment of customers.

### Market expansion strategy

If you're currently selling in a three-state area, a straightforward way to grow is to sell your product or services in two additional states. This strategy expands the size of your market. But to use this *market expansion strategy,* you need to make sure that your new market area includes the right kinds of customers and that some new competitor won't undercut your pricing or make entering the market in the new location difficult.

After assessing the new territory, decide what the main challenges of entering the market there will be. Then base your marketing plan on what you must do to succeed in the new, bigger market you want to pursue.

### Buzz strategy

The idea behind the *buzz strategy* is to create excitement about something new, hot, fashionable, or trend setting. Implementing the buzz strategy isn't as easy as it sounds — beware! However, sometimes a marketer has such a cool new idea that is so in synch with the times (and the current headlines) that it's a natural for buzz marketing.

If this strategy fits your product, put up cool or quirky YouTube videos, widgets, and blogs and post MySpace and Facebook pages. Plus send press releases to let the media know you're a good exemplar of a hot new trend. Also, consider doing some public speaking or product demos on college campuses, demos at trade shows and fairs, or whatever else you can think of to shamelessly pursue attention. (If you have a product you can give out, give it to up-and-coming celebrities who are also eager to create buzz.) The window doesn't stay open long, so hurry to make your mark before you're no longer the new thing.

If you aren't totally cool and hip and leading some new fashion or trend, a buzz strategy is not for you. Lots of marketing pundits are excited about the idea of spreading the word through youth culture — but it's a silly concept if your message is really just an advertisement in disguise. Kids aren't that easily fooled! You better actually *be* cool if you want anyone to view your YouTube video, friend you on Facebook, or download your widget.

## Setting specific objectives for your strategies

A *strategic objective* states something you hope that your business will accomplish in the next year as a result of pursuing a strategy. If you're pursuing an expansion strategy, for example, you may set some goals for the number of new customers you want to acquire in each of the new territories.

If you're pursuing a positioning strategy, on the other hand, quantifying your success may be harder. You may have to do a survey at the end of the year to ask customers what they think and feel about your product. One objective may be to convince a significant percent of customers that your product is better, faster, more sophisticated — or whatever the positioning goal is — than your competition. A second objective may be to increase your sales by a certain percent as a result of communicating your special position in the market to prospective customers.

Set specific objectives that flow from your strategy and that also reflect your resources, such as the number of salespeople or the amount of money you have to spend. Good objectives require you to stretch a bit — but not too much. They should energize and give a purpose to the rest of your marketing plan. For example, if your strategy is to gain market share and try to become one of the top three in your market, a good, energizing objective may be to increase your sales at twice the speed of the underlying growth rate in your market. (In other words, to grow twice as fast as the average competitor.) Trying to grow much faster than that may not be possible.

You also use your strategic marketing objectives in your sales projections (use CD0207 for that). One of your objectives must always be about sales, and this objective drives your sales projections. Pick a rough sales objective now, but expect to adjust it as you work on the tactical parts of your plan. Marketing activity is needed to generate sales. However, marketing activity costs money and takes time and effort, so you have to make sure that the sales objective seems realistic before you finalize it.

What are good marketing objectives? Whatever objectives you need to help you achieve your mission or growth goals. Your marketing objectives may be to

- Boost the performance of salespeople or distributors
- Change the way customers think of your offering (reposition)
- Cross-sell more products to existing customers
- Develop new channels of distribution (such as the Web)
- Educate customers about a new technology or process
- Expand into new geographic markets
- Fend off a competitor's challenge
- Find new customers
- Generate more or better leads for the sales force
- Improve customer service
- Improve the distribution of existing products or services
- Increase the average order size
- Increase the perceived value of offerings to counter a trend toward price competition

✔ Introduce new products or services

✔ Recruit new distributors or retailers

✔ Attract attention and create a buzz

✔ Reduce customer complaints

If you go through this list checking those objectives that apply to your situation, you'll probably come up with at least a few appropriate ones that you can use to guide your planning. If not, you can always make up some of your own. But make sure that you have clear objectives before you go into any planning process.

TIP

## Avoiding random activity

Planning exercises can easily turn into random listings of possibilities. The poor planners run out of insights, information, and time when they have to itemize the details of their marketing programs. Their thinking often goes like this:

> "What sorts of ads, mailings, or other marketing communications should we use? Hmmm. Dunno. Maybe we should just list a bunch, so we make sure that some advertising and mailings are included in the budget."

I guess that's a planning process, but not a very intelligent one! You can take many actions to promote your product or service. Often, people just try one thing after another, hoping to see sales increase without any real idea of what may work, why, and how. I call this *random marketing*. It goes kind of like this:

> "Hey, we need to do something to get more sales. Let's do some advertising."

Or maybe it goes like this:

> "Our competitors are offering coupons. Should we do some coupons, too?"

And so on. What about trying some telemarketing? Or print advertising? Or even television or radio spots? Direct mail may be better. Hmmm. Lots of choices. But which should you try? Is it entirely a matter of blind experimentation?

No. At least it better not be unless you have a lot of time and money to waste groping around in the marketing dark. Random marketing is like the old philosophical theory that if you put enough apes at enough typewriters for long enough, they'd eventually type a Shakespearean play by chance. Same with random marketing. Eventually, you might produce a winning program by chance. But you better be very patient! The only difference between the old ape-at-the-typewriter theory and the typical approach to marketing is that nobody is silly enough to actually try the ape experiment, whereas the majority of businesses try random marketing. And then people wonder why their plans don't produce satisfactory results.

# Running Goal-Oriented Marketing Experiments

There's always an important element of creative experimentation in any marketing or planning effort, but there's not random experimentation. When you experiment, you need to have specific marketing goals and a rough idea of the kinds of marketing activities that may achieve those goals. Then you can focus your creative experimentation on finding out how to better achieve those marketing goals by refining your ideas until you have a unique approach that produces a winning marketing program.

The formula you develop and continue refining through your marketing experiments is uniquely yours. No formula works for more than one organization; each business needs to find its own marketing zone. Yet your formula can and should rely on certain transferable elements — the fundamentals that hold up in all marketing programs. And the most easily transferable formulas have to do with marketing goals.

Specifically, you need to know that certain kinds of marketing initiatives tend to be appropriate for certain kinds of marketing goals and not for others. You can use that information to help you define the basic structure of any marketing plan or program — and narrow down those apparently random choices — simply by picking one or a few marketing objectives. Then, focus on the marketing techniques that are most likely to help you achieve those objectives.

# Planning Benchmarks for Marketing Communications

How much should you spend on marketing communications (MarCom) like advertising, the Web, mailings, telemarketing, or whatever you plan to use? Communicating with your market takes many forms in your plan and will probably be a major part of it. If you want to truly achieve your strategic objectives, you need to have a plan that communicates well and often.

On the bottom of the spreadsheet in CD0205, I include a row that calculates your total MarCom spending by adding up any rows above it that involve spending on direct communications within your market. As you work on your plan, keep a close eye on this number and make sure that it's a big enough percentage of your projected sales to actually give you a good shot at achieving those sales projections.

What's a big enough percentage to spend on marketing communications? "As much as you can afford" is one philosophy, but sometimes it's best to benchmark against industry norms rather than just maximize MarCom. If your company is an average size in your industry, then a spending level similar to the statistic from the industry closest to yours in Table 2-2 will probably keep you growing as fast as your competitors and the industry as a whole. To grow faster than your industry or to make up for being smaller than average, you probably need to allocate more money, perhaps even two to three times the average amount.

| Table 2-2 | MarCom Spending as a Percentage of Sales |
|---|---|
| *Product or Service* | *Spending* |
| **Services:** | |
| Insurance | 0.6% |
| Advertising | 2.8% |
| Freight | 1.2% |
| Cable/pay TV | 1.0% |
| Nursing homes | 3.4% |
| Hospitals | 3.0% |
| Investment advice | 6.8% |
| Personal services | 4.0% |
| Services in general | 2.5% |
| **Products:** | |
| Ice cream | 5.4% |
| Furniture | 5.0% |
| Clothing | 5.1% |
| Auto parts/accessories | 0.8% |
| Greeting cards | 3.3% |
| Software | 4.5% |
| Periodicals (newspapers/magazines/newsletters) | 5.8% |
| Food products | 9.4% |
| Toys | 18% |
| Computer equipment | 2.5% |
| Office supplies | 4.2% |

*(continued)*

**Table 2-2** *(continued)*

| Product or Service | Spending |
|---|---|
| Building supplies | 1.2% |
| **Retail stores:** | |
| Watch stores | 15.7% |
| Department stores | 4.3% |
| Furniture stores | 9.0% |
| Clothing stores | 3.2% |
| Hotels/motels | 3.9% |
| Insurance agencies | 1.6% |
| Banks | 3.8% |
| Stockbrokers | 2.0% |
| Consumer electronics stores | 3.8% |
| Variety stores | 2.0% |
| Gift shops | 4.5% |
| Grocery stores | 1.2% |
| Restaurants/bars | 4.4% |
| Retailers in general | 3.4% |

There's no harm in violating these norms, but I do recommend thinking about how your company's marketing communications expenses compare to others in your industry, and I want you to have a good reason in mind if you decide to be significantly different. For example, if you want to gain market share or grow your company's sales, you probably have to outspend the averages. But if your plan produces numbers that are dramatically different than the norms and you don't know why, then you really ought to go back and look to make sure that a good reason exists for the differences.

## For more information . . .

In this chapter, I queue up a number of tools, techniques, and benchmarks to help you with your marketing strategy and plan. Whether you just need to diagnose the situation or develop a full-blown plan, you should find plenty of guidelines in this chapter and its corresponding CD files. For more details on how to design and budget all the specifics of your plan, such as advertising campaigns, sales programs, and promotions, see the upcoming chapters that focus on each of these topics.

Often, a chapter in this book directly corresponds to a section on the market planning template and a section on the budget template, too. In addition, you can find complementary coverage of marketing plans in my other book in this series, *Marketing For Dummies,* as well as in *The Portable MBA in Marketing* (Wiley), a book I co-authored with professor Charles

Schewe of the business school at the University of Massachusetts Amherst. And, of course, I'll continue posting helpful content and links on the Web site that supports my *For Dummies* books (www.insightsformarketing. com).

I encourage you to seek additional resources as well. For example, William Cohen's *The Marketing Plan* (Wiley), although written for classroom use, has a number of good examples of marketing plans that I recommend as benchmarks. And *Kleppner's Advertising Procedure* is the classic text for marketing communications and advertising courses and a good general reference for planners (shop for a used, fairly recent edition on Amazon.com). In my experience, the more support and information you have on hand when undertaking a planning process, the better.

## On the CD

Check out the following items on the CD-ROM:

- Editable Marketing Audit (CD0201), a Word document
- Marketing Audit (CD0202), a PDF format version of CD0201
- Audit Score Form (CD0203), a Microsoft Excel spreadsheet
- Marketing Agenda (CD0204), a PDF format worksheet to use in a planning brainstorm session
- Marketing Plan Template (CD0205), an editable Microsoft Word file
- Marketing Budget Worksheet (CD0206), an editable Microsoft Excel template
- Sales Projection Worksheet (CD0207), an editable Microsoft Excel template

# Chapter 3

# Cutting Costs and Boosting Impact

• • • • • • • • • • • • • • • • • • • • • • • • • • • • • • • • • • • • • • • • •

### In This Chapter

▶ Considering low-cost ways to boost sales

▶ Stimulating word-of-mouth referrals

▶ Boosting impact by using persuasive information and creativity

▶ Increasing effectiveness by narrowing your focus

• • • • • • • • • • • • • • • • • • • • • • • • • • • • • • • • • • • • • • • • •

*I*n this chapter, I review a variety of ideas, tips, and examples that may help you improve your marketing effectiveness and efficiency.

This chapter is especially useful for people who are in a hurry to find something they can do that increases sales and profits. Sometimes you don't need or want to do a full-blown audit and write a new plan (Chapter 2) and instead just want to look critically and creatively at your business to see whether you can do any "quick fixes" to help performance. Usually, you can!

## Taking a Look at Low-Cost and No-Cost Marketing Ideas

You don't need to spend a lot of money on marketing. However, if you look at most of the conventional options, you quickly find the dollars adding up. That's why it is good to look at options you may not initially think about — and ones an ad agency may not think to mention to you.

### Transit advertising

It generally costs between $50 and $500 per month to have your advertising poster displayed on a bus or at a bus-stop shelter, depending on the size of the city. Usually, the minimum time period for this outdoor ad is three months.

Okay, it's not free, I agree — it's in the low hundreds to the low thousands, depending on the size of the audience. But it's a fairly small commitment on your part for a lot of exposure, and if your message clicks with the public, you can expect a good return. (I recommend a direct response format, with a Web site and toll-free phone number right there on the ad.)

An ad agency may direct you toward a local television ad, but that would cost ten times as much to create and place as a small-scale transit ad placement. The nice thing about marketing is that you always have alternatives that fit your budget.

## Publicity

What if you want to spread the word throughout your city for free? That's harder, but still not impossible. If you can think of an interesting news story about your product, people, or events, then you can put your time and energy into contacting local media and trying to generate some editorial coverage instead of advertising. (See Chapter 10 for details.)

You may not be a "hard news" story unless something bad happens (and honestly, I'd rather have no publicity than to see a headline about a fire at my office building!). But it's okay to be soft news. Local newspapers, radio stations, and news weeklies need a lot of filler stories with local or human interest. Here's where you come in. Let them know about a recent accomplishment or happening or offer your expert advice for home or business owners.

Publicity is free. I like free marketing. Don't you?

## Viral marketing on MySpace or Facebook

Here's another example of how to get free marketing. I helped a friend who was a marketing manager for a wholesaler of hair-care products do some viral marketing. The company, The Hair Factory, supplies hair for weaves and wigs to salons and uses a traditional catalog as its primary marketing method, supported by a telephone order center and a Web catalog that can process orders, too.

However, my friend wanted to find some creative ways to attract salon owners and build their customer base. For free. Hmmm. We had just done a series of photo shoots for the company's catalog and Web site, which gave me an idea. I created a MySpace page featuring some of the more interesting and artistic photographs, and sent friend requests initially to the models — many of whom were volunteers. They were so excited to see their model photos on MySpace that they told their friends about the page and soon more links were created. Gradually, salon owners got interested and picked up on the buzz — many of them had MySpace pages for their businesses, and they linked up to our page.

You can use a similar strategy on Facebook. Schools are learning that it makes sense to create their own Facebook page and offer links to alums. Private high schools and colleges that do fundraising are able to identify and build communications channels to potential donors this way. In fact, many products and services can have their own Facebook, MySpace, Friendster, or other online community. I have Friend links on my personal MySpace page to a number of businesses, along with the real human friends that make up the bulk of my Friend list.

For example, a local pizza shop friended me, and the owner seemed so nice and sincere that I accepted the link — and then went in to try the pizza. It was pretty good. Also, I have links to musical bands and other artists whose work I like and to some places that I like to visit or have good associations with (like the MySpace page for Harvard Square, which I feel friendly toward from my college years spent there).

Almost everyone is open to the right marketing-oriented links, but won't respond to obviously commercial and impersonal ones. It's tricky, but you *can* create a vital page for your business and make friends in cyberspace.

And yes, it's completely free! I like free. Don't you?

## Low-cost display ads in online communities

Insurance agencies seem to find www.friendster.com a great place to buy low-cost ads (which are displayed in a generously large right-hand column under the Suggestions header). The demographics of this online community favor auto insurance and other products for adults because members tend to be older than MySpace or Facebook members.

MySpace is a much bigger community, but it skews toward younger people, so it's better for consumer products than for business-to-business marketing or services oriented toward the middle-aged homeowner. Facebook is a young community, too, but every year, the average age of these online communities goes up by a year. Think about it. Soon, they'll tap into a full range of consumers and offer as good demographics as any marketing medium!

My advice to potential buyers of display ads on any of these pages is to visit the site, read their latest information about advertising options, and buy the cheapest, easiest entry-level ad. Test a message. See what happens. If you don't get a good response, try adjusting the message. You can run a half-dozen inexpensive experimental ads and see whether something clicks. If not, you haven't risked much of your budget. But if you find a formula that works, online communities are now so large that you can bump up the scale of your advertising and do some serious business on them.

## Text messages — a new viral marketing frontier?

You're a member of more online communities than you might think. I just got a text message on my phone that said, "Hi Everybody! I'm in a group show@ Gallery 51, 51 Church St, Montclair NJ reception Friday 6-9pm." It's from my friend James Adleman, a promising young painter. I own several large pieces by him, so it makes sense for him to include me in this informal news broadcast to all the phone numbers in his cell phone directory. Cell phone text messages are a very personal, informal medium, but for the right message (something your friends and acquaintances won't mind hearing about), they're a good way to do viral marketing. Check with your cellular telephone service provider to make sure that you have a plan with a cheap package rate for text messages; otherwise, they can be costly to send.

Of course, your phone cannot by itself reach a very large audience — unless you can get people to pass the word along, or you can get lots of people to give you their cell phone numbers. The latter strategy is working on college campuses for the broadcasting of security messages. One of my sons was working out in the gym at Seton Hall University recently when news spread rapidly about a request from the campus security office to stay inside the building. Someone had been spotted on the edge of campus with a gun. Nothing bad happened and the person was quickly arrested, but it was a good test of the school's new text message communications system. Thousands of people heard and shared the alert within a few minutes.

If you want to tell people about a special marketing event like a one-day blowout sale at your store, you may not get quite as much compliance as a public safety message does. However, the news is still of potential interest to lots of people, and you may want to enlist the growing power of telephone text messages to help spread the word. Although I don't know anyone who's tried this trick yet, I'm sure that we'll soon see special text message offers saying something like, *"Bring your phone in with this message to receive an additional 20% off our storewide sale 'til 9 p.m. tonight!"*

# The classic flier — tried, true, and free

It costs just a few cents to make a photocopy on colorful paper, and the turn-around at most copy shops is under an hour. *Fliers* — single sheets designed to be put under windshield wipers and doors or stuck to public bulletin boards and other public spaces — are a great way to get the word out locally for almost nothing.

Although some towns regulate fliers and will ticket you if you violate their rules, you can still distribute them in plenty of ways and in many places. Also, some stores (such as coffee shops, grocery stores, and convenience stores) have bulletin boards or other spots where they permit you to post approved notices. If you want to reach a local audience, a flier may be worthwhile.

 Simple is good: Copy your flier in one color and avoid complex designs. Select one or two simple, clean, easy-to-read fonts. Look at what others are posting in your area and try to make yours look a little more appealing and easy to read. Most fliers cram too much information onto the page. Design yours to be read in ten seconds or less, from a distance of 3 feet or more away. If you need to give a lot of information, refer to a Web site for followup or add a phone number for people to call. Keep it simple, and the classic flier will work far better.

While it will cost you a minimal fee to print fliers, the great thing about them is that you pay nothing for the exposure. They're placed in public spaces for free. Displaying advertising for free is very hard to do, so be grateful for this rare opportunity and treat it with respect. Appropriate (G-rated), friendly, professional-looking fliers are best and always be polite and respectful when looking for places to post or distribute them.

# The informational booklet or brochure

Many marketers forget about the value of technical or special knowledge. People don't want to be bothered with your sales pitch, but they sure love it when you offer to help them with their problem. And sometimes, the difference is just a matter of perception.

For example, I recommended that a surf shop create a tall, thin brochure-like publication (which they published inexpensively at their local copy shop). The cover was a picture of a long board — an old-fashioned surf board — along with the title "How to Find and Care for Classic Boards." The inside contained historical information about the long boards that once dominated the sport, tips about the different types and which ones are most usable or collectible today, plus care tips, a directory of places to find and trade used boards, profiles of the best early surfers and their boards, and other interesting information. The store's name, address, logo, and product line (which includes a good selection of used long boards) are modestly relegated to the back cover, so as to give the piece the feel of a real booklet, not an advertisement or brochure. The result of this kind of marketing material is something that people would pay good money for if it were sold in a bookstore. If you give it away for free, it will be very popular indeed.

A company in the lawn-and-yard-care business used a similar strategy: Recognizing that its clients were beginning to be concerned about chemical pesticides and herbicides, the company designed an informative booklet about organic lawns and how to care for them. The company gave it as a free gift to its current customers, and distributed it in local lawn and garden shops for a modest price. What a great way to establish your expertise and make yourself highly trustworthy in your local market!

In another example, a tourist-oriented restaurant in a resort community on the coast of Maine had hired an artist to design an appealing tourist map, which was printed on its paper placemats. Customers liked the map and often asked for a clean placemat on their way out. I recommended taking the art and printing it on a foldout brochure, along with promotional information and coupons to encourage a visit to the restaurant. The brochure doesn't have an advertising message on its cover. Instead, it says "Free Tourist Map and Coupons." The local Chamber of Commerce offered rack space, and now the tourist map is attracting customers to the restaurant. Better to use it to draw them in than to give it to them as they go out.

## The informational Web page or blog

Web sites are usually designed as if they're interactive sale catalogs. However, the sites that have the biggest and most consistent traffic are usually ones that give away useful information and are less commercial in nature. Channel 22 News in Springfield, Massachusetts, uses its Web site to inform the community about a remarkable range of topics. The site has a place where you can sign up for a dating service, as well as a great page for checking the local weather. The Web site also has the best listings of snow-day cancellations. It has informative content on how to install a hot tub or maintain a good lawn. It contains, really, just about everything. Getting married? Check the site for advice and tips. Looking for a perfect gift? Go to the site's gift section — which, by the way, is a money-maker because local businesses purchase small display ads there. But most of the site is free content that exists purely to attract and retain visitors. The idea is to create a user base that is loyal to the site and the TV station that sponsors it.

I use a similar strategy for one of my own Web sites — in fact, the site that supports readers of my marketing books. If you go to www.insightsfor-marketing.com, you'll see that the right half of the page features free articles you can download. The idea is to be an informative resource by giving away information about marketing, which ensures high traffic and decent visibility in search engines. I view it as a free way to build awareness of my books on marketing. Sure, I do give away information for free, but what does it cost me to post it on the Web? Almost nothing. My hosting charges are under a hundred dollars per year, so why not create a public resource? And all I want in return is some visibility. It's a *much* cheaper way to build brand awareness about my books than any form of paid advertising or direct mail.

Maybe you could do the same on your Web site. What special knowledge and information do you have that prospective customers might appreciate your sharing with them?

If you're an expert on something — anything — you might consider a blog. Once a week, a local owner of a garden center posts a new blog about some seasonal challenge for gardeners. In spring, the blog may contain tips on which shrubs to prune now and which ones to leave alone until after they flower. In fall, it might cover bulb planting and how to put your lawn to bed for the winter. Blogs are easy to create and post if you use a blog template and hosting service, such as the one offered by Google. You don't need to do HTML programming. You just need to have some interesting and/or useful things to say. If you're unfamiliar with this (completely free!) new medium, start reading other bloggers' work and get a feel for it before designing your own.

## Pay-per-click advertising (keyword ads)

Pay-per-click advertising isn't free, but it's very economical and you can easily control your costs. You can turn it on or off depending on your budget and results. And you can keep fiddling with your selection of key terms, the price you bid for a click on a key term, and the phrase that pops up to promote your link.

You need a Web page to link to, so if you don't already have one, you will have to spend some money to create one. But Web pages don't need to cost an arm and a leg. You can create your own simple one from an inexpensive template. (Google and many other companies offer them.) So even that requirement isn't a major barrier to using pay-per-click advertising.

I give you more information about how to use this powerful and inexpensive medium in Chapter 5. You can also go to the section of Google's or Yahoo!'s Web site that explains how to use its key-term advertising services. Pay-per-click advertising isn't rocket science, but it can help a marketing program take off.

## Pay-per-click advertising for the dogs?

Happy Hound is a daycare and boarding facility for dogs. Located in a warehouse in Oakland, California, it serves busy dog owners who drop off their pets on the way to work. The dogs have a great time playing in the warehouse. Suzanne Golter founded the business a few years ago and right away faced the classic entrepreneur's marketing problem: How to attract customers economically and quickly enough to cover her overhead. Warehouse rent is expensive. She needed clients.

She found her marketing zone after experimenting with a variety of advertising. Print ads in national magazines catering to pet owners were expensive and not local enough; they mostly reached people too far away to use her service. Newspaper advertising would have been better — more local — but it was also somewhat costly, and she felt her customers were too busy to read the newspaper. The best

tool she found — now her primary marketing method — was Google AdWords, which allows you to create small ads that appear in response to appropriate key-term Web searches. You can choose the geographic area, so she only had to pay for ads that ran within driving distance of her facility. In the early days, 90 percent of Happy Hound's business came from these simple, modestly priced Web ads.

Now, of course, word of mouth from happy Happy Hound customers tends to bring in referrals, so the business doesn't have to advertise as heavily. Once a local service business gets established, advertising probably should drop to secondary status and word-of-mouth referrals ought to become the primary source of new customers — assuming, of course, that service is good and people are happy enough to tell their friends and neighbors about the business.

## *Widgets, gadgets, and the like*

You may hear excited marketing chatter about *widgets*. Widgets look like tiny square Web pages that sit in their own window on another Web page. Sometimes they're obviously commercial. (eBay has widgets that show specific eBay listings and their status, for example.) Often, widgets are informative, entertaining, or fun. (Some of them are games, for example.)

If you search on the Web, you can easily find a variety of companies offering software you can use to build your own widgets, which may be a good idea if you're clever with your electronic fingers. If you come up with something that is really appealing, people may seek it out and put it on their home pages. Cool!

More likely, however, is that widgets will become yet another kind of paid Web ad — more interactive and interesting than most, but sold as ad space by the same players you go to now for pay-per-click listings (especially

Yahoo! and Google, the latter of which is promoting widgets under the name Gadget Ads as I write, although it won't surprise me if the name and details change as they work out the kinks in this new advertising medium).

# Word of mouth or referral marketing

If your service is good enough, all you need is one customer. This customer will be so impressed that he'll tell others to give you a try. And they will tell others, who will tell others. And soon you'll have more business than you need, without ever spending a dime on marketing.

Your quality better be notable and your people skills flawless, or customers won't talk you up.

I once was hired by an industrial company that was owned by a brilliant chemist. His clients were other companies, mostly manufacturers. He had several dozen good customers, but wanted me to audit his marketing to see whether he could grow the business more rapidly. I set out to audit his marketing activities by asking whether I could meet his sales force.

"We have no salespeople," he said.

I was surprised, but tried again. Could I review his mailings and print ads? "We don't do any of that," he admitted, looking somewhat embarrassed.

Next I asked about trade shows and directories. No, none of that, either. A Web site? Um, sorry, but no.

It turned out that this business was growing and making a profit with no marketing program at all. It had started with one loyal customer — a personal connection of the owner — and referrals had built it from there. I was amazed. This marketing was the simplest, cheapest program I had ever encountered. The trick to it was that the owner and his staff were extremely smart and helpful, and people really liked doing business with them. I finally threw up my hands and said I couldn't help. I suggested he call his customers instead and let them know he was looking for some new business. They quickly spread the word, and soon he had as much new work as he could handle.

I hope you can apply that story about the power of referrals to your own business. What can you do to make a more positive impression on each of your customers? How can you become their favorite vendor, service provider, or store? If you're better than 90 percent of your competitors, word of mouth will naturally lift your sales and bring you new business. All you have to do is do your job well and make an effort to be friendly and likeable whenever you interact with customers.

## Events, parties, and charity fundraisers

New retail stores sometimes throw Grand Opening parties, which attract attention and draw in the curious. I like parties. They're events, and people go to events. All you need is some helium-filled balloons, beverages, and finger foods on trays, and you can hold your own party. To pump it up, you can invite a local group of musicians to perform or tie into an art event. (If you let local artists display their travel or nature photos in your office or store, they'll show up for the party with friends and family members.)

Another good way to attract people and make your business visible is to offer space and support for a local charity to stage a fundraising or community event. Pick a charity that is compatible and of interest to your prospective customers, of course. Then let the enthusiasm draw a crowd.

Soft-sell at events and parties to keep the event from feeling too commercial. It's more than enough to get people to your place of business and let them meet you and your staff. Let them connect the dots later. I promise they'll remember you.

Sponsoring a local sports or charitable event is another way to make yourself visible in the community and to build goodwill. Mega-brands pursue these goals with multimillion-dollar TV and print ad campaigns, but the smaller and/or local marketer probably does better image building through events than through brand advertising. And the price is right — opportunities range from free to modest contributions or fees. And it feels great to see your company name on kids' sports uniforms or on the list of hosts or sponsors of a local charity.

## Better looking basics: Stationery, business cards, and brochures

I can't believe how poorly most businesses dress! They may have expensive ad campaigns or flashy Web sites, but if their mailings and business cards are poorly designed or cheaply printed, they're undermining their investment by not doing the basics well.

Take a hard look at your business card. Does it really present you and your business in the best possible way? Does it say "Wow!" or does it just mumble? Please don't ignore the cornerstones of business communication. Make sure that you always make a powerfully positive impression. See Chapters 6 and 7 if you want some how-to advice to bump up the impact of these low-cost but high-value marketing tools.

Another hidden problem in most marketing programs is a lack of consistency in image and presentation. If you don't present your brand name and related information in a consistent manner, both visually and verbally, you're not making the impact you ought to. Often, you can improve marketing response rates and boost sales just by reviewing the way you present your business in all existing formats, forums, and media. Go for a consistent impressive look, and good things will follow.

## Asking for the business

Another common marketing mistake is to fail to ask people to make a purchase. View every human interaction (whether in person, by phone, mail, or e-mail) as an opportunity to make a sale. It amazes me, when I consult, at how these opportunities are often wasted. Are you asking for the sale whenever possible, and using proper sales techniques when you ask? If not, check Part V of this book and look for ways to bump up your sales efforts.

Maybe this point is obvious, but a sales call is, at least in the short term, free. Yes, I agree that if you staff up with salespeople who receive a salary and/ or commission, the sales staff isn't free — but I'm talking about you or other staff sometimes popping your sales hat on and getting out there to make a few calls. That kind of marketing doesn't entail paying commissions to salespeople or sales reps. It just involves your remembering to ask for their business on a regular basis. My theory is that everyone in the business ought to do a little friendly soft selling. Everyone needs sales, right? Well, then they can help you find them. Making sales is everyone's responsibility. If you can instill that value, you can generate a lot of business that otherwise would be left unharvested.

I could go on for many more pages on the subject of low-cost ways to boost sales and maximize marketing impact. In fact, I have! CD0301 is a printable tip sheet with a dozen ideas you can check out. Maybe one of them will work for your business. Have a look!

# Harnessing the Power of Information

Information is usually free. Yet this commodity of the information age is rarely leveraged to full effect by marketers. I can't believe how fluffy and insubstantial most marketing communications are. Open any piece of promotional mail or visit any business's Web site to see what I mean. Do compelling, convincing, exciting, hard facts jump out at you? No? Well, they should. Powerfully presented information has the power to make your marketing communications much more effective.

Here are some tips for pumping up your marketing communications with well-presented information:

- ✔ Select your strongest fact or argument and emphasize it consistently.

- ✔ Prune your writing down so that you make your point clearly and simply.

- ✔ Strengthen your main point with three or more supporting facts or arguments.

- ✔ Use a *creative* approach to make your main point so that *people are not bored* by it!

Most ads are mediocre in their performance. They do okay, but they're not stars. Same with sales letters, sales presentations, Web pages, and so on. Marketing is a lot like most other areas of human performance in that there is a dominant midrange of intermediate level performances, and not that many high-end examples. I bring up this point because of the cost impact it has.

To illustrate the opportunity, I'm going to reach for the very first letter I find in the In Box on my desk. Hmmm. It's an oversized white envelope bulk-mailed to me from State Street, which I know is the latest brand name of a bank where I have some accounts. (My bank was acquired by a bigger bank, so my statement envelopes have taken on a new look recently.)

Now, what does my marketing eye make of this mailing from State Street Bank? Well, for starters, it isn't very attractive. The envelope looks like it is made of the cheapest possible paper, and it's very plain and boring. No information appears on the front other than my address and the return address; the back is completely blank. Tearing it open, I find a folded set of pages that are labeled Account Statement and have technical information about my holdings. The only other information provided is, "For Account Inquiries Call 1-800-xxx-xxxx."

This mailing is a wasted marketing opportunity! Plenty of space is available on the envelope, as well as within it, to print informative content about what this bank's other services may be, how it can help me, or what advice or tips it may have to make my financial life better and more secure. And what would it cost to add some of that information that could cement their relationship with customers and possibly cross-sell other services? Nothing. The mailing goes out every month anyway.

The next envelope in my In Box is, I'm amused to see, another statement from another bank where I do business. I open it and find that, in addition to my statement information, the bank includes a couple sentences about various special accounts it offers and who is eligible for them, along with a customer relations number. That's better! A little information can go a long way in the world of marketing.

Here are some questions to help you assemble hard-hitting facts that can bump up the impact of any marketing or advertising you do:

✔ What technical specifications or qualities can you mention in order to make your offering look as good as possible compared to the competition?

✔ What qualifications or experiences does your company or team bring to its work that might impress potential buyers?

✔ What special degrees, memberships, awards, or other honors have members of your team received?

✔ Who is already using your product or service? Get permission to name names or, better yet, ask for quotes or testimonials.

✔ What news coverage have you received that you could cite?

Facts and evidence, such as product specs, expert recommendations, media coverage, or customer testimonials, have tremendous impact. They can increase the effectiveness of your marketing communications and thereby reduce the amount you have to spend on communicating. More effective equals lower cost. It's a powerful equation. Take a look at your marketing and sales and see where you can add more evidence and information.

# Exercising Creativity: Ideas Are Free!

Creativity is the silver bullet of marketing programs. It can slay overspending and bring new life to your sales and profits. Maybe instead of searching for ways to cut costs or new media that are cheaper to use, you should go back to the drawing board and come up with some creative marketing concepts. It's like minting money in your basement — except it's completely legal.

A candle retailer in Durham, North Carolina, wanted a print ad that reminded consumers that candlelight is nice for the dinner table. Instead of the obvious (a photograph of a nicely set table with a candelabra in the middle), the company went for a stark white ad showing nothing but a generic light bulb. If you look closely at the bulb, it has written on it, in dull black ink where the technical specs usually go (in a circle at the top), the message, "How romantic can a 60-watt dinner be?" Good question! It gets you thinking in a creative way about how to stage a romantic dinner — and whether you need to stop by Pinehurst Candles and pick up some tapers for your table.

Creativity doesn't have to be clever. In fact, headlines with clever puns are rarely as effective as the copywriter thinks they're going to be. (Usually, the joke turns out to be on the marketer.) Creative concepts simply need to get the message across clearly and well. For example, a local insurance agency might have as its message that it doesn't just sell business insurance, it provides the benefit of 40 years of experience and expertise to its clients. Great! Service and support can make the difference. But how do you communicate this message creatively enough that it grabs consumers' attention and makes the point without your having to buy endless advertising and billboard space to repeat it?

Okay, get creative. How about a visual image to make the point? I'm seeing a spokesperson, someone who looks helpful, sage, and business-like. This wise mentor-like insurance consultant is, hmmm, leaning over someone's shoulder, pointing something out to him as he examines a complex document. The grateful customer is smiling, nodding, and saying, "Thanks. I was wondering how to control our rising insurance costs! This looks perfect!" Perhaps a high-quality posed photograph of this scene could be used in their ads and brochures?

That idea is called a creative concept. I'm not boasting — it's not really all *that* creative. Not compared to a Jackson Pollock canvas, for example. But it's sufficiently creative to bring the message to life with words and imagery.

Thinking visually is often a good approach when you want to harness the power of creativity to make your advertising more effective. Studies generally show that print ads that are between $1/4$ and $3/4$ art (a drawing, diagram, map, or photograph) have much more impact than ads that are mostly or all copy (words).

You can use creativity in all media, not just in print ads. Pump up your Web site the same way you would a print ad — except use streaming video instead of static art. (See Chapter 5 for more on visual appeals.) Also, make sure that your brochures, logo, business cards, billing statements, and, in fact, all communications that reach customers or prospects are creative enough to draw the eye and attract attention.

A dull speaker puts the audience to sleep. And dull marketing gets even less respect. By the way, that sentence uses a metaphor, and metaphors are a powerful creative tool for marketing. I will give you more tools and techniques for creativity in Chapter 12, but even if you don't read that chapter right away, you can start to harness the power of creativity by using simple, powerful metaphors to bring your message home more effectively.

Here's an example: The Australian winery Wolf Blass wanted to convey the sense that it's a bold leader in the industry. It decided to get this message across with a simple metaphor — the winery compared its brand to an eagle. The name "WOLF BLASS" is always shown in gold capital letters with a gold line drawing of an eagle spreading its wings directly above. The message is also reinforced with words — the tag line that always appears next to their logo reads, "Australian wine at its peak."

Can you compare your brand, product, or service to a bird or animal? If so, then this visual may be a good way to get your message across. For example, the camel epitomizes sustainability because it can store and conserve water for its desert habitat. Perhaps a camel would be a good image to associate with a company that does energy audits and consults on green construction methods? See whether you can come up with a good metaphor for your marketing message.

# Narrowing Your Focus to Cut Costs and Maximize Impact

In Chapter 1, I introduce you to the concept of a marketing zone — the set of formulas that you develop for optimizing your marketing and making it reasonably predictable and reliable. I also share the important insight that good marketing needs to have a tight focus and not be spread too thin. When you find your zone and get your marketing program well tuned, you'll discover that you're focused in two ways: You know what your message is, and you know what your primary medium is for delivering it. This focus is the secret to economical marketing. It produces marketing programs that generate a lot of leads and sales from relatively little effort.

Unfortunately, most marketing is not well focused on either of these areas. Or is that a fortunate thing? Maybe so, because it means you can follow an obvious path toward better performance and lower marketing costs.

## Focusing your marketing message

What exactly is the benefit of your product or service? Why should people buy from you?

If your answer varies or is lengthy, confusing, unconvincing, or uncertain, then you need to focus your message more sharply. I have to be brutally honest with you: I don't think your message is clearly defined or communicated with sufficient consistency. I think your marketing communications lack focus. A lack of focus is a problem for 99 percent of my clients, so I imagine it could be for you, too.

Take a look at any well-positioned consumer brand for inspiration on how to focus your message. They often are good examples of highly focused marketing that hits the same powerful positioning message over and over.

And you don't have to be a multibillion-dollar consumer products giant like Frito-Lay or Procter & Gamble to use this strategy. For example, the brand of bottled water called Pure Mountain Spring Water is, according to its Web site (puremountainspringwater.com), a fourth-generation family business that bottles water from a pristine reservoir on Cobb Mountain (in California's Lake County). All its packaging says the same thing: Pure Mountain Spring Water. Its bills (to customers who have the water delivered to their homes and offices) also repeat the product's claim to fame, because the company name, Pure Mountain Spring Water, is apparent on every communication. You can't help but get the message. The marketing message is 100 percent clear, just like the water. No competing messages or confusion is allowed to cloud it.

This water is. . . . Well, I don't need to repeat that marketing message, as you already know it by heart. But do your customers and prospects know *your* message by heart? Think about it. Do something about it.

To make sure that you're focusing your message and basing it on a strong foundation of compelling evidence, open file CD0302 and take a look at the Message Pyramid, a simple way to diagram your message strategy. I filled it in for my example, Pure Mountain Spring Water, so that you can see how you can use this tool to clarify and focus a marketing message. Give it a try!

## *Focusing your marketing program*

In Chapter 1, I introduce the concept of a well-focused marketing program and diagram it as a pyramid. The idea is simple but powerful: At least a quarter of your effort and spending should be concentrated on the single most effective marketing activity, or your program will be too scattered and unfocused to be effective. When you figure out what the right focus is, your marketing runs smoothly and profitably, and you enter what I call your marketing zone.

The reason you need to focus your marketing program on one primary method and several secondary methods is that this approach is the most cost-effective and efficient way to market. It is difficult to be noticed; it is hard to be heard. There is what marketers call "noise" in all the communications channels you're using to try to reach prospective customers. Lots of information is competing for their attention. You have to focus your program if you want to rise above the background noise.

For example, running a few 30-second radio ads a week probably won't produce any significant impact, because people won't really pay attention. You probably need to run a few dozen to get your message across, but you won't be able to afford it if you're also spending money on billboards, a direct mailing, several new Web sites, and an event at the same time you're trying to hit the market with radio ads.

If you lack tight focus, narrow your program and concentrate more effort and resources in one lead marketing method. I have a hunch you'll see more bang for your marketing buck as soon as you identify the most productive marketing activities and focus your resources on them.

Don't get me wrong: You still need to have a lot of things going on at once in most marketing programs. Your business cards and letterhead need to look sharp and should use the same version of your logo and tag line as your latest catalog or Web page does. Your packaging should be carefully designed to maximize appeal (if you sell a packaged good). Your house list of customers needs a friendly mailing, telephone call, or e-mail at least once a month, and so on. You always have to juggle many activities and media, but you need to decide which are the most important — and be tough as nails about defending their dominance.

Give your primary method between a third and a half of your attention and budget, or it won't have enough fertilizer to grow healthy sales and profits for you.

# On the CD

Check out the following items on the CD-ROM:

- ✔ Tips for Boosting Sales (CD0301)
- ✔ The Message Pyramid (CD0302)

# Part II
# Advertising Management and Design

# In this part . . .

Do you ever advertise? If not, I can honestly say that you better think about starting because there are few businesses that couldn't benefit from well-designed, carefully placed advertising. If you do already use this powerful medium, then you no doubt know how expensive it can get and how hard designing an ad that really achieves its business objectives can be. Careful planning — which I show you how to do in Chapter 4 — is the answer to these problems. Ads can accomplish a lot of profitable objectives, but only if you clearly define them upfront and then design your campaign appropriately.

Ads absolutely must be well designed. They need to look good, read well, sound great, catch the eye, make a lasting impression, and be the stuff of dinner conversation. In short, ads have to be powerful. In Chapter 5, I share my best ideas and techniques for building powerful ads that really make an impact on your customers and on your sales. Promise me that you'll read it carefully and that you won't ever run an ad that lacks power and punch.

# Chapter 4

# Planning and Budgeting Ad Campaigns

## In This Chapter

▶ Calculating a practical average cost per ad

▶ Calculating your ad budget as a percentage of your overall sales

▶ Adjusting your budget based on gross profit

▶ Planning your ad campaign

▶ Preparing a budget that achieves high ad frequency

▶ Designing business-to-business ad plans and budgets

▶ Preparing an objective-and-task budget

$B$efore you start designing specific ads, you really need to create an advertising plan. In this chapter, I help you plan how much you want to spend on advertising and how you ought to spend it.

You can easily spend more money than you've imagined in your wildest dreams because ads can be very expensive — but please don't! In this chapter, I show you how to set some practical limits on your advertising campaign to make sure that you're laughing, not crying, all the way to the bank.

## A Practical Approach to Ad Budgets

I feel like I need to start this chapter with a bold, flashing WARNING! sign in the middle of the road. If you're approaching advertising as a midsized or small consumer business or as a midsized business that sells to other businesses (B2B), you have to proceed with special caution. Why? Because all the expert advice and conventional wisdom about advertising is based on what works for giant consumer brands.

I don't know why all the advertising textbooks are based on what's best for Sony, McDonald's, Toyota, and Coca–Cola when most businesses need a very different approach, but that's how it is. In this chapter, I break with tradition and show everyone else how they need to approach advertising.

Your CD contains a White Paper I wrote titled *Budgeting for Advertising: A Practical Approach* (CD0401), which explores the difference between a corporate ad campaign for a chain of restaurants and a local ad campaign for a single family-owned restaurant. The corporate approach has several qualities that the local restaurant owner should be wary of:

✔ Large scale (multiple stores throughout a region or a country), which makes frequent, expensive TV ads practical and effective for the corporate marketer

✔ Deep pockets, which means that the corporate marketer can choose to invest in extra advertising without immediate payback

✔ A focus on expansion, which gives the corporate marketer more reason to invest in pure brand-building without the need for immediate sales and profits to show for it

When you operate at a relatively small scale and want to make profits every year, you can't just scale back the corporate advertising budget. Most businesses would need to spend their entire annual advertising budget to create just one high-quality, 30-second TV ad and run it a handful of times. That ad would be useless because you need to run ads many times in order to make an impact. The most important rule for practical small-business advertising is *Use cheap ads so that you can run them frequently without going broke!*

## Setting your ad budget

Imagine that you're the owner of a local restaurant — a steak house, a seafood joint, an upscale business lunch place, or whatever would be most successful in your local market. To start with, you need to consider your advertising plan in the context of the overall budget. Is the business profitable? If so, then some of that profit ought to be directed into advertising.

Advertising is a business expense, so it comes out of pretax profits.

If you can afford to put 5 percent of your gross sales into advertising *without posting a loss,* then plan to do so. If not — if you have a profitability problem — then stop worrying about advertising and start looking hard at your cost structure. Make necessary cuts first. Get the business at least to break even. If this means scaling back and reducing your payroll, moving to a smaller location with cheaper rent, or otherwise changing your business plan, then make these needed changes first.

Advertising is powerful — but not powerful enough to dig you out of an unprofitable business model unless you have a lot of extra cash to invest and are *sure* that your business will be profitable if you increase the size of your customer base just a little more. Meeting these conditions isn't easy. Often, when people try to spend their way out of a loss, they find they have to spend more on advertising than they had initially expected, and the losses get bigger and swamp them. Remember that you should be *spending gross profits* on advertising and making sure that the underlying business model is sustainable.

With that caution in mind, I'm now going to show you how to budget and plan an annual ad campaign, using a local restaurant business as my working example.

Table 4-1 shows the annual income statement for such a restaurant. (It's a simplified budget, so please don't use it as a template for doing your business accounting. See *Accounting Workbook For Dummies* by John A. Tracy and speak to your accountant if you don't already have a budgeting process.)

| Table 4-1 | Calculating a Percent-of-Sales Ad Budget | | |
|---|---|---|---|
| | *Year 1* | *Year 2* | *Year 3* |
| Goal: 10% growth, family-owned restaurant: | | | |
| **Sales** | **$1,366,770** | **$1,503,447** | **$1,653,792** |
| Food costs at 36% | $478,370 | $526,206 | $578,827 |
| Packaging at 6% | $68,339 | $75,172 | $82,690 |
| Labor at 25% | $273,354 | $300,689 | $330,758 |
| Overhead at 20% | $259,686 | $285,655 | $314,220 |
| Total Operating expenses | $1,079,748 | $1,187,723 | $1,306,495 |
| **Gross profit** | **$287,022** | **$315,724** | **$347,296** |
| Advertising set at 5% of sales = | **$67,770** | **$75,172** | **$82,690** |

The two key lines in Table 4-1 for setting your ad budget are *sales* and *gross profit.* Total sales multiplied by 0.05 tells you what your 5 percent target is going to be. Gross profits tells you if you can afford to spend 5 percent of sales. In the case in Table 4-1, 5 percent of sales is considerably less than gross profits, so the ad budget is affordable and I would recommend investing in it in order to help the business achieve next year's sales target of 10 percent growth. (Remember to adjust the percentages to reflect your own expenses.)

If the 5 percent goal isn't affordable (gross profits are too low to cover it), you may be forced to reduce your ad budget. Be a pragmatist and cut back — that's just how it goes. However, also make sure that you adjust your sales projections for the coming year, because less advertising means lower sales. And reducing your sales forecast will, of course, reduce your gross margin (because some expenses are *fixed* — meaning that they don't vary with sales). Therefore, you also have to make some *cost cuts* in order to salvage your next year of business. Cut costs until you can project a healthier gross profit for next year. Don't try to advertise your way out of a losing business plan — it takes more than advertising to succeed; it also takes firm financial management.

## Planning your ad campaign

After you're confident that you can afford to put at least a few percent of your sales into advertising, you're ready to think about how to spend that budget. Here's a simple, practical approach to planning your ad campaign:

1. **Decide how many ads you need to place over the course of the year and pick a goal for this variable.**

   For most businesses, the goal should be to run more than 100 ads per year. By number of ads, I'm referring to frequency of exposure. You can accomplish the same frequency with one ad, run 100 times, as with five ads, run 20 times each. Which is best? It will depend on how effective the first ad is and whether you need to replace it. You can work out such details later in your process, but for now, just focus on budgeting enough to run a high number of ads.

    If you're uncertain about how many ads you need to run, don't feel bad; this decision is tough, and even experts at big ad agencies have no hard and fast rules. However, keep in mind that major, big-budget ad campaigns try to expose prospective customers to ads very frequently — perhaps many times a day. (Witness the frequent repetition of TV ads.) If you're a normal — that is to say, not a huge — business, you can't do that. But what *can* you do? Can you at least expose people to your message once a week? How about two or three times a week? That may be an affordable goal. (After all, a single billboard can expose commuters to your message once every workday.) If high frequency proves not to be affordable for you, then narrow your focus to a smaller target market, which allows you to run ads that cost less because they reach a smaller audience. You're better off reaching a small audience often than you are reaching a huge audience just a few times. It *does* take repetition to have an impact. And it takes repetition to make an impression. In fact, you really need to repeat your message frequently. Okay, you get the point!

2. **Divide your overall budget by your frequency goal.**

   This result tells you what your average ad ought to cost. If you buy ads the way big corporate advertisers do, you'll blow your budget on overpriced ads and won't be able to afford to repeat your message frequently. That's why you need to do this simple math before you shop for ads. In the example of a restaurant with an ad budget of about $68,000, a frequency goal of at least 150 ad placements would mean that the average ad cost needs to be around $450 ($68,000 ÷ 150).

3. **Armed with the knowledge from your analysis of what your total budget is and what your average ad cost ought to be, explore the options available to you in your local market.**

   As you examine options, look for media that reach *your* customers well. For example, a newspaper that reaches the majority of homeowners in your city or town is a good place to advertise things homeowners buy, such as furniture, lawn care, or dinners out (when they get sick of cooking in). A national magazine on home remodeling isn't as good a match for you if you have a local business, because many of its readers are outside your market area.

Table 4-2 is an example of a spending plan based on a budget of $67,700 and an average ad cost of around $450 so that the business can run at least 150 separate ads over the course of the year. Actually, this plan will achieve considerably higher frequency — probably twice that much — because it includes some package buys. That's fine. There's no harm in exceeding your frequency goal — just make sure you don't come in under it. In this example, I used ad prices for a typical small city, but pricing will vary depending on the size of the population in your local area.

Contact your local media and ask for quotes or rate cards to get actual ad pricing. Most ads are sold by salespeople — real human beings who can talk to you on the phone, answer your questions, and sometimes even negotiate a good deal if you ask nicely. So don't be shy. Spend a day or two calling and e-mailing to find out what the options are within your market area and price range.

Keep in mind that the rate per ad should come down proportionately with the frequency. Also contact publications close to their closing date for insertion orders. Many times, they're not at full capacity and are more willing to cut you a deal.

| Table 4-2 | Ad Plan and Budget for a Local Restaurant | | |
|---|---|---|---|
| **Type of Advertisement** | **Cost*** | **Frequency** | **Total Cost** |
| Daily newspaper 3 column inch display ad (40K circulation) | $50 | 40 | $2,000 |
| Daily newspaper 9 column inch display ad | $265 | 20 | $5,300 |
| Newspaper insert (color card) | $2,000 | 11 | $22,000 |
| Internet radio ad package (through TargetSpot), monthly | $2,500 | 5 | $12,500 |
| Google localized key term search advertising, monthly cap on costs of $300 | $300 | 10 | $3,000 |
| Back of bus poster, monthly, per bus | $300 | 36 | $10,800 |
| Sponsorship of weekend crafts fair, with signage on site plus radio mentions (estimated number of ads) | $5,500 | 21 | $5,500 |
| ValPak single panel coupon in cooperative mailing to local households** | $600 | 11 | $6,600 |
| Total*** | | 154 | $67,700 |
| Annual sales | | | $1,366,770 |
| Ad budget as percent of sales | | | 5.0% |

Notes:
* Cost adjusted for any quantity discounts.
** Does not include cost of redeeming coupons, which will depend on the nature of the offer. See Chapter 8.
*** Total does not include package buy of radio spots, so actual frequency will be higher.

A spreadsheet based on Table 4-2 is provided on your CD (file CD0402). None of the cells are locked, so you can edit it to fit your own ad plan. If you enter your annual sales in the correct cell, a formula will calculate the percent of sales your ad spending works out to, so you can keep adjusting your plan until you hit your percentage target.

My budget for this family-owned restaurant is based on a mix of public advertising (bus posters and signs at an event), Friday and weekend newspaper display ads, experimental Web-radio ads, Google key term ads, plus a newspaper special insert and coupon mailings approximately once a month (see Table 4-2). The local market will be fairly well saturated with advertising. The marketing zone pyramid (see Chapter 1) for this business is based on using newspaper advertising as the primary method, with two other types of ads (event sponsorship, bus posters) in secondary supporting roles, plus by-mail coupons as the third supporting method. The Google keywords advertising and Web radio ads are somewhat experimental, as I'm imagining the restaurant is a traditional business. However, if either of them really makes an impact, I'd recommend giving them more of the budget next year and reducing the newspaper and bus advertising correspondingly.

## Adjusting the ad budget for a B2B plan

If you're working on a B2B (business to business) marketing plan, you should use the same method and logic described in the preceding section, but should favor professional venues for your advertising instead of consumer-oriented ads. You won't participate in a mailing of coupons to homes, but you'll probably want to pay to be listed in online business directories. Similarly, you should substitute advertising in business and trade publications for the newspaper advertising. And you'll probably spend less overall on advertising because you'll want to budget something for personal selling, trade shows and exhibitions, or other business-oriented marketing activities. However, the same basic rule applies: Work up a budget that is pragmatic and sustainable because it's funded out of your gross profits and make sure that you buy inexpensive ads so that you can afford to run them frequently.

B2B ad plans take a secondary seat behind the sales plans if personal selling is important to the business. Your sales force ought to be paid largely on commission (to reduce your risk), and commissions can range from 10 to 25 percent depending on the industry and business. The high commissions mean the cost of sales is much higher than with advertising — but usually price and quantity make up for the high cost of sales in a B2B plan.

If you're budgeting sales force commissions plus overhead (which encompasses items such as sales collateral material and travel expenses), then you're probably going to need to keep advertising to a more modest level — somewhere around 1 to 3 percent of sales.

To get started, I suggest you work up an ad plan based on 2.5 percent of gross sales and see what it looks like. Often, B2B marketers can get away with half as much advertising as consumer marketers, so you can start with this amount as your working assumption until you gain enough experience to know what your marketing zone formula actually is.

# Tailoring Your Advertising Plan to a Specific Goal

The preceding section covers my modified version of a classic percent-of-sales budgeting process. The modifications I made had to do with keeping it in line with your profits, and making sure that you had realistic expectations about what types of ads you can afford given your scale of operations. Other than these adjustments, the method is quite common and traditional and many businesses have used it with success.

Now I want to share an alternative method that is a bit more sophisticated, and may be worth the added trouble. If you want to dig into the differences between ad options and refine your plan based on which give you the best return on investment, you may want to use a more sophisticated method: the objective and task method of designing an ad plan and budget. This approach is common among large corporate advertisers instead of smaller businesses, but you certainly can use it — and you may want to at least take a look at the approach before finalizing your plans.

You're not advertising for the right reasons if you're thinking things like

- ✔ "We do some advertising just to keep ourselves visible, but I don't think it affects our sales."

- ✔ "We try to match our competitors' advertising because customers expect it."

- ✔ "We've always done advertising; I don't know if it really works, but we're afraid of what might happen if we stop."

If you aren't sure why you're advertising or what you'll accomplish with it, you may need to do a careful analysis of your situation and market and build a new advertising budget and plan based on your specific goals or objectives.

Table 4-3 lists examples of objectives or goals that advertising can help you accomplish. To use a goal-based approach to advertising (also called *objective-based* or *objective-and-task-based advertising*), select a strategic goal such as one listed in Table 4-3.

| Table 4-3 | Examples of Ad Goals and Indicators |
|---|---|
| *Goal* | *Indicator* |
| Boost sales | Sales rise when and where the ad runs. |
| Generate calls | The telephone rings off the hook in the week after the ad runs. |
| Generate by-mail responses | Responses come in by mail in large numbers the week after the ad first runs. |
| Introduce new product | Requests for and press coverage of the new product increase significantly right after the ad appears. |
| Switch customers from competing product | Sales go up next month as a result of switching. |
| Encourage word of mouth | Current and past customers begin to talk, stimulating sales to people who say they "heard about you from someone they know." |
| Increase your share of market | Your sales grow faster than the leading competitors' sales over the course of a year. |
| Recruit new distributors | You hear from multiple distributors who are interested in working with you. |
| Help build sales by building image or reputation | Sales grow gradually but definitely do grow, along with rapid improvements in image and enhanced reputation. |
| Attract more upscale buyers | You sell higher-priced products or find that you can raise your prices or no longer have to negotiate as many discounts. |
| Attract a different group of customers | Your sales to the new group increase over the course of a year. |
| Cross-sell new product to current customers | You sell more of the new product to your current customer base during the year than you did last year. |
| Get more shoppers to visit your store(s) | Monthly store traffic and sales figures increase. |

After you have a clear goal or purpose for your advertising, identify appropriate indicators to track your success. Your sales figures are probably going to be an important measure, but profits may also be important, as well as more specific things, such as whether you succeed in raising your prices or increasing the average size of a sale. Think about what you want to accomplish and be prepared to measure it so that you can see whether you're making progress toward your goal.

Notice that every objective in Table 4-3 links to a specific outcome that you can track to see whether you achieved the objective. If you see movement in the measure, then the ad is working toward its objective. If you don't, then the ad isn't working, and you need to improve it or scrap it in favor of a new design.

The ultimate objective, of course, is to generate sales from your ads. For example, if you run an ad designed to get more people into your store, the ultimate objective is to increase sales in that store. So you need to measure the ad by its impact on sales, as well as on more specific and short-term measures, such as the number of people visiting a store.

Also notice that I added a desired outcome in each of these descriptions of an advertising objective in Table 4-3. Each statement includes some what-to-do information and also some indicator of how you know whether it's working. I want you to be this specific when you define your own advertising objectives. That way, you can create or purchase advertising that has a very clear purpose in mind, and then you're able to watch its performance and see whether it's doing what you said it ought to. One of the most fundamental rules of good management is that accountability is important — and advertising is certainly not above this accountability rule.

## Budgeting based on goals

The concept of budgeting based on goals is simple: Decide what you want to accomplish and then design an ad campaign that will achieve your goals. It won't work that way in reality, unfortunately, but it's a great theory. If you can apply this idea even partially, it can strengthen your advertising budget and plan.

Here's how to budget based on goals:

1. **Set your objective.**

   For example, you may choose the goal of expanding the customer base for a local restaurant by attracting a business lunch crowd to supplement your traditionally busy dinner seating.

2. **Clarify the gap between current and desired results.**

   For example, a restaurant owner may decide to create a three-fold increase in lunchtime business, while sustaining the current level of dinner business.

3. **Make a list of types of advertising that may be effective in achieving your goal.**

   For example, you may decide to hire someone to drop off menus and coupons at office buildings in your area in order to encourage local employees to eat lunch at your restaurant.

4. **Think about the scale of advertising needed to achieve your goal.**

   Is the gap between your current sales and your goal a large one? If so, then you need to scale up your advertising in order to fill this gap. You'll probably need to bump up your sales by a factor of 25 to 50 percent at a minimum.

5. **Set a target for your overall budget that is appropriate to (proportional with) the scale of your goals.**

   Don't set your sights high and your budget low, or you're bound to be disappointed.

After you've gone thoughtfully through these steps, you'll have a clearer idea of what might need to change in your approach to advertising. You'll have some ideas about new and different types of ads and/or media to use, and you'll have a general sense of whether your historic levels of advertising are appropriate or whether you need to bump up your budget in order to accomplish an ambitious goal.

The strategic thinking involved in goal-based budgeting is especially helpful when you're trying to achieve something new and different with your advertising. However, coming up with a specific budget level through this goal-based approach isn't easy. I recommend starting with the more specific and practical percent-of-sales method described in the section "A Practical Approach to Ad Budgets" earlier in this chapter and then using a goal-based analysis to refine your budget and focus your approach to advertising.

# Using an Advertising Objectives Worksheet

While the goal-oriented approach is especially useful when you're designing individual ads, writing an effective ad is a lot easier when you have a clear goal or objective in mind. For example, if I'm a B2B supplier of industrial machinery and my goal is to boost sales of my newest product, I need to remember this goal as I design ads. An ad that tells the history of my company may be impressive and confidence-inspiring, but it doesn't address the goal of pushing the new product into the market. Instead, I ought to plan some show-and-tell ads that convince prospects that this new product is superior. I may also want to think about a special offer, such as a one-month free trial. These ideas are focused on the goal, so they make more sense than a general ad about my company.

To help you give your ads a purposeful focus, I include an Advertising Objectives Worksheet on the CD (CD0403). Print multiple copies of it and use it for brainstorming as you think about what your ads should accomplish.

The worksheet in CD0403 forces you to design your ad campaign one ad at a time. Each ad should stand on its own as a goal-oriented plan that makes both strategic and economic sense. Use the worksheet to estimate the costs and results of each ad. Plan to run the ad and others like it enough times to achieve your overall objective. The worksheet keeps you honest by forcing you to make a reasonable estimate of what each ad can accomplish. Its bottom line is the sum of the impact of each individual ad or flight of ads. Adjust the mix of ads in your worksheet until you're satisfied that you have a good selection of ads that achieves your goals efficiently (with a good return on your advertising investment).

The Advertising Objectives Worksheet is a helpful tool for analyzing specific ads and for summing up their overall impact on your marketing program. For the sake of analysis, an *ad* means a specific advertisement run in a specific medium a specific number of times. So, in a budget for my own training-materials company, for example, I may define ad No. 1 as "4-x-4-inch ad on Conflict Assessment, three months in *Training* magazine." And I may define ad No. 2 as "Direct-mail script #22, to house list with new catalog." To keep track of these specifics, I write a clear description of each ad in the Description column of the spreadsheet.

When you use the Advertising Objectives Worksheet on your computer, you'll see (to the right of the Cost of Ad column) that the spreadsheet calculates the return on investment for each ad. If the result is 1, the ad breaks even, which means that its expected revenue-generating power is equal to its cost. If the result is above 1, you're making a profit on the ad. If you aren't sure which ads (combinations of a specific ad design and insertion in a medium of your choice) to use the most, then look at this column and repeat the ads with the highest returns on investment.

If you aren't sure what to enter under the Reach (number of prospects) column in the worksheet, ask whoever sells space or time in the advertising media of interest to you. Almost all media you buy ad space from will have statistics on whom they reach, and they almost always give away detailed profiles of audience or readership for free to anyone who's interested in advertising with them.

Note that the worksheet defines reach as the number of *prospects,* not just the number of warm bodies. Sometimes these numbers are the same; sometimes they aren't. For example, if you're promoting a product that mostly women buy, then you want to enter the number of women (your prospects in this case) who read a magazine into the Reach column, not the total number of people in the magazine's readership.

## *Preparing a month-by-month ad plan*

The Advertising Objectives Worksheet can be helpful as you work up a list of advertising plans for the year. After you've done your research on ad options and prices and have thought about what sorts of ads you need to run and how many of them you need, you should have a pretty good list. (It's never perfect — you'll no doubt revise it many times as you see what results you achieve during the year.) With this preparation, you can return to your overall ad budget and prepare a more accurate and thoughtful version of it.

You have two options now. You can go back to the simple ad budget format in CD0402 and revise it based on any insights your goal analysis gave you. Or if you want to create a more complex and detailed plan, you have the option of using the Advertising Budget Worksheets in CD0404.

The Advertising Budget Worksheets in CD0404 are two linked Excel spreadsheets. The first spreadsheet (see Tab 1) asks you to enter spending levels per month for all the different types of ads you plan to run. (Leave some of the rows blank — nobody should use all the options in this worksheet at the same time!) After you fill in the monthly worksheet, Tab 2 will automatically produce a summary in the form of an annual budget. Handy, isn't it?

You may find as you use the worksheets in CD0404 that your monthly plans produce an overly expensive annual budget. Keep an eye on the bottom line total for the year and make sure that it's reasonable. If you aren't sure what a reasonable overall ad budget might be, see the section "Setting your ad budget," earlier in this chapter, and set a percent-of-sales goal (roughly 5 percent for consumer marketing, roughly 2.5 percent for B2B marketing). Then review your goals and gaps and adjust accordingly. But don't forget that you have to fund the ad plan, so it ought to be less than gross profits. If not, worry about your costs and come back to your ad budget later.

## *Staying flexible throughout the year*

Sometimes I hear from readers who say something like, "Okay, I've created a detailed ad plan and budget, but I'm still not sure it's right. How can I be certain I've done it correctly?"

My answer usually shocks them. The fact is, you *can't* be sure your budget and plan are correct. There are no certainties in advertising. That means you need to stay flexible, keep an eye on performance, and adjust your plan from time to time throughout the year.

Here are some ways you may want to adjust your plan:

- If sales are disappointingly low, consider cutting back on general brand-building ads while simultaneously increasing your sales promotions and direct response ads in the hope that they'll quickly boost sales.

- If one of the ads you run doesn't seem to be working, drop it from your budget and increase your spending on a more effective ad.

- If sales are higher than you expected and you're unable to increase your capacity fast enough, cut back on your advertising and channel some of that money into hiring more people, ordering more materials, or whatever you need to do to meet demand.

These examples are adjustments that marketers can make at any point during the year.

Sometimes ad reps (the people who sell advertising space or time) try to lock you into big contracts by offering enticing discounts. But is the commitment worth the additional discount? Remember you're trading flexibility for price. I favor flexibility, especially if I'm trying a new ad campaign and am not sure how it will go. But don't forget that a few ads won't be enough in any medium or ad venue to make an impact. Midsized and small businesses are always at a disadvantage because they can't advertise at the high frequency that marketing giants can. Avoid spreading your ads too thin. Run at least a dozen ads in a row in the same place (for example, the same newspaper or Web site). So long as you think you're getting a response, keep advertising in the same place.

# On the CD

Check out the following items on the CD-ROM:

- Budgeting for Advertising: A Practical Approach (CD0401)

- Annual Advertising Budget and Plan (CD0402)

- Advertising Objectives Worksheet (CD0403)

- Monthly & Annual Advertising Budget Templates (CD0404)

# Chapter 5

# Shortcuts to Great Ads

**S**imple, inexpensive approaches to ad design are best for most marketing plans, because the goal is to keep your design and prepress costs low. (I recommend you cap them at 5 percent of your ad budget.) That way, most of your advertising budget is spent on actually getting those ads out in front of potential buyers. If your ads aren't award winners, that's okay. Just make sure that they're professional and simple enough that the message gets through loud and clear. And make them visually appealing because that's usually the secret to noticeable, memorable ads.

In this chapter, I help you conceive of good ads and mock them up or (in some cases) design them fully, using nothing fancier than a basic computer running Microsoft Word. Word has a decent and simple-to-use drawing toolbar, plus a lot of basic templates, and it can produce output in PDF format, which a growing number of printers and ad departments are happy to accept.

## Following Do-It-Yourself Shortcuts

One of my favorite ways to think about a new ad I need to design is to leaf through a copy of *The New York Times Sunday Magazine,* studying the ads and pulling out examples of ad layouts that I think may fit my needs. (I like looking in the *Sunday Magazine* because its advertising space is expensive, so I usually find a lot of carefully designed ads that inspire me. However, if I am designing a mailing, I prefer to go through the junk mail I receive for inspiration.)

Of course, you can't just cut someone else's brand name out of an ad and paste yours in. But you *can* get lots of starting ideas for different ways to communicate your message and achieve your advertising objective. (Make sure that you have a clear objective for your ad — something simple and persuasive to communicate.)

## The tried-and-true visual appeal ad

If you look at a large number of print ads in any well-read consumer or professional magazine, you'll begin to see some basic ad templates repeated over and over, each time with a fresh new combination of imagery and language. Most commonly, many consumer magazines run one- or two-page full-color ads featuring a striking or beautiful photograph with a simple headline that usually contains a play on words to help catch and hold attention (but you don't have to have a cute headline — serious is fine, too). The ad always includes the brand name and the tag line explaining the brand's basic brilliance and appeal. (If you don't already have a clear statement of what makes your product or service compelling to buyers, think about that and write a simple, compelling, one-sentence description of why your brand is great.) At the bottom, the ad may have a sentence or two of explanatory copy. Figure 5-1 illustrates a basic layout sized for a full-page magazine ad.

The basic visual ad template in Figure 5-1 works for almost everything — including clothing, automobiles, cosmetics, travel destinations, business services, and life insurance. Just vary the image and wording to fit your product (the illustration in Figure 5-1 would be good for a travel or tourism theme). The layout may work for you, and you can adapt it to a Web ad, brochure, postcard, or poster, too.

To make a visual appeal ad, start by seeking a photograph (or other illustration such as the original oil painting by Harold Newton used in Figure 5-1) that is glue to the eye — and also make sure you can somehow relate the image to the essence of your appeal. For example, if you sell computer maintenance services to businesses, you might choose the message, "We keep you performing at your peak" and illustrate it with a beautiful photograph of a noble snow-covered mountain peak rising out of cloud-covered lowlands.

But where will you find that stunning photo of a mountain peak? I thought you'd never ask! Go to stock photography Web sites (see the upcoming list) and rifle through them to see whether something strikes your fancy. Then use your headline to relate the image to your message.

If you decide to use a stock photograph in your ad, contact the stock photography house directly to find out what it will charge for your intended usage. The cost typically ranges from as low as $100 to as high as $1,000, depending on what you have in mind. I usually budget $250 up front for a photo, because that amount seems to be about the average for my work in the past.

**Figure 5-1:**
A basic
layout with
headline,
illustration,
caption,
body copy,
and logo.

You can view and license the rights to photographs at Web sites such as

- ✔ **Jupiter Images:** www.ablestock.com
- ✔ **Corbis:** www.corbis.com
- ✔ **Comstock Images:** www.comstock.com
- ✔ **Photolibrary:** www.photolibrary.com
- ✔ **Getty Images:** www.gettyimages.com
- ✔ **Fotosearch Stock Photography:** www.fotosearch.com
- ✔ **iStockphoto:** www.istock.com

# Become a desktop publisher?

Increasingly, entrepreneurial marketers are designing their own print ads and submitting them in the Acrobat Portable Document Format (PDF) output option that all graphic design programs, and even Microsoft Word, support. (You may bump into the term PDF/X, which refers to certain standards for how you save the PDF file so as to make it more printer-friendly. If you're unsure of what the publication or printer requires, ask for instructions before you send the file or hire a prepress service bureau to prepare your file for submission.)

Consult the people at the publication you want to advertise in (or the printer you want to hire to produce your brochure or catalog) to find out the easiest and most inexpensive way to submit your ad designs. But don't let them talk you into buying an expensive new design program you don't know how to use — just ask them whether they can accept PDF files from whatever program you already know how to use.

Glossy monthly magazines may not accept a PDF file. Oops! For example, all the Condé Nast magazines (such as *The New Yorker*, *Vogue*, and *Gourmet*) require you to submit your ad as a TIFF/IT-P1 (Tagged Image File Format/Image Technology) file because the company's digital printing processes work well with this format and errors are kept to a minimum. However, you, as a desktop publisher, can't easily produce such a file. If asked for a specialized file format such as TIFF/IT, you'll need to find a provider of prepress services. (You're not alone in this need; most ad agencies and graphic designers contract out for prepress services, too.) Send your file in its normal format (for example, an Adobe Illustrator file when saved has a `.ai` extension; Photoshop files use `.psd`), and prepress services or a friendly local graphic designer will, for a modest fee, convert it to the TIFF/IT format the magazine requires (and also allow you to proof and correct it).

Search the Web for "prepress services" for quick access to hundreds of companies that provide such services. Note that you can also ask a prepress service provider to help you with a PDF file so as to ensure the best possible color reproduction and avoid errors with your type.

Many local and smaller publications (including some magazines and newspapers) offer design and prepress services to the advertiser — sometimes for free! Just give them the design concept, with the images and language you want included.

To get you started, I include *a library of photographs you can use for free as a buyer of this book.* They're in the folder labeled CD0501. Within this folder are several dozen varied images in high resolution JPEG format, which means they're suitable for use in any magazine or newspaper or for the cover of a catalog, brochure, or postcard. This paragraph is your permission to use them. I took all these images (because I happen also to be a professional photographer), so I can give away the rights to my readers if I so choose. All I ask is that you include in small type the following line: *Photo credit: © Alex Hiam.* Have fun playing with words and images!

Lots of good photographs appear on the Web and in magazines and books. Use magazines like *National Geographic* or *Life* or do a Google search for images to look for the sort of image you want and then go to a stock photography company to find a high-resolution version for which you can purchase usage rights. But don't try to use "found" photography in your ad unless you track down the owner and get written permission. Purchased photographs from the stock photography suppliers aren't very expensive, but defending a copyright lawsuit is.

And don't forget the obvious: A good, clear photograph or drawing of your product is sometimes the best art for an ad. If you have a product that's even slightly photogenic, maybe you can just use a photo of it and not bother with purchasing any other art.

To take a photo of your product yourself, use a high-end digital SLR camera — borrow one if you don't own one — and plenty of light. Professionals usually drape a white cloth under and behind the product, making sure that no obvious wrinkles appear, and then use two light sources, one from either side, a little to the front. Check for glare spots and move the lights or diffuse them through a screen of thin white cloth so that you don't have white-outs on your product.

If you're using a photograph of an industrial or business-oriented product, surround it with white space (a white background cloth for photography will facilitate this) and then drop in arrows and text boxes to point out and describe three to six features that make the product useful and unique. A clear, clean, photo-based ad that emphasizes information and specifications is often the best approach for business-to-business sales. If you do want to include a beautiful image of a tropical beach ("Let us show you how to work less and spend more time on vacation") or a mountain peak ("Here's how to make sure your company reaches its peak performance zone"), keep the pretty picture and explanatory headline in the top third of the ad so that the product and its specifications can take up the bulk of the space.

## Some basic ad templates

The following sections offer you some basic designs that you can use as a starting point for your own ads. Each design is a fairly common type of ad that can work quite well when you drop in the appropriate words and images.

If you have some ideas about what you want your ad to achieve, try laying it out in one or more of these templates to get a decent rough cut of a design quickly and easily. All the following templates are on the CD as Word files that you can copy and edit.

### *Image ad template*

CD0502 has a basic Word template similar to the ad shown in Figure 5-1, for laying out an ad designed to communicate your brand's image to strengthen awareness and interest in your brand. If your objective is brand building, this format may work for you. Find a great image to help you show others what you think makes your brand appealing or special (see the list of Web sites in the previous section for sources of photos) and then tie the image to the brand with clean, simple language in your headline and copy.

Many successful image ads use a central metaphor or simile tag line to connect the product to an unlikely object, place, or event, which may then become the central photograph or drawing in the ad. For example, a marketer of birthday or party supplies may want to say that her Instant Party Kit is "Like a Carnival in a Box." With this simile in mind (this tag line is a simile because it uses "like" — otherwise it's called a metaphor), you can visualize ad concepts, such as an illustration showing a Brazilian carnival scene, visible through the cracked-open lid of a plain brown cardboard box. (Figure 5-2 shows a simple line-art conception of this ad concept. I created it in a few minutes entirely in Word just to show you that you can do more designing than you might think with this ubiquitous program.)

After you visualize such an image, how do you bring it to life in your ad? You need to track down a suitable photo from a stock photography house (see the earlier section "The tried-and-true visual appeal ad" for a list) and negotiate usage of it. This photo may cost a couple hundred dollars or more, so make sure that you like the photo and believe the ad will be valuable enough to justify the investment!

Next, create a clean line drawing of a three-dimensional box with the lid cracked open and combine this with a sliver of your photo. How? You have several options:

✔ To do it yourself, use a drawing program on your computer (such as Adobe Illustrator or Canvas), or a photo-editing program, such as Photoshop, if you're more familiar with one.

✔ Hire a graphic designer to create the visual for you if you don't know how. Community colleges are a great source of aspiring graphic and Web designers who will work at a reasonable price because they need resume-building experience.

✔ Get a newspaper, magazine, or Web ad seller to do the graphic design for you for free, as part of their support services for advertisers. It's always worth asking.

To come up with a good comparison for a metaphor or simile image ad, start by naming one or more qualities of your product that you want to communicate in the ad. Next, brainstorm other things that exemplify these qualities. An elephant represents a long memory, for example, so an auto mechanic service that maintains full service records in its database may want to use an image of an elephant sitting behind a service counter. The headline could be, "We Remember," followed by body copy saying something like, "When did you last change your oil or charge your AC? What grade of oil got the best mileage in your car? Where did you put those snow tires? Do you still have any warranty benefits? What can you do when you lose your car keys while visiting Aunt Matilda, two states over? Whatever your problem, however foolish you think your question may be, don't hesitate. . . . *Call us.* We remember!"

**Figure 5-2:**
An example
of a small
print ad
that uses
a simple
metaphor
with a visual
to catch
reader
attention.

Each order of
**Instant Party Supplies**
is like a
*CARNIVAL in a BOX!*
www.instantpartysupplies.com

Okay, you get the idea. Now use these examples to come up with a comparison for your own ad campaign.

### Informative ad template

CD0503 is a template for an ad that emphasizes information about the product. What are its important features or benefits? How does it work? If you have a good story about your product, this ad design allows you to tell it clearly and well (see Figure 5-3).

You can lay out an informative ad in lots of ways. If you feel that the design in Figure 5-3 is a bit too technical, try the option in CD0504, which floats a series of product or usage photos around a column of simple explanatory copy.

**Figure 5-3:**
The informative ad template emphasizes information that helps the reader see why your offering is special.

To design an effective informative ad, first make sure that you're clear on what's special and important about your product from your customer's point of view and then select three or more facts that communicate this benefit convincingly. For example, if your service is faster than your competitors', use facts like the following:

- Average response time for new service requests: 3.5 hours

- Winner of multiple industry awards for the quality and speed of our service

- Money-back guarantee if we take more than 24 hours to respond fully to your request

These facts make the case in a compelling manner, and each supports the core claim to fame the ad is trying to communicate.

Don't let your facts wander off topic, or you dilute the ad's impact rather than strengthen it.

### Call-to-action ad template

Another option is to design your ad so that it asks the viewer to leap into action and request information or make a purchase right now. CD0505 and Figure 5-4 show a basic call-to-action ad template that you can use to stimulate leads or sales by adapting it to your product.

Before you do, think hard about what incentives you can give the viewer to act immediately. Your objective is direct action, so you need to include some extra benefit or reason for them to act, beyond the basic benefits of your product or service.

**Figure 5-4:**
A call-to-action ad asks the viewer to make a purchase right away.

# Main Headline (Short & Eye-Catching)

## *Secondary headline* (explanatory, draws reader in)

Call to action in a short, clear opening paragraph saying exactly what you sell and why they should buy it right now.

Supporting information giving benefits, testimonials, or other evidence to help close a sale or stimulate a visit to your Web site.

Additional benefits or special offer associated with this ad to encourage them to take action immediately. **Number to call.**

Illustrative photo or drawing, black and white or gray scale art

Small, short caption

## Company Name Here

www.yourwebsite.com
Toll-free phone number

You can ask the viewer to take action in a lot of ways, but these types of ads generally have several elements in common:

- A strong basic appeal with both emotional and intellectual reasons to choose the product or service

- Added incentives to buy right now, such as a special time-sensitive discount or free add-on product or service included in the offer

- Direct request or command to act; for example, to call a toll-free number or go to a Web site and enter a special code to take advantage of an offer

- Clear, frequent, and varied options for contacting you and placing an order or requesting more information

Try to include plenty of options or choices in your ad because choices tend to increase the response rate. CD0506 is a template for a call-to-action ad that's, in essence, a minicatalog, showing multiple products from which the viewer can select.

# Creating Ad Concepts for Fun and Profit

The ad templates in the previous section are layouts that show you how to create an ad in two dimensions using text and images. But every good ad has an important third dimension: the *conceptual dimension*. Your ad needs to engage readers on the conceptual level by grabbing their attention, stimulating their senses, or engaging their creativity. It needs to make them think, feel, laugh, or maybe even cry.

The conceptual dimension of advertising is what gives an ad power. A clean layout and design help the concept jump off the page or Web page and into the viewer's mind, but only when you have a conceptual design for the ad in the first place. I'm going to take you beneath the surface of your ad to help you explore the conceptual dimension of your design.

Some ads start with a basic objective and graphic design, whereas others may start with the concept and then let the form follow naturally. Designing ads is a creative job, so don't feel you have to do it in any particular order.

How do you find a great ad concept that will give your ad design that extra zing needed to really make it work?

Creativity is a good source of conceptual design. Think of something special that's easy and cheap to do, and you'll have a high-impact ad for less.

Of course, that's a tall creative order; otherwise, everyone would already be doing it. So I better give you some help. I have two cool ideas that aren't over-used. They're adaptable general approaches that give your ad more stopping power and hold attention:

- ✔ In my first idea, I create ads that evoke a strong sense of mood by using words and/or an image associated with that mood.
- ✔ In my second idea, I create ads that communicate a mind-catching thought in the form of a wise quote.

In the following sections, I show you how to use these two shortcut design concepts. They're very flexible and adaptable. In fact, these concepts fit every business. You can easily adapt them to many media (that means you can use the same design concept for a brochure, Web page, catalog, post-card, or poster, as for your print ad).

## The mood ad

The premise of the *mood ad* design is that you can position your product or service in an appealing way by setting an emotional tone. You can accomplish the same goal in many ways — for example, a picture of a playful child conveys a happy, playful mood better than a thousand words. (By the way, the folder labeled CD0501 includes some photos of happy children you can use in your ads.)

To design a mood ad, ask yourself this simple question: "How will our product or service make the customer feel?" Your answer gets at the emotional benefit you offer. Often, the feeling or mood conveyed by the ad is an important part of making the sale.

Figure 5-5 contains an example of a mood ad for an insurance company (but please open CD0507 to see it in color). This ad combines an image of a gold pocket watch with the headline "Loyalty" set in a classic-looking type (Rockwell) to convey a mood of quiet reflection about traditions, heritage, and passing your values down to the next generation of your family. The goal of this ad is to capture the best mood for talking about life insurance — a topic that can be hard to broach without setting a mood first.

This ad for Coulter Insurance illustrates several points of good ad design. First, it takes an indirect approach to asking for business because more straightforward pitches, such as, "You're going to die and if it's anytime soon, your family will be mighty ticked off at you if you haven't bought a good life insurance plan," don't work very well. Also, the ad in Figure 5-5 not only sets a mood that makes talking about the subject of life insurance easier, but it also creates an analogy between the prospective customer and the valuable antique gold watch: "Help them [referring to the prospective customer's family] learn the value of loyalty by setting a fine example yourself" is a subtle call to action that is made palatable by the fine example of the valuable watch in the illustration.

Also notice how the copy in the Coulter Insurance ad has been overlapped with the gray of the photograph and laid over a series of soft vertical lines to create a strong vertical design element that draws the eye from the watch to the words. This pull of the eye is an example of what designers call *flow*. The goal is to create enough visual tension and interest that the eye enters, then travels around, the ad in the order you've chosen.

**Figure 5-5:**
This ad uses an heirloom pocket watch and the word "Loyalty" to convey a mood that might get people thinking about buying life insurance (see CD0507 for color version).

**Loyalty**
*is passed down through the generations*

Help them learn the value of loyalty by setting a fine example yourself.

**Coulter Insurance**

*Term, whole life and investment instruments for the discerning customer since 1939*

In addition, the copy has been kept to a minimum, allowing the picture and headline to do most of the talking. Visual appeal is the key to success with almost all print and Web ad designs. (If you like the photograph of the watch, you can use it in your own ad — it's in the folder labeled CD0501.)

Figure 5-6 also uses a photograph to convey a mood, combined with a headline (which, in this case, appears below the photo in place of the traditional small caption). The ad uses a simple, obvious descriptor of how the customer is feeling: happy. But it adds a bit of intrigue with the idea of a "happy secret," and the viewer wonders what this happy secret could be. It's not explained fully (it's good to challenge the imagination), but the secret must be found at Euphoria Day Spa.

This design could be the basis of a magazine ad (in which case, you'd probably want to add the name and address, plus a small coupon or other call to action, at the bottom of it). Or it could be the front page of an elegant brochure or the front of a glossy card with services and rates listed on the reverse. If used for a brochure or card, you may want to carry over the theme by using a header, such as "Discover your own happy secrets," on the next page to get the eye to flow into the listing of services. (By the way, this ad uses Humana Serif for the word "happy" to make it pop joyfully from the block lettering of the Bank Gothic type behind it.)

Naming and illustrating a good mood, such as happy, loyal, or relaxed, is a simple way to give your ad power. Sometimes I have experimented by taking a word like "reliable" (to describe a business service, for example) and looking up synonyms, such as "dependable," "careful," and "trustworthy." You can add these words to your design if you want — for example, a local moving company may have a photograph of one of their trucks with all these words around it, like a picture frame. This concept uses a word or words to evoke a strong feeling and to associate it with your product or service.

I once used the mood ad concept to advertise a service plan for a company that sold capital equipment to businesses. Those at the company felt that their service plan offered better support than their competitors' plans did and wanted to convey this advantage. The key word they felt captured their attitude toward customer support was "concern." They were concerned about each customer and stayed in close touch with each one to make sure that everything went well. Figure 5-7 shows a basic layout concept for a service-plan brochure that uses words to convey the feeling that the company stands behind each customer and takes a personal interest in his success.

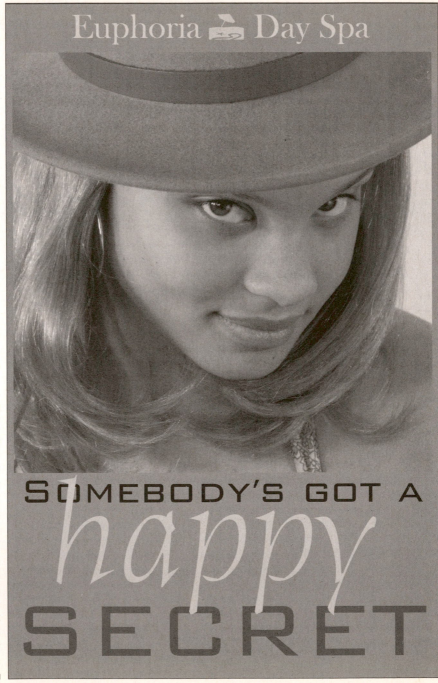

**Figure 5-6:**
This print ad or brochure cover conveys the mood of someone whose spa visit has left them feeling beautiful, relaxed, and self-confident (see CD0508 for color version).

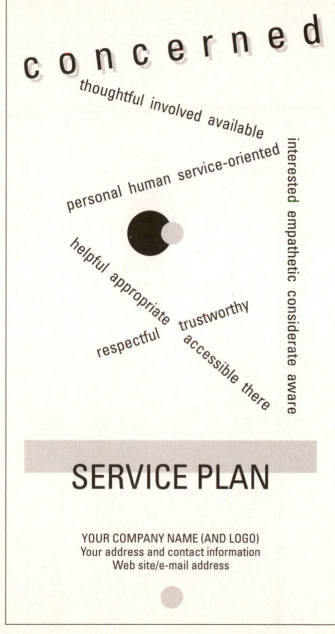

**Figure 5-7:**
This
brochure
cover
expresses
positive
feelings
associated
with good
service.

Perhaps you want to create a mood ad of your own. Many possible feelings or meanings exist beyond the ones I illustrate here. And while I generally favor a strong visual image as the basis for ad design, there are exceptions to this rule. The brochure cover in Figure 5-7 makes do with creative use of text without a photo or other visual image. Can you design an ad or brochure that uses text to set the mood or define the character of your product or service? It is an interesting design challenge that might help you strengthen your understanding of your product's appeal — and perhaps even create something strong enough that you can use it in your next campaign! Here are some thoughts to get you started:

- ✔ Wrap words around an illustration to frame it.

- ✔ List words in a long string to form unusual and powerful body copy or script.

- ✔ Ask a question and then let viewers answer it by checking boxes next to words ("Is your ISP reliable? If so, then surely you'd describe it as careful, trustworthy, stable, available, safe, unfailing, helpful, and supportive. What? Didn't check all those boxes? Maybe you'd better send us an e-mail. That is, presuming your current service will let you.")

- ✔ Make a collage of words or a string of words (like in the design for a brochure cover in Figure 5-7).

- ✔ Create a simple crossword puzzle of the words that describe your product.

These design concepts all harness the power of the written word. Words are extraordinarily powerful: They can create a definite mood or feeling about your business or its product or service.

## The wisdom ad

The wisdom ad is another simple-to-design, but potentially powerful, ad concept. The premise of the wisdom ad design (which you can use for any media from display ads to direct-mail letters, brochures, catalogs, and sales collateral) is that people like ads that give them the gift of wisdom. People value wisdom because it's in short supply.

So where can you find servings of wisdom to include in your ads? My strategy is to go to the classics. People always like a great quote from a master writer or thinker, so a wise thought from literature can give your ad stopping power and increase its value to readers.

Figure 5-8 shows an ad that uses a quote from a famous detective of Victorian-era stories, Sherlock Holmes. The ad is executed in simple black and white for inexpensive back pages of magazines or for newspapers. This style of ad replaces the traditional headline with a thought-provoking quote. (If you use short quotes and attribute them accurately to a famous author or fictional character, you don't need to obtain reprint permissions. You can find thousands of quotes to choose from in any dictionary of quotations.)

TIP

The ad in Figure 5-8 uses a quote to draw reader attention. Many people like such quotes and may even clip the ad just to help them remember the quote. A short message to the reader ties the quote into some positive attribute of the marketer's offering. The approach used in Figure 5-8 is a lot easier than writing a compelling headline or coming up with an original hook. All you have to do is find your hook in the form of an appealing quote and then tie that quote in to your products or services.

When you design an ad using a quote, pay attention to the little details that tighten the links from your offering to the quote. In Figure 5-8 I drew an easy-to-recognize silhouette of Sherlock Holmes to add visual appeal, plus the reverse (white letters on dark field) phrase "We agree!" in large type to add another eye-catcher to the design. To further refine the design, I set all the copy in an old-fashioned-looking type called Baskerville, choosing the semi-bold option for its stronger lettering. You'd have to be an expert on type fonts, as well as a Sherlock Holmes buff, to realize I am making a subtle reference to the story about this Victorian-era detective called *The Hound of the Baskervilles,* but everyone will recognize that the type matches the general style of the illustration and quote. (For your creative inspiration, I include an editable Word file of the second ad on your CD as CD0508. You have my permission to use the illustration and copy for your own ad, if you wish.)

As the two variants of the Sherlock Holmes ad illustrate, you can explore many options once you have a concept. I recommend trying multiple designs and layouts until you come up with one that really seems to work.

Figure 5-9 shows another way to use a famous quote to draw attention and get people thinking about your offering. The ad uses a photo of a thoughtful young man whose eyes, you may notice, are looking downward toward the thought-provoking quote and the body copy about the online course offerings of the advertiser. The viewer tends to follow the gaze of the person in the photo to the headline, which makes viewer attention flow from the photo to the quote and then into the substance of the ad's body copy.

"It has long been an axiom of mine that the little things are most important."

*- Sherlock Holmes*

That's why we:
- grgfdgytgf fgh hyuukghk  jguihojhjlkf
- dfgfd  ytty  asdrhtj h jkiylghj kiry jkljlkvbnvaabt xvsdraab
- 655 fdyjh par fyutjf mjyfui

OUR COMPANY NAME. Getting the little things right, so you don't have to. Call or email for a free quote and audit today, or visit our Web site for more of those all-important details.

Contact info    contact info                               **LOGO**

**Figure 5-8:**
Print ads relating the timeless quest for truth with the quest for better products.

"The real question is not whether machines think, but whether *people* do."

- B. F. Skinner

**Eliot College** offers distance learning for anyone who is thirsty for knowledge. Visit our Web site for a full listing of courses and majors, from The History of Literature to The Future of Computing. At **Eliot College** we answer B.F. Skinner's question every day. Do you?     www.eliotcollegelearining.com

**Figure 5-9:**
This ad uses another famous quote to draw the reader in.

# Making an Impact by Using Visual Shortcuts

In the preceding sections, I share concepts and designs that start with an inspiration for advertising copy (or the written word), then add an illustration to support the text. However, sometimes it works better to start with a visual image (such as a photograph you really like), and then find words to support it. An ad based primarily on visual appeal can transform an ordinary marketing message into an extraordinary one.

In the following sections, I look at strategies for creating powerful ads, catalogs, brochures, Web pages, or other marketing communications in a hurry or on a tight budget by using beautiful visuals.

If you want to make a big impact with a gorgeous photograph but need to work fast or are on a tight budget, you probably don't want to hire a professional photographer. Your best bet in a hurry is stock photography, and you can find many vendors on the Web, so don't be afraid to go shopping for a great image. (See "The tried-and-true visual appeal ad" in the beginning of this chapter for some links, or visit `www.insightsformarketing.com` for updated links.)

Think about the visual appeal of your ad this way. Every year, people buy expensive calendars featuring fine photography and hang them up where they look at one image for a full month. These same people are routinely exposed to many hundreds of ads each day but do their best to ignore and forget them. What's the difference between the calendar they pay for and treasure and the ads they ignore? One has beautiful photographs; one doesn't. So if you want people to treasure your marketing communications instead of ignore them, try giving people what they want — something beautiful.

## Using a beautiful landscape photo

My office has a pretty big library of books on marketing and advertising, and I just went through the indexes of a bunch of them looking for the word "beauty." It's not there. Go figure. What I figure is that most people aren't designing their marketing materials (or even their products) to be beautiful. They're trying to make ads effective, clever, informative, or persuasive, but not beautiful. So you can use a beauty-based appeal with the confidence that you won't have a lot of competition in using this shortcut to great advertising.

You can offer customers beauty in plenty of other ways, as well. You don't have to confine yourself to photographs! A beautiful storefront, office space, or even an especially elegant business card can create an aesthetic impact that pleases and impresses prospects and customers. Yet how many of the spaces where businesses receive or serve customers are actually made to be truly beautiful? A flowering plant or small garden, a gorgeous painting, photo, or art poster, a fresh coat of paint, and a little trim — all are small investments in adding beauty to the customer's world.

Here's an ad concept: Why not select a really attractive photo of a beautiful natural landscape? The headline can say, "Have a Great Day!" In the bottom-right corner, you can put "Brought to you by . . ." and add your logo or company name, plus a short one- or two-sentence update on what you're doing or any new upgrades or additions to your product line. Start this copy with "Now offering . . . " or a similar phrase.

Keep the ad copy minimal and let the beautiful photo be your gift to customers and prospects. Don't clutter your photo with too many advertising messages, either. A beautiful ad achieves the objectives of burnishing your brand image and generating goodwill among customers and prospects, and both of these objectives can help you close sales and retain customers later on.

## Portraying an attractive person

People look at other people. We're socially oriented; we can't help it. In particular, photos of people playing, laughing, and having fun tend to attract viewers. Also, photos of children and babies are naturally attractive. And handsome or attractive people tend to draw and hold attention. (The ads in Figures 5-6 and 5-9 take advantage of the eye appeal of a photo of an interesting person.)

But don't make the mistake of thinking that a sexy, provocative-looking model will sell your product. Sexy images aren't very effective in advertising unless your product actually offers sex appeal. So go ahead and look for sexy photos if you're selling cosmetics or lingerie, but for most marketing needs, stick with photos that are interesting, but not overly sexy.

One way to use the natural appeal of people is to have a head-and-shoulders photo of an interesting or attractive person, using her as your spokesperson for your print ad. The spokesperson can say something in first person, like "I'm glad I switched to (name of your company or brand)." Placing that message in a bold headline, over an interesting, animated face, draws most viewers down to the copy to see why the person is happy she switched to your product.

Another classic concept is to have models using the product rather than just showing the product by itself.

People bring ads to life. Whenever possible, include photos of interesting people to draw the eye and engage the viewer.

## Inserting a humorous cartoon

Humorous cartoons clipped out of newspapers or magazines cover many office bulletin boards and home refrigerators. People like a good cartoon. So another simple way to attract viewers to your print ad is to include a good cartoon.

This idea is easier than it sounds. Web sites like Cartoon Bank (`cartoon bank.com`), cartoonist Randy Glassbergen's site (`www.glasbergen.com`), Pritchett Cartoons (`www.pritchettcartoons.com`), cartoonist Carol Simpson's site (`www.carolsim.com`), and cartoonist Ted Goff's site (`www.newslettercartoons.com`) cue up thousands of humorous cartoons and give you the option of licensing them for professional use in an ad, newsletter, mailing, e-mail, blog, or Web page. Have a look. You just need to think of some way to relate your product or service to a humorous cartoon, and you have yourself a great ad concept!

# Giving Postcard Marketing a Try

The old-fashioned postcard is an interesting option for advertisers to consider. If you have or can buy a good mailing list of prospective customers, then a color postcard may be the cheapest and easiest way to get your ad message out.

Designing a postcard is a lot like designing a print ad, except that the photo is on one side (often along with a headline), and the body copy is on the other side. If you've already designed some good ads, you can easily adapt them to the postcard medium. And lots of templates and services can help make designing and mailing a postcard easy.

Figure 5-10 shows a simple postcard designed to be sent to homeowners to promote a heating and air-conditioning company's spring cleaning special offer. CD0509 shows you this postcard in color, and CD0510 is a Word template for both the front and back of the postcard. The back is important because it contains the details of your offer — but notice how I keep the copy short and simple in the template. You should assume that the reader will only give the text a quick glance.

If you want to minimize design time, you can find plenty of postcard templates online. Type "postcard marketing" or "postcard templates" into your search engine and see what comes up. Firms such as Postcard Mania (`www.post cardmania.com`) offer one-stop shopping for postcard designs (including the art), plus printing and mailing services, although usually you have to provide the mailing list.

If you don't have a list, you can buy one — search the key term "mailing lists," and you'll be amazed at the number of companies offering names and addresses for use in marketing!

Some of the postcard marketing firms, including Postcard Mania, offer mailing lists along with design, printing, and mailing, so they're truly one-stop shops. And because these companies specialize in postcards, their designs are better than average.

Fresh paint, check!
Fresh lawn, check!
Fresh air? Hmm...

**Figure 5-10:**
This postcard design is best appreciated in full color; see CD0509.

A good postcard needs to be visually appealing and bold, and to have interesting and useful information — but not too much information. Keep it simple!

The standard postcard (which takes a postcard stamp in the United States) is 4.25 x 6 inches, which isn't a lot of space for a marketing message. Yet it can economically communicate a single, timely message and is more likely to be read than most mailings because the message is right there on the outside and the recipient doesn't have to open it. For these reasons I recommend postcard mailings at least a few times a year for most businesses.

You can print postcards in small quantities, but you get a much better price if you have them offset printed by the thousands. Figure around $300 per 5,000 postcards from high-volume postcard printers, such as Postcard Mania. That's just the printing costs for a big box of them. Now you need to mail them.

It takes a long time to hand-address and stamp 5,000 cards, so if you have anywhere near that many good names and addresses, consider contracting out for the mailing services, too.

Postcard stamps (for 4.25-x-6-inch postcards) are set in the United States at about two-thirds the cost of a regular first class letter stamp. At time of writing, they cost $0.27 (but not for long!). To mail 5,000 postcards, the cost (at time of writing) would be $1,350. However, if you pay for a mailing list plus mailing services, you add another 15 to 20 cents per card. I'm going to call it an extra 24 cents to hedge against stamp inflation and estimate that a mailing of 5,000 postcards will cost you about $2,500 if you contract the entire project out. That's 50 cents per postcard, delivered to a purchased list. Not bad! However, you don't actually need to mail all 5,000 cards unless you can obtain 5,000 good names and addresses. Remember that your base price just for the printing is a few hundred dollars, so you can just as well mail a couple hundred by hand to your own house list, give out another hundred cards to customers and prospects, and save the rest for next year. And the year after. . . .

# Using Web Pages as Ads

You don't necessarily have to confine your ads to the printed page. Think broadly about your choices and don't be intimidated by the prospect of designing ads for viewing on a computer screen instead of a printed page.

Many companies are springing up to offer simple ad templates for Web advertising. Some of these companies are resellers of Google products, which leads me to ask, why not just go straight to Google? For example AdReady (www.adready.com) offers an easy interface for creating ads, which may speed the effort for someone unfamiliar with Google products. On the other hand, if you're willing to do a bit more work, you probably can build the same ads directly on the Google site.

So buyer beware — you may not be getting quite as much as you think you are when you open an account that promises free ad templates and great Web advertising results. Make sure that you like the templates and support you're receiving and that the pricing isn't too much higher than Google's base prices.

You can get an almost instant Web site up and running in myriad ways, so you really need to think of Web sites as an easy way to post a highly interactive, content-rich advertisement. Marketers are eventually going to see Web sites as fluid, frequently changing, powerful advertisements. You may as well get ahead of the curve and start putting up Web sites to help communicate your advertising messages. There is no reason on earth for your Web presence to be confined to one central, static "corporate site" when Web space is unlimited and lots of Web traffic exists.

For example, if you are in the heating and air-conditioning business, you certainly need (and probably already have) a Web page with a domain name based on your company name. This central corporate Web site is like a brochure describing your business — who you are, what you do, what your credentials are, what your happy customers say. (Yes, be sure to include testimonials on your central Web site — see Chapter 14 for how-to details.)

However, this corporate Web site should just be the spoke of your Web marketing wheel. You should use pay-per-click advertising on Google and Yahoo! to direct local searches to your Web site, plus the occasional paid ad or directory listing on high-traffic sites that reach your customer base.

And then you should consider specialized Web sites and/or blogs that relate to research topics of interest to your customers, such as

- How to reduce energy costs and usage for existing home or office heating and AC systems (complete with a downloadable audit form bearing your company logo and contact information)
- How to prepare your AC and/or heating equipment for the off season
- Spring cleaning for AC, including how to get ready for a summer of fresh, clean air (and why better quality air is also more economical to the homeowner)

These topics sound like good article topics for a magazine, don't they? That's the idea. You can create a Web page or blog that is essentially an interesting, informative article for homeowners (Google and other vendors offer simple templates; check them out!). Homeowners have an interest in such topics, and they'll search out your content and study it (assuming that you do your homework and give them informative, useful content, illustrated with photos from your own job sites to make it visually appealing, too).

Keep informative topic-oriented Web sites from looking overtly like corporate Web pages or promotional pieces. Present your content like editorial content, but, of course, give credit and a link to your business. For example, a "Sponsored by COMPANY NAME" and a Web link and phone number for more information could be visible at both the top and bottom of each page.

Don't forget to look to other sources for content as well. Whether or not you write it, being the source of useful information is key. Look to other vendors and businesses and credit them when you use their content. (Don't forget to ask permission first.)

If you want to do these editorial Web pages in-house, consider using any of the widely available Web page templates from vendors such as Register.com (www.register.com, my personal favorite). It offers do-it-yourself sites, build-it-for-me sites, hosting, and other needed services at modest prices. Yahoo! and Google also support the do-it-yourself Web designer with reasonable products. And a growing number of easy-to-use Web store templates can get you up and running quickly — see Register.com's ProStores and check out PayPal (www.paypal.com) for other easy and inexpensive ecommerce options.

# On the CD

Check out the following items on the CD-ROM:

- ✔ A library of photos for design use (CD0501)
- ✔ An image ad template (CD0502)
- ✔ Informative ad templates (CD0503 and CD0504)
- ✔ Call-to-action ad templates (CD0505 and CD0506)
- ✔ Insurance company ad (CD0507)
- ✔ Sherlock Holmes ad template (CD0508)
- ✔ Postcard design sample (CD0509)
- ✔ Postcard front and back templates (CD0510)

# Part III
# Power Alternatives to Advertising

The 5th Wave                    By Rich Tennant

"That's very innovative, but I'm just not interested in buying a box of Girl Scout Cigars."

## In this part . . .

Ads are powerful, but they aren't the only way to attract business. Other elements of your marketing communications are vital, too. In this part, I show you how to present your brand identity consistently in everything you do, starting with the basics of business cards, letterhead, e-mails, and faxes. I also explore the important new topic of presenting your brand on the Web, and I guide you through the rewarding challenges of designing effective brochures, blogs, and press releases.

# Chapter 6

# Branding with Business Cards, Letterhead, and More

- - - - - - - - - - - - - - - - - - - - - - - - - - - - - - - - - - - - - - - - -

## In This Chapter

▶ Clarifying your brand identity

▶ Designing your business name and logo

▶ Creating a successful business card, letterhead, envelopes, and e-mails

▶ Strengthening your presence on Web sites and blogs

- - - - - - - - - - - - - - - - - - - - - - - - - - - - - - - - - - - - - - - - -

*W*hen presenting themselves at arm's length through marketing materials, people are far, far less professional. Try to keep in mind that your business card, letter, brochure, catalog, or other materials represent you to potential customers. Most businesspeople tend to impose a lower standard on these materials than they would on themselves if they were there in person. But in truth, an even higher standard is necessary and appropriate. Why? Because you aren't there to make your case. And if you have sub-par materials, people will assume that you don't take your business seriously enough to invest in good collateral.

In this chapter, I show you how to take a close look at how your brand looks, starting with an examination of the brand identity and then making sure that your business cards, stationery, labels, envelopes or boxes, faxes, and e-mails all convey your identity clearly and well.

## Who Are You? Establishing Brand Identity

Who are you? Your name and face are instantly recognizable to anyone who knows you. People who don't know you can easily begin to recognize you from your unique combination of name, face, and voice. You have a clear identity as a human being — so clear that telling you apart from anyone else on the planet is easy.

Well, maybe I'm exaggerating. If your name is John Smith, then you may not be too distinctive by name alone. But add your face to the name, and now you're truly unique. People are expected to be unique and easy to identify. It's confusing and even upsetting when someone doesn't look like a unique individual. No one wants clones running around — they seem creepy. I should know: I'm a twin. When I stop to get a cup of coffee at the general store in the small town where my brother lives, I usually create social chaos. People come up to me and say hello, and I have no idea what to say back. Or they look at me quizzically, turn away, and then look back, not quite sure whether they know me or not. You want to make sure that your product or service is so clearly identifiable and so well known that you never have such problems in your marketplace.

To evaluate the strength of your corporate identity, consider the following questions:

✔ Does your letterhead look unique, and is it easy to identify at a distance, like from across the room?

✔ What adjectives would someone use to describe your company if she could work from only a copy of your letterhead?

✔ Does your logo look more attractive and professional than your competitors' logos?

✔ Does everything you send through the mail, fax, and e-mail show your logo and identifying information in a clean, consistent, and attractive manner?

✔ Do you include your *corporate identity* (logo, name, and so on) on all packaging and products in an appealing and consistent way?

✔ Do you and all other representatives of your company carry attractive business cards in a proper case to give out whenever you have an appropriate opportunity?

✔ Do your e-mails include your corporate logo, name, and contact information consistent with your letterhead and business cards?

✔ Is your *identity* (your name, logo, and overall look and feel, or brand personality) consistent on the Web as well as in printed material and signage?

These questions help you identify immediate issues or opportunities in how you present your identity to the world. Marketing is in the eyes of the beholder, so you must make sure that everyone interacting with your firm or any of its products, services, publications, Web pages, ads, or other marketing materials sees your unique identity clearly and fully.

The best-looking logos, the most appealing names, and the strongest presentations of identity are usually associated with winning companies and brands. Like it or not, appearances matter. I always urge my clients to make sure that they look like the company they want to be, not the company they were three years ago when they last ordered stationery. There is no harm in updating your logo and materials, and you often have much to gain. Don't be afraid to change the way you present your business or brands.

In the remaining sections of this chapter, I ask you to take a close look at some of the most important elements in your public presentation of your marketing identity.

# Managing the Presentation of Your Brand Name

Whether you're selling your business or a specific product, your name and logo are key. Coca–Cola has a striking identity: The brand is easy to recognize anywhere, any time. The Coca–Cola Company writes its name in a distinct way that makes its name into a logo design, and it always has color. Plus, the company puts its name everywhere in a clear, consistent manner so that consumers can't possibly forget it.

Nike uses another strategy. The company doesn't always write its name the same, but it always has the distinctive swoosh logo nearby. The swoosh brands every product the company designs and also appears on the company's letterhead, business cards, and Web pages, giving the company one of the best-known brands in the universe. Are you as clear and consistent as Coke or Nike in the way you present your business name or brand identity? Hmmm. Maybe not. In this chapter, I help you work on that.

Close your eyes for a moment and try to visualize the logo or name of your local telephone company, bank, cable TV company, and local taxi company. How many of these logos and names pop right to mind, appearing clearly and easily in your mind? Not all of them, I bet. Depending on where you live, maybe one or two logos or names are so well designed and consistently portrayed that you can actually visualize them instantly without a hint or other aid. (Bank of America has a particularly strong brand identity, and the company is careful to always use the same strong blue and red in its signs and printed materials to help make it instantly recognizable.)

# Assessing your identity

Take some time to make sure that your marketing identity looks really good. A good marketing identity is one that

✔ Makes a strong, positive impression on all who see it.

✔ Portrays you, your firm, service, or brand as you aspire for it to be. This way, as your

business grows and achieves higher levels of success in the future, it will grow into, not out of, your logo and look.

✔ Is highly memorable and easy to recognize, even from a great distance.

✔ Is consistently displayed wherever you have an opportunity to do so.

To pump up your identity, give your company, product, or service a clear, clean, visual signature. Always write your company's, product's, or service's name the same way. This means using the same type. Pick a font and style you like and stick with it (see Figure 6-1). If you don't know how to design a great signature or logo, hire a graphic designer who can show you a portfolio of really impressive logo and identity work.

If you insist on a do-it-yourself logo in order to save money, here's the shortest and simplest set of instructions for creating your own:

1. **Finalize your name's appearance.**

   If your business name presentation varies, choose one version and stick with it from now on. For example, Valley Landscape Services, sometimes known as The Connecticut Valley Landscape Service or CT Valley Landscapes, should choose one clear, simple version of their name, such as Valley Landscapes.

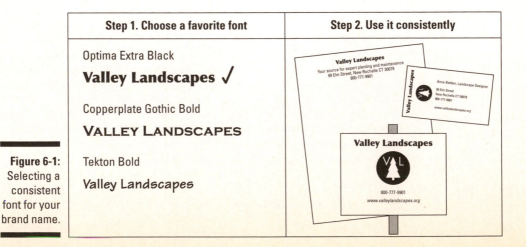

**Figure 6-1:** Selecting a consistent font for your brand name.

| Step 1. Choose a favorite font | Step 2. Use it consistently |
|---|---|
| Optima Extra Black **Valley Landscapes** ✓ Copperplate Gothic Bold **VALLEY LANDSCAPES** Tekton Bold **Valley Landscapes** | |

2. **Use Word's library of fonts or the sample sheet at your local printer to choose a typeface you like for your name.**

   Avoid highly unusual, fanciful, or hard-to-read types. If you aren't sure which you like best, print a sample sheet of several of your favorites (see Figure 6-1) and sleep on the decision overnight.

3. **Select a simple, clean, small visual image or symbol if you want to add a visual element to your identity.**

   Pick clean black line art. Sources include

   - Your local print shop

   - Dover Publications (`www.doverpublications.com`), which offers CDs and books of copyright-free line art; search for clip art and copyright-free images in this publisher's catalog

   - Online services such as Stock Photo (`www.stockphoto.com`)

   Or just use the first letters from your name to create a simple logo.

   Figure 6-2 combines a very simple image of a tree (which I drew in a few minutes with Word's drawing toolbar, using three triangles, a rectangle, and a circle) with the first letters of the company name to make a distinct symbol that you can combine with the name for better recognition and recall (see Figure 6-2).

**Figure 6-2:**
A clean, memorable identity for use on stationery and signs.

**Valley Landscapes**

4. **Make sure that your name and image are unique.**

   Yes, you do need to avoid using a name and image that resemble another business logo. Check your region's phone directories, do a Google search, and also check that your name and design aren't already trademarked. (In the United States, go to `www.uspto.gov/main`, click Trademarks and then click Search TM database to do a free search.) If somebody else is already using the same name and/or a similar design, revise yours to something that is unique. (At date of writing, I see that nobody else is using Valley Landscapes, so this design is in the clear.)

5. **Pick a smaller, less bold version of your logo type, or a simpler, more common type (such as Helvetica or Times), to use for your address, phone number, Web address, and e-mail.**

6. **Work up one to several standard arrangements of your logo (name and graphic elements).**

   How will you lay your name and graphic element out on business stationery, business cards, magnetic signs for your vehicles, and the banner of your Web site's home page? (See the upcoming sections "Selling Your Business Cards and Designing Your Letterhead and Envelopes.") Also, will you want a colorful version of your identity for places where color printing is easy? The Valley Landscapes design in Figure 6-2 would look great in forest green, wouldn't it? But I'd confine the green to the name and logo and use plain old black ink for the address and contact information to keep it simple.

   To bump it up another level, you can try versions with several colors — but usually this experimentation gets overly complicated. Complex is bad when it comes to logos. Think about the power of the Coca–Cola identity. If Coca–Cola needs only red and white, then I think Valley Landscapes can get away with using only green and white, don't you?

If you're visual yourself and willing to fool around for an hour or two in whatever drawing or design program you have access to (or just make do with the Drawing tab in Word), you can create a wonderful variety of identities in a hurry. Most such programs have libraries of line art; even Word has a rich variety of symbols in some of its fonts. Figure 6-3 is a simple logo design I made entirely using Word's text boxes and fonts. (To appreciate the use of color, see CD0601 for a viewable PDF of this logo.)

**Figure 6-3:**
A simple
identity
using widely
available
typestyles
and
symbols.

# Business Name

Bringing the world to your doorstep

If I wanted to make this design my official logo for my business, I would either print all my cards and stationery on a good in-house laser printer or hire a designer to take my design concept and work it up a bit for me. Or maybe I'd just bring it to a print shop and ask them to finalize it for me. Many printing shops offer free or almost-free design services as a way to get you to give them your order, and bringing them a strong design concept is the best way to ensure that they give you back something that really works for you.

The technical editor for this book, who is a professional designer, explained to me why it's helpful to pass your logo concept on to an expert for finalization. I'm going to share her note with you because it shows how much is involved if you really want a high-end, professional logo: "When I design a logo for someone, I am keeping in mind every intended use for that logo. Will they be putting it on a tradeshow banner, maybe embroidering a polo shirt? Designing a logo for these uses requires a professional that can supply several file formats, one of which had better be an .eps file that is scalable. Not to mention, the font should be converted to outlines so there is no room for error (such as a substituted font) when your logo is reprinted somewhere. It is understandable that someone may start with a homegrown logo, but they had better invest in doing it right for the long-haul very soon."

# "Selling" Your Business Cards

Your business card is often the first contact someone has with you or your business. Sometimes your business card is the only marketing communication that a prospect has, so you want to make sure that it follows the rules of good marketing communications by building both emotional and rational involvement. That means it needs to communicate the information that a prospect needs to figure out what products or services you have and how he can contact you easily. Also, make sure that it contains your Web address.

## Making a good overall impression

Don't forget that your business card has to appeal to prospects on a basic emotional or intuitive level, too. Imagine someone looking through a pile of cards that includes many competitors of yours. Why would a prospect choose yours? What about your card makes it call out to people? A strong logo and clean design are a good start.

Basically, your card needs to make a powerful, positive, personal impression. However, most cards don't. Most are quite dull. Even the ones that are clean and professional generally emphasize information and ignore the need to make an impression.

To make a good overall impression, strive for a sophisticated, professional image — with something different, such as a better-quality paper, a more beautiful logo, an unusual vertical layout, a useful fact or inspirational quote printed on the back, or an attractive use of color to highlight your company name or logo. Above all, focus on a well-presented company name and logo.

Hold on! Just because you want to make a powerful, personal impression with your card, don't do anything crazy. You don't want to make a *negative* impression! An overly colorful, flashy card with a photograph plus gold-, red-, and green-colored print is not the way to attract attention. Keep the design clean and professional.

## Deciding on design details

When designing your business cards, remember that you want your card to make a good impression and to include enough information so that contacting you is easy. But at the same time, you don't want to overload it with so much information that the card is confusing. CD0602 illustrates four ways to lay out a standard business card, each of which is clean, simple, and eye-catching. Even though business cards are small, you can design them in lots of creative ways. It really comes down to what you like and what fits your business image best.

The standard size for business cards in the United States is 2 x 3½ inches. Businesses traditionally use printers to make business cards and stationery. They have their cards *offset printed* (printed from a plate in ink on a large printing press), as opposed to photocopied, largely because printing is more durable when handled a lot. Now you also have the choice of desktop publishing your own business cards and stationery, so I cover both options for you.

### Choosing flat or raised ink if using a printer

You can get business cards printed in either flat ink or raised ink. *Flat-ink printing* is just the standard printing. In *raised-ink printing,* the printer uses an ink, dusts it with a plastic powder, and heats it in an oven that melts and expands the powder, giving the type a raised look and feel. Almost all printers offer both types of printing for business cards, and the choice you make is largely one of taste. Personally, I don't like the look and feel of raised cards, but many people prefer them.

Here's my favorite, if you want serious elegance: Ask your printer to help you find a specialist who will make a *die* (metal stamp) of your logo and have it *embossed* (so that it sticks up a little bit) on your card, along with flat-ink printing of the business name, tag line, and your name and contact information. Embossing takes longer to make and is considerably more expensive, but it really stands out.

### Setting your margins for the printer

You need to design only one master version of your business card, and the printer will take it from there. Most printers are happy to accept a PDF file produced by Word or any of the desktop graphic design programs.

Whatever you use, make sure that you keep the print from being too close to the margin. Printers like to have space from the edge of the design to the edge of the paper. The amount of space needed varies from printer to printer — anywhere from $1/8$ inch to $1/4$ inch. To be safe, leave $1/4$ inch in all directions (see Figure 6-4) because paper can sometimes shift from side to side when going through the press, and this amount of space ensures that the cutter won't clip off any text that's too close to the edge of the card.

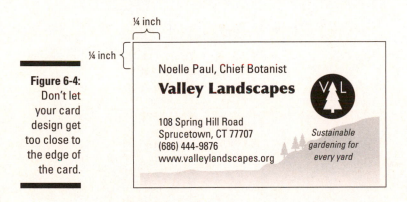

**Figure 6-4:**
Don't let your card design get too close to the edge of the card.

¼ inch

¼ inch

Noelle Paul, Chief Botanist

**Valley Landscapes**

V A L

108 Spring Hill Road
Sprucetown, CT 77707
(686) 444-9876
www.valleylandscapes.org

*Sustainable gardening for every yard*

### Pondering paper stock

Have the printer print your business cards on a heavy paper, such as #65 cover stock. Also, use matching (lighter but similar looking) paper for your stationery and envelopes so that people will see them as part of a clearly defined professional presentation and image (see Figure 6-5). Some papers differ in weight but match in color and finish, so you can easily match your cards with the lighter paper of your letterhead.

Some printers offer package discounts on letterhead, envelopes, and cards when you order them together, so getting them all printed at the same time is often cost-effective.

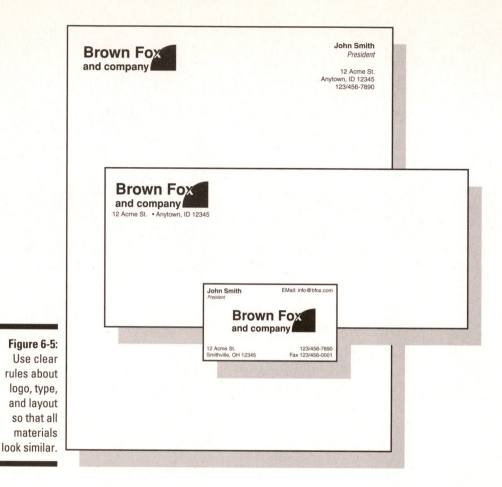

**Figure 6-5:**
Use clear rules about logo, type, and layout so that all materials look similar.

# Who needs a printer when you have Word?

Most people don't realize that Word software includes a number of service-able business card templates. These templates are cleverly hidden away in the Label Tools area (look under Tools⇨Labels), but they're easy to find once you know what you're looking for.

Here's how to design your own business card on the Microsoft Office software that almost certainly is running on your computer right now (If not, borrow somebody's computer that has this software.):

**1. Choose Tools⇨Labels.**

In some versions, you must choose Tools⇨Letters and Mailings⇨ Envelopes and Labels.

2. **Click Options in the Labels dialog box.**

3. **Choose a business card option from the lengthy menu and click OK.**

   I recommend starting with the first one, 5371 Business Card, because it's a clean and simple standard to work with.

   Word returns you to the Labels dialog box and automatically fills in the details of your selection. Your cursor is positioned for you to enter your name and address information to create a 2-x-5-inch table-like page with your choice of copy (words in the size and font style of your choice) on each card.

4. **After you type the lines of text you want on the card, highlight each line in turn and choose a type style and size.**

   Forget about any art. You can't paste a logo or other art into a dialog box because Word won't allow it (for reasons beyond me — why the heck not?!?). So you'll have to wait on your graphics.

5. **Proof your text and then click OK.**

   A new Word file opens with a page full of business cards, set up to match Avery 10 business card sheets, which you can buy at any decent stationery or office-supply store.

   Once you have built this file of ten identical business cards on a single sheet, you can manipulate and save it just like any Word file. Click and drag or insert art (including a logo design, if you have one). Manipulate the text as needed. Then print, and you're in business.

To print the cards yourself, use Avery business card stock unless you want to run your own card stock through your printer and then measure and cut your own cards by hand. You can do this process all yourself, but it takes a sharp paper cutter and some patience, and the Avery products are so easy to use that they're worth the extra cost. I recommend the cards on a peel-off back over the perforated ones — the latter just don't look very professional.

To get the cards made up for you, just take a CD with the template file to your local copy shop and find out what the employees can do for you. (If they don't take Word files, you can generate a PDF file out of Word and give them that.) Every shop is different, and some shops have their own business card software and want to reset the design, so talk to them and do whatever seems reasonable and within your budget. But *please* stick to your design convictions. Don't let them talk you into a boring, generic, stock design. Promise? Good! However, if the print shop you work with is willing to give you a quote on designing and printing cards based on your design, by all means let it quote this service. If it's affordable, and you need lots of cards, then I recommend letting the print shop take over. Do-it-yourself cards are great when you have no printing budget, but at some point, you'll want to upgrade to professionally designed and printed cards.

# When you have trouble . . .

If you have trouble opening the Word template in CD0603, go directly to www.avery.com, click find a Template, click Templates for Microsoft Word, and do a search for the cards you've purchased by product number or just select Business card wide, ten per sheet, for the generic template in which you can enter your text.

To print a PDF of your formatted template, click the PDF button in Word or choose Print⇨ PDF in the Print Dialog Box and then Save as PDF. If this process doesn't work, search "save as PDF" in your Word Help. There is a lot of variation in the versions of the Word program, but this function is somewhere in yours — don't worry!

To see what a business card template produced in Word looks like, see CD0603. You can print on Avery card stock directly from this Word file, or you can print it as a PDF to create a file that your local print shop can work from. The lines indicating the dimensions of individual cards won't show up on the PDF (see CD0604 for an example), so you can either add some trim lines in the margins or ask your print shop to work with the file and set it up however they prefer.

Here are some additional sources of online information and templates for designing your own business cards:

✔ **VistaPrint** (www.vistaprint.com) offers colorful card designs to which you simply add your text. The prices are low because the company uses digital laser printing. It's not a bad way to get starter cards if you don't have the time or skill to develop your own logo and look quite yet.

✔ **Microsoft Office Online** (http://office.microsoft.com/en-us/ templates) gives you access to a huge variety of designs that you can quickly download and adapt to your needs in Word.

✔ **PrintingForLess.com** (www.printingforless.com) is a one-stop shop where you can select a template, add your text, and place an order for as many cards as you need. Templates for brochures, stationery, catalogs, and many other printed products are available, so it's easy to choose a semi-custom look that is consistent across all these products — but only if you continue to shop with this company.

✔ **Hewlett-Packard** (www.hp.com/sbso/productivity/office/ buscards.html) offers a page of good quality card templates maintained by Hewlett-Packard (which makes many of the printers used for desktop publishing of marketing materials). All you have to do is double-click the card you like and the file downloads to your desktop. You can then open and edit it in Word and print it using the Avery business card paper specified on the site. These templates are easy to use and allow you much more design control than the template pages maintained by printers.

CD0605 shows a card design I created using one of the HP templates from the Hewlett-Packard Web site. I liked the vertical format and the stripe on the side, but I ended up adjusting the size and location of text boxes and replacing the stripe provided with one I constructed myself because the original had a funny irregularity in it. Sometimes you have to fiddle with templates to get a card that satisfies you, but it's still worthwhile to start with a template because it can reduce design time significantly.

Notice that the card design on CD0605 doesn't have a $^1/_4$-inch margin all around it. Instead, the green stripe is supposed to *bleed,* as printers say — in other words, it goes to the edge of the card and so must be printed slightly over the trim line. Bleeding is easy when using the Avery templates, which is why some of the HP templates use this design feature. Run one sheet to check your alignment and then adjust your template if need be until you get the desired ink or toner coverage.

Figure 6-6 shows the two business card designs I created using free Word and HP templates. They're rendered in black and white here, but, of course, you can do color versions of them in "real life" if you want to. I think green is a natural color for Valley Landscape's identity, don't you?

I've gone into quite a bit of detail about the mechanics of designing and printing business cards. Once you've mastered that chore, you'll find you have a lot of transferable skills and knowledge that allow you to tackle other essentials, such as stationery and brochures, with greater ease and confidence.

**Figure 6-6:**
Cards
designed
with free
Word and
HP tem-
plates for
desktop
printing.

# Designing Your Letterhead and Envelopes

As with business cards, letterhead and envelopes may be the first encounter someone has with your business, and first impressions are obviously important. But even if customers have done business with you for some time, the look and feel of your stationery has a subtle but powerful impact on their attitude toward you. Good letterhead can help retain a customer or stimulate a referral. So, like with business cards, letterhead is a surprisingly important marketing investment. Make sure that you have a clean design that impresses customers favorably.

As with your business cards (see the preceding section), you can order these items from a printing house, or you can do them yourself. Word has envelope and letterhead templates (see the Tools menu), but you can easily create your own template in Word, too, because all you need to do is use text boxes.

To create a text box in Word:

1. **Display the Drawing toolbar if it's not already there by choosing View➪Toolbars➪Drawing.**

2. **Click the AI symbol to draw a text box that you can write in and format and resize and drag your text around the page at will.**

   To draw a text box, click the AI icon, position your cursor on a black section of your page, and then hold down the Select key while moving the cursor diagonally. Release the cursor and then the Select key. To expand or change the size of the text box, position your cursor outside of it, then move your cursor over one of the small squares embedded in the frame of the text box. When the cursor changes form and is directly over one of these boxes, click your mouse or mouse pad and drag the frame of the text box and then release your finger from the cursor button.

   Add multiple text boxes if you need to break Word's rules of formatting — for example, to move words close to each other or overlap them.

Traditionally, letterhead was printed in black ink, and the company name and address were centered at the top. You don't need to respect this tradition; anything that looks good and fits your image well is fair game. Just remember to leave room for the letter, invoice number, or fax number on the stationery you design and to confine the design to the left third of the envelope (because the remaining area needs to be reserved for stamp and address). Color is fine, too. And unless you do business on a fairly large scale, you can desktop publish your stationery (a color laser printer is my preference for durability), which means it need not cost you expensive printing bills to have colorful stationery. You can also use Word templates to make up labels in any size you need, with matching identity and color scheme.

CD0606 is a PDF file showing a creative, colorful letterhead design based on the logo from Figure 6-3. CD0607 is a Word version of the same design, in which you can edit the text and adjust the color scheme as you desire, in case you like the basic design concept and want to use it as a template for your own letterhead.

In CD0607, the font types I used for the logo, Arial Rounded and Brush Script, won't display correctly unless you have those particular types in your font library, too. Sometimes you have to go online to find and purchase a particular font if you need it for a design and don't already have it. However, all fonts come through fine in PDF files because they're converted to art objects in the format.

## Conveying your image through paper and print

Your image in your business card, letterhead, brochures, and Web site (plus signs, trade show banners, and any other marketing materials) should reflect who you are and what you do. If you're a stockbroker or a business consultant, you may want to have an established, conservative look for your design, ink, and paper selections. Communicating a sense of stability and longevity can be important in these fields. What sorts of type, ink color, and paper leave this impression the best? Perhaps Times Roman lettering, centered in a traditional style at the head of the paper, printed in conservative black ink on an old-fashioned creamy paper made with cotton fiber and a subtle watermark. Such paper is more expensive than lighter, more modern papers but is consistent with a conservative, solid, sophisticated image. (Make sure that you order blank sheets, too, to use for second pages, because a regular piece of white paper doesn't match.)

Here are tips for how to choose an appropriate style based on your profession:

- **Law firm:** Stick with a conservative top-centered layout for stationery using Times New Roman, Baskerville, or Century for your type. Avoid color and design-oriented logos. Just present the partners' names in a firm, traditional, trustworthy font.

- **Massage therapy:** Balance the idea of being trustworthy with the idea of being helpful and healing. A rounded block-letter type of font meets these two goals. (Ask your printer to show you what Euphemia UCAS Bold and Helvetica Neue look like.) Consider a logo featuring a pair of hands palms-down, as if in the midst of a massage. Avoid strong or bold colors, but a subtle use of soft pastels may be good. Include credentials on business cards to increase the sense of professionalism and trustworthiness.

✔ **Construction:** Avoid the temptation to use large type, a strange mix of bright colors, and a simplistic icon of a house or other building. And please, no icons of hammers! I rarely see a business card that looks adult or professional in the construction business. Try to break with tradition by using 11 point Times New Roman, Arial, or any simple, traditional font. Instead of a simplistic piece of clip art for a logo, either have a sophisticated logo designed for you or just use your business name as the logo (in 16 point type — not any larger, please). The goal is to avoid looking like you couldn't get any other job, so you went into construction.

✔ **Insurance:** Start by reading the advice for lawyers. Insurance agents should be almost as conservative in their logo designs as lawyers. However, it's helpful to add a list of the types of insurance you provide because many people are uncertain about who sells what in the insurance industry. Also, if you've been in business for a long time, add "Since 1975" or whatever the date is, which helps position yourself as trustworthy and professional.

Notice that I did not recommend a wild and crazy design for *any* of these professions. Whatever you do, stick to a clean, professional look. Even if you're nontraditional in person, be fairly traditional on paper. Otherwise, you'll scare people off before they get a chance to know you.

You need to project a clear, strong personality each and every time you present your business. Capture and convey your brand personality on your letterhead, envelopes, and business cards. Even if you don't work with an expensive designer, take the time to explore many options and make a thoughtful selection of paper, ink, type, and logo (if you use one). Extra care and a little extra investment here go a lot further than most people realize to help make sales and marketing successful.

Here's an idea you can act on easily, with or without a designer's help. Go to a larger print shop and select a distinctive paper for your business — something that you feel has a unique, appropriate, and appealing look and feel to it. Then order letterhead, business cards, envelopes, and even labels all on this distinctive paper. This subtle design element can boost the image and appeal of a business.

## Keeping visual control in faxes and e-mails

Many businesses use decent letterhead but send faxes using a generic cover sheet with designs. (Please avoid the templates in Word!) Other businesses create inconsistent and unprofessional-looking faxes.

You can simply use your letterhead for faxes, centering the header FAX MEMO at the top of the page, with the date centered in smaller type below it. Then use the standard memo format of left-justified for the To:, From:, and Re: lines, including both the name of the person the fax is to and her fax number. At the bottom, beneath your signature, provide your own fax number if the contact address on your letterhead doesn't include it. You can also say in a Note at the bottom, "3 more pages to come" or whatever, to make sure that the recipient receives all the pages you send.

Nowadays, e-mail is favored over fax, so you need to give more thought to how your e-mails look. For starters, I recommend using your business domain name for e-mails, too, so that every e-mail address reinforces the business identity. This change is easy to do because host servers generally offer e-mail options. Check with your Web host for details, or if it's not helpful, switch to someone else.

Next, consider creating a standard identity and look for e-mails. However, to keep it simple (and avoid being screened by many receiving servers), this look should not include art elements like a logo or specific type style and color. In other words, your basic e-mail identity should be boring. Sorry, but the text that e-mails are made of isn't intended for use in graphic design. If you want to make it pretty, you have to resort to the methods used for designing Web sites — and I'm not going to go into HTML coding, how to post a logo file on a server and call out to it from within the code of an e-mail, and other oddities of making e-mails pretty, because e-mails with HTML coding and fancy designs get filtered so often these days. I suggest you just create a standard set of text lines for your business identity and contact information, plus a short marketing phrase describing what you do or what makes you great, and paste this signature into the bottom of every e-mail you send. (You can also include a link to your Web site, but it, too, may trigger filtering in the more finicky systems.)

To bump up your e-mails beyond this basic format, consider getting a product such as Email Templates (www.emailtemplates.com), an add-on for your Microsoft Outlook programs that gives you lots of capabilities for sending personalized e-mail marketing messages to your contact list, including some HTML template options. (Keep in mind that simple text e-mails do tend to avoid filters much better than fancier ones.)

# Maintaining Your Identity on the Web

I want to compliment UPS for being a good example of how to present a corporate identity on a Web site. If you go to www.ups.com, you see a beautiful version of the UPS shield-shaped logo displayed prominently in the upper-left corner. The logo seems to pick up a little light from above and positively shines out at the audience. Click any of the many tabs to navigate through pages for different countries and services, or go to the corporate page, and this nice version of the UPS logo is always there to greet you. That's how Web sites should handle logos and identities, but most sites don't do it nearly that well. Does yours?

In a more personal example, the Web site that supports this book, `www.insightsformarketing.com`, uses a consistent banner that appears across the top of every page, where the Insights for Marketing name and distinctive logo are displayed along with a short descriptive phrase. (We use the same identity strategy at all my business Web sites; Trainer's Spectrum at `www.tspectrum.com` also has a banner where the identity appears on every page. Notice that it uses a variant of the eye and triangle logo, which signals that it's in the same business family as my marketing site.)

Whether you confine your logo to the top-left corner (like UPS does) or use a full-width banner at the head of every page (the way my sites do), the goal is the same: Anyone navigating your site ought to have their recollection of your identity reinforced constantly. Web pages allow for excellent graphics with high resolution, strong colors, and good backlighting on the viewer's computer screen, so use them to present your logo attractively. Every Web page can help build the strength of your marketing identity. Make sure that yours does!

Many Web sites overcrowd the identity by trying to squeeze too much information or too many tabs at the top of the page. Make sure that you leave an inch or two in all directions around your name and logo. Also, set it against a contrasting background so that it isn't washed out by the background color.

A *Web blog* is a Web site maintained by an individual who posts frequent text entries of commentary and news and may also post digital photographs, music, or streaming video. Entries are commonly displayed in reverse-chronological order. Blogs focus on a topic of interest to a group of readers, who are expected to revisit often in order to see the latest posting. Most blogs are personal activities, but you can write a blog to forward your professional interests and promote yourself and your business. For example, at the time of writing, Nathan Bransford of Curtis Brown Limited is using a blog effectively. He's a literary agent (someone who represents authors and takes a percentage of their publishing contracts), and his blog attracts considerable attention both from authors and editors. See `http://nathanbransford.blogspot.com`.

Blogs are a simple, quick, free way to put your content on the Web, and increasingly, I'm seeing small businesses (as well as large ones) turn to blogs for Web marketing. In fact, some small business owners and entrepreneurs are using blog-hosting sites to create their main Web presence — the blog takes the place of a more traditional (and complex) Web page. I recommend portal host sites for blog creation, such as `www.blogger.com`, which make it startlingly easy to get a blog up and running, and can create an attractive banner at the top of your blog with your identity in it. For example, at the time of writing, the blog at `http://sfbaywhalewatching.blogspot.com` has a handsome blog created on Blogger that looks a lot like a corporate Web site, but was much easier to create and is simple to update with new information.

You'll always need a business card and stationery, but increasingly, you'll find that e-mail, Web sites, and blogs are a great way to interact with prospective customers and build awareness of your brand identity. Seems like new media just add to the old, instead of replacing them, which means more opportunities for marketers to make a splash.

# On the CD

Check out the CD for the following materials:

- ✔ Sample business card designs (CD0601)
- ✔ Sample logo design made entirely in Word (CD0602)
- ✔ Business card sheet for printing with Avery stock (CD0603)
- ✔ PDF version of business card sheet (CD0604)
- ✔ Colorful business card made from a free HP template (CD0605)
- ✔ Sample letterhead design with strong visual appeal (CD0606)
- ✔ Editable Word version of sample letterhead design (CD0607)

# Chapter 7

# Creating Eye-Catching Brochures, Catalogs, and Spec Sheets

*I*f you sell something expensive or complex, then you need a detailed brochure and perhaps additional information in a binder or pocket folder, on a CD or DVD, or in an informative Web site. If your offering is fairly simple but you want to make sure that prospects are impressed, excited, or trusting enough to buy from you, then you need a smaller brochure that emphasizes design and visual appeal over information. And no matter what your business, a collection of press clippings, an informative or interesting booklet, a great promotional video, or other supplementary marketing materials can be helpful, too.

In this chapter, I help you work on brochures, spec sheets, catalogs, and booklets, all of which are essentials of a good marketing program. I also touch on modern CD, DVD, and Web versions of the introductory brochure, which are, in my opinion, the most exciting new direction in brochures. Finally, I encourage you to get creative in your design and approach. Hundreds of millions of brochures are in print right now. Most end up in the recycling pile. This chapter shows you how to make yours stand out!

# Considering Your Needs

A brochure, spec sheet, and flier are really just variations of the same theme. In all these marketing materials, you include essential information about your offerings, plus additional information and images to attract and hold interest. And you make sure that you present your brand identity correctly and memorably (see Chapter 6). Here is a quick decision-making guide to help you select the format you need right now.

## The simple one-page spec sheet or flier

If you need only one page of information and plan to place it beneath a letter or in a pocket folder, then you can just design a one-page spec sheet (for technical information) or flier (which contains more interesting information and/or images than a spec sheet).

CD0701 is an example of a colorful one-page promotional sheet that explains a product sold to the training departments of large employers. As you can see from this example, limiting yourself to one page doesn't have to cramp your style. You can use many techniques to make it into an appealing marketing message, complete with product specifications and benefits, a photograph of the product, and a call to action saying how and why to purchase.

## The multipage brochure

If you have more information and need multiple pages or if you expect to fold the material for mailing or displaying in a rack, then create a brochure layout and design. Another consideration to keep in mind is that brochures — when done well — can look more sophisticated and professional than sheets. Something about the folding or binding says that you took care to create it, and it invites the reader to open it up and see what's inside.

CD0702 is an unusual brochure designed to convey a sense of creativity (because it's for creative design services, it needs to look unique). It is designed to be printed on one side of a tabloid ($8\frac{1}{2}$ x 11 inch) sheet and then accordion folded into four tall, narrow panels. CD0703 shows what that same brochure looks like when unfolded by the prospective customer. It's printed on stiff enough paper that it can be stood up like a Japanese screen.

For a more conventional example, see CD0704, a brochure template for a business-to-business marketer to use. This three-panel design is printed landscape (horizontally) on standard $8\frac{1}{2}$-x-11-inch paper, with two inward folds. This brochure has two sides so that when it's folded, each of the six panels, front and back, is used. Replace the text with your own. (Some of it is filled in with nonsense right now.)

Microsoft Word includes templates for a variety of brochures. Each version of Word hides these templates somewhere different, so I'm not going to give you specific instructions for finding them. Instead, I suggest you type "brochure" into the What Are You Searching For? window in Word Help and let your program tell you where to find them.

The more visual your brochure, the better. If you can't think of any good photographs, and a cartoon (see Chapter 6 for sources) won't work either, then consider using colorful rectangles or triangles, which are easy to draw using the Word Drawing toolbar. (See the many options under Basic Shapes, the pop-up menu that is symbolized by a circle, square, and triangle in the Drawing toolbar.) Or use a large star in a cheerful color or a gradation of two colors (available in the Stars and Banners menu of Word's Drawing toolbar).

Figure 7-1 is an illustration of the outside three panels of a standard brochure made for 8½-x-11-inch printer paper. I used only the standard options and menus in Word to draw this illustration, just to show you how easy it is to make strong, eye-catching designs. For display in this book (which is printed in black ink), I used shades of gray, but I would choose appealing colors if I were designing an actual brochure for desktop or print-shop production. (If you make up your own brochure, take care to line up folds and leave room between them for a margin around every illustration and block of text.)

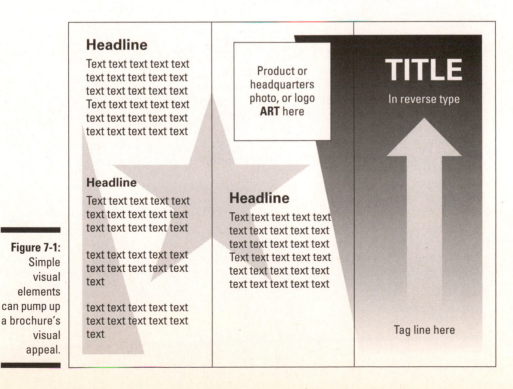

**Figure 7-1:**
Simple visual elements can pump up a brochure's visual appeal.

## Catalogs and booklets

When you want to include a lot of information, such as descriptions of multiple products, a brochure may get a bit overstuffed, so you probably need to make a catalog or booklet instead. What's the difference? In producing them, not much. Both a booklet and a catalog contain multiple pages that are bound together by center-folding and stapling or by the spiral binding or glued *perfectbinding* method. (Perfectbinding is how paperback books are made; see the sections "Captivating Catalogs" and "Marketing with Booklets and Books" later in this chapter.)

When multipage publications focus on portraying and selling an assortment of products, they're usually called *catalogs*. So if you have an assortment of products, you probably need a catalog. But don't overlook the less common option of a *booklet* or a book. (A booklet is a center-folded and stapled short book, which you can make more cheaply than a traditionally bound book.) For example, if you run a boatyard, you can compile a booklet on how to maintain your boat, geared to boat owners.

Booklets and books can work wonders in generating interest in what you do and in positioning you as an expert in your field. (If you're daunted by the prospect of writing a booklet, hire a writer to help you.)

# Becoming a Brochure Wizard

"We need a brochure." That's the most common request a marketing consultant or designer hears from clients. Seems like everybody needs a new brochure, and I think I know why: The old ones aren't working.

People are rightfully unhappy with their brochures because most don't accomplish what a good brochure should. A good brochure

- ✔ Gets prospects excited about doing business with you
- ✔ Communicates enough information to support a purchase decision
- ✔ Communicates enough feeling to create a strong, positive impression or image
- ✔ Serves as a simple minicatalog that describes your various products or services
- ✔ Supports *all* your marketing activities by serving as a handout for salespeople, a great mail piece for prospecting, a useful update for existing customers, a giveaway at events or trade shows, the perfect accompaniment to a formal proposal or press kit, and so on

Whenever you present yourself to the public, you can use your brochure to break the ice. Because brochures can be such effective icebreakers and sales-makers, you may want to create a line of brochures — one for each purpose, service, or product, plus a general one that presents your company well. Single-purpose brochures are more effective and easier to design well, so I usually recommend creating a separate brochure for each major need or purpose.

## Brochure design considerations

I recommend keeping a file folder somewhere in your office labeled something like "Brochures I Like." Whenever you see an appealing brochure, toss it in that folder. That way, when you have to think about designing your next brochure, you can empty the file folder and look at lots of appealing approaches. One of them may inspire you.

### Function and purpose

Just like an ad (see Chapter 5), a brochure should have a clear message and audience. Who are you designing the brochure for? What do you want to tell them? What do you want to do? If you think these questions through before you start, your brochure will be more effective and focused than most.

### The major design elements

Next, think about the major design elements of a brochure. Most brochures present a narrow front panel first. This panel needs to have a simple, clear, large headline, along with enough visual and/or verbal information to make it clear who should read the brochure and what it contains.

You can use the front panel like a book or magazine cover, with a title at the top, plus art, and a few short lines advertising the contents. Or you can include some of the content on the front cover — but if you do, make sure that you leave some room for a large-size (25 point or bigger) title and a large version of your logo or other visual element. See Figure 7-2 for the major design elements of the outside of your brochure.

If you plan to use the brochure for mailings, make sure that you design it to meet postal requirements. Avoid oversized brochures, which cost considerably more to mail. A standard three-panel brochure printed on $8\frac{1}{2}$-x-11-inch paper makes a good mailer. The middle outside panel should be set up like a business envelope, with your name and address in the upper-left corner (see Figure 7-2). Word has a number of brochure templates that meet this requirement. (Find the ones in your version of Word by searching for "brochure" in the Help dialog box.)

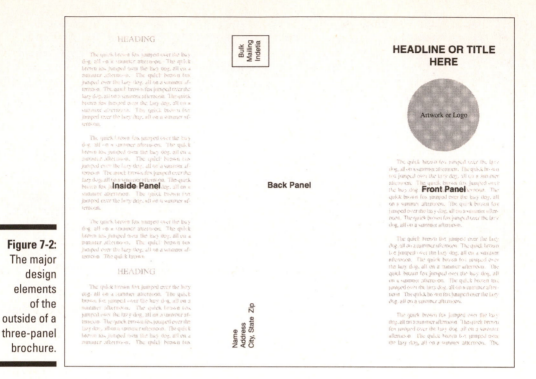

**Figure 7-2:**
The major
design
elements
of the
outside of a
three-panel
brochure.

## Infinite materials at your fingertips

Brochures are unusual in the variety of options they present. You're working not just on one piece of paper but on as many as you want to include. And you have the options about how you fold the paper and whether you include more than one sheet.

In addition, you have more options for materials than you do for ads or letters. Brochures can be printed on regular or coated paper, but you can also get creative and use unusual cover stocks or even foil paper, embossed covers, clear or opaque covers, inside sheets, and so on. In fact, if you don't mind assembling brochures by hand, you can even include unusual materials, such as cloth. (How about a silk sheet between the cover and the first page?) Nothing's stopping you from using a leather or wood cover either, although I don't recommend using exotic materials unless they tie into your image or relate to your product line (for example, a hardwood floor installer should certainly consider a varnished wood cover). Brochures give your marketing imagination plenty of scope!

## Sizes and shapes

I suggest looking first at simple, inexpensive, standard design options before going crazy. They're economical because they use standard paper sizes. And you can vary these paper sizes by folding them in different ways so that you still have plenty of room for creativity. The standard precut paper sizes in the U.S. and Canada are

 ✔ Letter (8$\frac{1}{2}$ x 11 inches)

 ✔ Legal (8$\frac{1}{2}$ x 14 inches)

 ✔ Tabloid (11 x 17 inches)

Of these three standard sizes, the first two are the most common and the easiest to work with. I recommend working within the possibilities that these two standard sizes present unless you have a good reason not to.

The first option is to use standard 8$\frac{1}{2}$-x-11-inch paper, which you can work with horizontally or vertically (see Figure 7-3). With a little imagination, you get five excellent brochure layouts out of this standard paper size: horizontal half-fold, accordion-fold, and tri-fold, and the vertical half-fold and fold over.

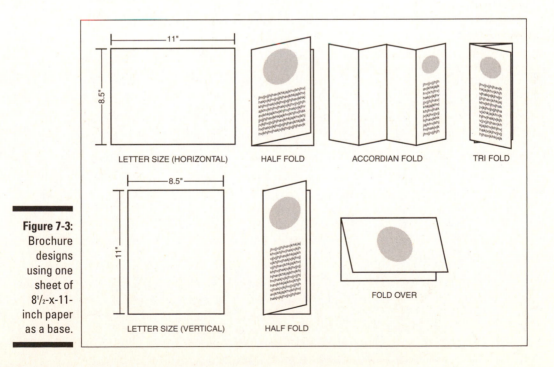

**Figure 7-3:** Brochure designs using one sheet of 8$\frac{1}{2}$-x-11-inch paper as a base.

LETTER SIZE (HORIZONTAL)  HALF FOLD  ACCORDIAN FOLD  TRI FOLD

LETTER SIZE (VERTICAL)  HALF FOLD  FOLD OVER

Similarly, you can fold a standard legal-size sheet of paper measuring 8½ x 14 inches in many ways to create different brochure layouts. Figure 7-4 shows the same five options executed with legal-size paper. Because of the longer length, the various folds create completely different brochures from the ones made with letter-size paper. For example, compare the horizontal half-folds in the two figures. The smaller letter-size paper gives a vertically oriented page, whereas the longer legal-sized paper gives a chunkier, magazine-style page with the same horizontal fold. I recommend creating two or three columns of text on these wide pages and interspersing art (photos, diagrams, or figures of some sort) to break up the text — just as many magazines and newspapers do.

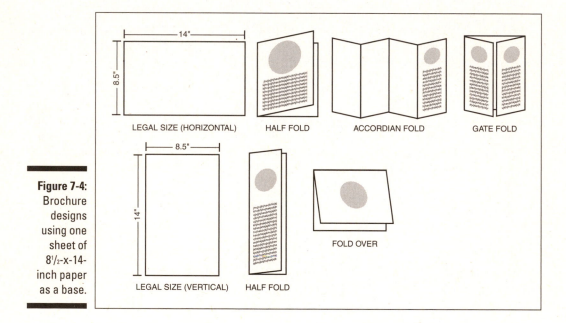

**Figure 7-4:** Brochure designs using one sheet of 8½-x-14-inch paper as a base.

LEGAL SIZE (HORIZONTAL)   HALF FOLD   ACCORDIAN FOLD   GATE FOLD

LEGAL SIZE (VERTICAL)   HALF FOLD   FOLD OVER

Between these two standard (and therefore inexpensive) paper sizes and these five different folds, you have ten different brochure options. Each fold makes a unique page size and therefore supports different approaches to page layout and design. In designing your brochure, think like a painter who first decides which size canvas to work on.

Sometimes you want your brochure to have an unusual shape or size to help it grab attention or make a statement. In this case, the added expense of a nonstandard paper size makes sense. For example, a car dealership may print an oversized, heavy, glossy-coated stock brochure cut in the shape of a car. The cover may show the owner, key salespeople, and key service people as if they're riding inside the "car," viewed through the "windows" of it. Such a brochure costs more than an ordinary one, but may be worth the expense if the brochure is highly appealing and memorable.

If you intend to mail your brochure, make sure that it meets postal regulations and fits in a standard-size envelope. Otherwise you have to find unusual envelope sizes and pay extra postage. Start with a search at the printer for unusual envelope sizes; that way, you don't get stuck with a great design that you can't match with an appropriate envelope.

## Paper characteristics

Paper usually comes in bulks of 500 sheets called a *ream. Paper weight,* or basis weight, is the weight in pounds of 500 sheets of 17-x-22$\frac{1}{2}$-inch paper. The paper weight designation doesn't change when paper is cut down to smaller, more common sizes for sale. A ream of 20-pound paper (written 20#) is a lighter paper than, say, 24# paper, although, of course, an 8$\frac{1}{2}$-x-11-inch ream of 20# paper doesn't weigh 20 pounds.

Lighter weight paper, such as stationery paper, is called *offset paper,* and heavier card stock, such as the paper used for business cards, is called *cover stock.* You can use either type for a brochure. Try folding and handling different types and weights of paper before you decide what to use. But remember that if you intend to do mass mailings of your brochure, the heavier papers may cost more for postage. Weigh and price the postage on several options before you make your final decision.

Also consider the finish or texture of the paper you use. Paper with a texture or grain feels nice but may not be advisable if your brochure has photos because the texture of the paper will break up the ink for the photo, making it look coarse or muddy. If you're reproducing a lot of photos, stick to paper with a smooth surface to keep them sharp and clear.

## Layout tips

Local printers usually use one of several programs for page layout: Adobe InDesign, Adobe PageMaker, or Quark XPress. Your printer has at least one of these programs. In some cases, these programs can read layouts that were constructed in other programs, but check with your printer beforehand to find out what the shop is capable of.

Increasingly, printers can work from Word files, which is helpful for occasional designers who don't want to buy and master a new program. Newer versions of Word incorporate a basic Adobe Acrobat output capability that allows you to convert your Word file to Acrobat's format (Portable Document Format, or PDF) — which printers are also increasingly willing to use. The printing industry is more accommodating to Word users than it used to be, and you may be able to design a serviceable brochure or flier in the basic word-processing program that your computer already has and then have a local printer produce it directly from a CD or e-mail attachment. This option is definitely progress for budget-conscious marketers!

Also, affordable desktop printers are improving every year. I have an incredible Oki single-pass laser printer that does high-quality color printing and can handle 11-inch-wide sheets — which means I can run tabloid pages and even oversized tabloid sheets through it. I make a wide variety of booklets, catalogs, product sheets, and brochures in-house and prefer to do runs of under 100 copies myself. I get more control, lower cost, and excellent quality this way. (HP now makes a relatively inexpensive tabloid printer that is great for homemade brochures.)

When laying out the text and artwork for your brochure, keep in mind that printers need a *gripper margin* — the blank space that's needed on the edges of a document so that the printing press can grab the paper and pull it through the press. Usually, the gripper margin is about $^3/_8$ inch, but it varies, so check with your printer for specific needs. The gripper margin area needs to be totally free from text or images. (If you want the ink to *bleed* or run to the edge, the printer will have to print on larger paper and cut it down after printing.)

Next, think about how you want your text and artwork to lay out on the paper. You won't find any absolute rules for how many illustrations or pictures you can use in any one brochure, but you can follow these general guidelines:

- ✔ **Shoot for a balance between text and artwork or photos.** Too much text can be boring, and a well-placed photo or illustration can break it up nicely. Use at least one visual element on every other page or panel.

- ✔ **On the front panel of your brochure, place an image and/or an opening statement or paragraph to catch your readers' attention.** This front panel needs to draw readers to the brochure and make them want to check out the information inside. You have to catch many people's attention with this important panel, so consider how people will receive it. If it's in a display rack, will the rack hide most of the cover? Maybe you want to design it to compensate for the rack.

- ✔ **Consider using a strong photograph both for your cover design and as a visual theme for the entire layout.** CD0705 is a brochure template you can use, with the cover featuring a striking photograph that is repeated in variations inside. Figure 7-5 shows a gray-scale version of this brochure's cover, with the strong photograph featured in its design. Also, graphic design elements refer to the photograph. Chapter 5 reviews sources of photographs, including the one used in this brochure.

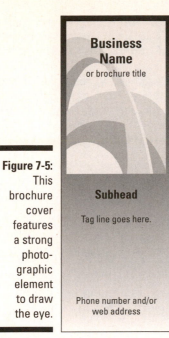

**Business Name**
or brochure title

**Subhead**

Tag line goes here.

Phone number and/or
web address

**Figure 7-5:**
This
brochure
cover
features
a strong
photo-
graphic
element
to draw
the eye.

✔ **You may hear your printer refer to *serif* and *sans serif* typefaces.** Serif typefaces have little feet-like appendages on their ends, whereas sans serif typefaces don't have those feet. (This paragraph is in a serif typeface.) Think about a combination of serif and sans serif type in your document. For example, use a sans serif type for your headings and serif for the body copy.

✔ **You measure type in point size.** For example, ten-point type is a small point size:

The quick brown fox jumped over the lazy dog.

A large point size is 24 point:

# The quick brown . . .

✔ **Make sure that the body type is readable; the size should be no less than 10 to 12 point.** Consider your audience. If the people reading this brochure are elderly, use a bigger type size, such as 14 to 18 point. Also avoid large areas of *reverse type* (where the type is white or a light color on a dark background) because it's much harder to read.

✔ **Try to stick with one or two families of fonts within a brochure.** Too many font styles can look sloppy and confusing. Each family has many styles (for example, **Bold,** *Italic,* narrow, and Underline in the Times New Roman family), so you have plenty to work with. And don't forget that you can change the size to add variety. For example, you can use all the following variations in size in a single brochure — the largest for major headers and other sizes for minor headers, the body copy, and the fine-print details.

Helvetica 10 point

Helvetica 12 point

Helvetica 14 point

Helvetica 16 point

# Helvetica 24 point

✔ **Mix up straight paragraphs with other ways of laying out text, such as checklists, tables, and columns.** The changes of pace you create keep the text appealing.

## Headline type

Headline type is made for just that: headlines. It's usually bigger, sometimes bolder, and sometimes more ornate than the regular text.

Headline type isn't meant for the body of the article — it would be too hard to read. Its purpose is to grab the reader's attention and draw her into the article below.

Headline type is usually used on brochure covers and paragraph headings. (I find I've been using Optima Extra Black fairly often lately for brochure headers as I find its look appealing.)

## Body type

Body type is used for the body of the text. Because it needs to be simple and easy to read, it's usually (but not exclusively) restricted to serif fonts, which are easier on the eyes, especially at smaller type sizes.

Times New Roman is the classic body copy and most readable of all the fonts. Garamond is an elegant alternative. Helvetica and Arial (both sans serif fonts) are more clean and modern, and they're attractive, too.

## Type alignment

The way type lines up on the paper supports an image or conveys a feeling. For a formal, conservative look, use *justified type* (where both the left and right sides of the type align at the margin). A *ragged right margin* (text not lined up on the right; used in this book) gives a less formal look. You can also center titles, and sometimes you can justify the text on only the right side, like when it floats in open space with a photo or box to the right of it. Figure 7-6 shows you what each of these options looks like and how printers and designers refer to each option.

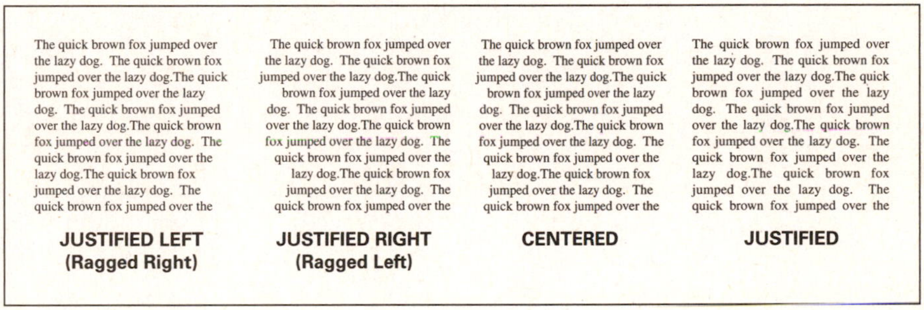

**Figure 7-6:**
Your options
for aligning
type on the
page.

The quick brown fox jumped over the lazy dog. The quick brown fox jumped over the lazy dog. The quick brown fox jumped over the lazy dog. The quick brown fox jumped over the lazy dog. The quick brown fox jumped over the lazy dog. The quick brown fox jumped over the lazy dog. The quick brown fox jumped over the lazy dog. The quick brown fox jumped over the

**JUSTIFIED LEFT**
**(Ragged Right)**

The quick brown fox jumped over the lazy dog. The quick brown fox jumped over the lazy dog. The quick brown fox jumped over the lazy dog. The quick brown fox jumped over the lazy dog. The quick brown fox jumped over the lazy dog. The quick brown fox jumped over the lazy dog. The quick brown fox jumped over the lazy dog. The quick brown fox jumped over the

**JUSTIFIED RIGHT**
**(Ragged Left)**

The quick brown fox jumped over the lazy dog. The quick brown fox jumped over the lazy dog. The quick brown fox jumped over the lazy dog. The quick brown fox jumped over the lazy dog. The quick brown fox jumped over the lazy dog. The quick brown fox jumped over the lazy dog. The quick brown fox jumped over the

**CENTERED**

The quick brown fox jumped over the lazy dog. The quick brown fox jumped over the lazy dog. The quick brown fox jumped over the lazy dog. The quick brown fox jumped over the lazy dog. The quick brown fox jumped over the lazy dog. The quick brown fox jumped over the lazy dog. The quick brown fox jumped over the

**JUSTIFIED**

## Text wrapping

With *text wrapping,* the lines of text end right where they bump into artwork. Word offers a variety of text-wrapping options in its Formatting area. (If you don't know where that is in your version of Word, search for the term "text wrap" in your Word Help and follow the instructions from there.)

You can choose to have the art bump the text so that the text wraps around or beside the art, or you can make the art float independently. (The same basic options exist in any design program.)

# Copy or print?

One of the first things you have to decide when creating a brochure is how to produce it. Traditionally, this decision means whether you have it copied or printed, but today the main choice is between offset printing (on traditional, large printing presses) versus using your printer's high-quality toner-based printer (this is usually called *digital printing*). Alternatively, you can also consider making it yourself on your own ink-jet or laser printer (usually called *desktop publishing*). Some factors to consider when deciding how to produce a brochure include

✔ Whether or not you have large runs of 1,000 pieces or more; if you have 1,000 pieces or more, having them printed is better than copying them.

✔ Having small runs (under 1,000 pieces) printed usually isn't cost-effective. The price per unit goes down as quantity goes up. Digital print or desktop publish instead.

✔ Offset printed pieces tend to have better quality, especially when you have a lot of photos in your marketing piece. However, newer digital and desktop printers fill this need at quantities between 1 and 100 quite well.

✔ Will people look at the brochure once and then throw it away? Offset (commercial) printing is far more durable than photocopying or inkjet printing because the ink sinks down into the paper, locking it in and making it impossible to remove. However, a good color laser printer will give desktop printed brochures almost as much durability as offset printed brochures.

✔ If you want to minimize costs for small numbers (under 100), why not just design the brochure in Word and print it on brochure paper on your inkjet or laser printer? Doing it yourself gives you the ability to adapt the design to your immediate needs.

## Color

Adding color to your brochure grabs the viewer's attention and makes the brochure more appealing to the eye, but for commercially offset printed brochures, each added color requires an additional print run and thus adds cost. You can add color in different ways, such as by using

✔ **Pantone Matching System (PMS) colors:** Printers use a universal ink color system called the Pantone Matching System. This system allows printers to match ink by referring to swatches that show the color along with the exact mixture of inks needed to obtain that color. So if you want to add color to an offset brochure, you need to ask a printer to let you see a set of PMS color samples so that you can select from it.

✔ **Four-color process:** In this process, printers achieve full color by separating the image into four basic colors: cyan, magenta, yellow, and black. Printers shoot film of the image in each of these colors and break the colors down into tiny dots (or increasingly, they ask for four digital files from you to substitute for the old-fashioned films). These dots, when arranged next to each other, create the full color effect, and you can see the arrangement of dots only with the aid of a magnifying glass, or *loupe*. The effect of the four-color process is excellent — it can reproduce fine art or photography quite accurately. But four-color printing is expensive because of the extra filmwork or digital separations involved, as well as the need for four runs through the press.

✔ **Alternatives to four-color process printing:** Some alternatives allow you to have a variety of colors but still keep costs down. When using PMS colors, screen the color(s) at different percentages. For example, your brochure may have only two ink colors, such as black and blue. Use the blue screened back to 80 percent, 60 percent, and 20 percent to give the impression that you're using four different blues when you're actually using blue at 100 percent, 80 percent, 60 percent, and 20 percent. This way, the printer can do all the blues on one run through the press. And although the shades of blue plus the black give the feeling of five colors, the brochure needs only two runs — one for black and one for blue.

✔ **Raster Image Processing (RIP):** Another alternative for avoiding the high cost of the four-color process is to have your publication RIPped to a color copier or high-end digital laser printer. Some printers have their computers hooked up to color copiers and can RIP your file to the copier and get a similar product to four-color copying. This process is especially good when you need less than 100 brochures. You pay an initial RIPping cost and then pay for each page printed at the cost of a color copy.

✔ **Inkjet and color laser printing:** For very small runs, you can use any decent desktop printer. For example, many of the HP inkjet printers can produce a good quality color brochure using HP brochure paper. You have to print and fold them yourself, so I wouldn't make more than 10 or 20 at one sitting, or you'll go nuts. But for small runs, the desktop option is great.

When laying out a brochure for any of these printing options, avoid large fields of solid color because they add to the cost of a printed piece, and some electronic printers have a hard time keeping the ink consistent throughout the field of color. In some cases, you can screen large solid colors to give them more consistency (for example, use blue at 85 percent instead of 100 percent — it will still look like dark blue but will print more consistently and with less trouble). Also, watch out for any printed areas that reach (or bleed) all the way to the edge of the paper. To print to the edge of your sheet of paper, the printer has to print a larger sheet and cut it down — and that adds up to extra costs for you.

## *Artwork*

Illustrating a brochure adds visual appeal and, if the illustrations are appropriate, makes it more persuasive. "Seeing is believing," as the saying goes! But just as with type design, you need some basic technical knowledge before you're ready to select artwork for your brochure. The catch is that how you want to produce the final output partially determines how you choose and prepare your graphics in the first place.

When you design a brochure or other printed product, keep in mind that the artwork needs to be in a file that has reasonably high resolution: 300 dpi is the standard for most printing jobs. Pictures for the Web need to be low resolution: 72 dpi is standard for Web images.

The rule is 300 dpi for your printed photos and 72 dpi for Web photos. However, I assume that you *are not changing the size of the picture* to any significant degree when you print it. If you do, the resolution doesn't automatically adjust with the size. The amount of data in the image file is the same no matter what size you make the picture in your printed product. You can get in trouble if you give your printer a JPEG file of a photograph you took that is saved at 300 dpi, and then you tell the printer to blow it up to twice its current size. Now the resolution is cut in half. Oops. When you shrink an image, you run the opposite risk — you may make it higher resolution. If a 4-x-6-inch photograph at 300 dpi is used to fill a 1-x-1$^1$/$_2$-inch hole in a Web page design, it will load slowly because it still has all the data with which it started. Graphic designers resize images and adjust their dpi in order to fit the design and medium (resizing is easy in programs like InDesign and Photoshop). I'm not going to cover these technicalities here. I'm going to suggest instead that you ask your printer (or Web designer) if your photograph is the right size and resolution, and if it isn't, ask her to help you adjust it.

Your printer or designer may ask you whether you're going to provide a bitmapped image or a vector image. Most photographs are bitmapped. Logos created by graphic designers are usually vectored. Here's a brief overview of the two options so that you'll know what your printer is talking about when the question comes up:

✔ **Bitmapped images (or raster images):** When you bitmap an image, you digitize and store the image, using small squares (pixels) arranged on a grid to represent the image. Bitmapped images are fine, as long as the image stays at the same size or smaller. If you blow it up, though, the small squares grow larger, making them noticeable and giving the image a poor appearance. CD0706 compares a bitmapped image with a vector image to show how they look when enlarged beyond their original size.

✔ **Vector images:** Designers use vector images to get around the problems of blowing up bitmapped images by using mathematical equations to represent the lines and curves in artwork. The art stays clean and clear at any level of enlargement because the computer program literally redraws it to the new scale. Most logos are vector images because they're reproduced in many different sizes for different uses.

The examples of bitmapped and vector art, shown in CD0706, are both examples of line art. *Line art* consists of any black-and-white image with no gray areas or screens. These images can be anything from line drawings to black-and-white logos.

You can also print forms of art other than line art — in other words, art that has grays or shades of color in it. (Photographs are a good example.) But, wouldn't you know it? Doing so adds more technical issues. Avoid using anything drawn in pencil, such as drawings or sketches, because these images are difficult to reproduce. If you have to use a pencil drawing, the printer may suggest making a *halftone print* of the image to save the gray areas from burning out. (A halftone print is a high-quality option using screens; your printer will know all about it.) Follow this advice and don't grumble about the minor added expense.

## Photography

Traditional printers usually like to work from black-and-white photos that you supply (assuming that you want one- or two-color output). Color photos, especially *low-contrast photos* (photos that don't have a lot of difference between dark and light areas), tend to muddy up when you reproduce them in black ink. But sometimes you have to use color photos because that's all you have or because your source is color photos from other marketing materials, such as your Web site or a PowerPoint sales presentation.

Do your best to find and use high-contrast photos (with lots of difference between the dark and light areas). High-contrast photos have more definition and reproduce better.

If you or a photographer are planning to take pictures of your products, facilities, or people, make sure that you use a high-contrast film (one designed to produce sharp, clear images). In general, slower films (ones with lower American Standards Association, or ASA, numbers) give higher contrast and sharper images. When shooting with a digital camera, you can set the ASA anywhere you like. However, the principle remains the same: You need plenty of light! If you're able to shoot at fairly low ASA, then your digital camera's sensors are telling you there is enough light for a publishable photo.

## Clip art and stock photography

You can use copyright-free images, such as clip art and photos, when budget constraints eliminate the possibility of hiring professional illustrators or photographers. These images are copyright free, so you don't have to pay royalties or get special permissions to reproduce them. They're usually available on disk or CD, and you typically pay a modest fee to the publisher. And you may also find some stock photography Web sites that are running promotions in which they're offering some images for free as a way to attract new customers — if so, grab some art while you can! The company Hemera (www.hemera.com) is one of the stock photography houses that sometimes runs promotions.

## Crop and fold marks

Crop and fold marks tell printers where they need to cut or fold a marketing piece. You need to mark these instructions on your original piece with a *hairline* — the smallest weight printed line possible — to ensure accuracy.

The following list briefly explains the standard terms and symbols that you need to know to communicate with your printer or binder:

✔ **Crop marks:** *Crop marks* are guides that show the printer where to cut a page. If you need to print your brochure on larger paper and then cut it down (like when the ink bleeds all the way to the edge of your page or when you specify a nonstandard size), the printer uses the crop marks to cut in exactly the right place.

✔ **Fold marks:** *Fold marks* tell the printer where to fold the paper. But make sure that he understands which *way* to fold the page!

✔ **Score marks:** *Score marks* indicate where the printer should *score,* or lightly cut, the paper. When using heavy paper, you sometimes need to score before you fold in order to get a clean, crisp fold. In that case, you need to mark the fold line as a score line, too.

✔ **Perforating marks:** You use *perforating marks* when a brochure includes a coupon or postcard that you want people to tear out. Perforating marks show the printer where to make the *perforations* — a series of short cuts in the paper.

In addition to providing marks to show where you want folds, scores, and the like, you should also make a mock-up of your brochure. It doesn't have to be fancy. Cut and tape it together. The point of a mockup is to show the printer how the finished product should look in three dimensions. The mockup will help the printer interpret your marks and instructions and avoid confusion.

## Making Digital Brochures

In my firm, we often include a CD or DVD along with the printed materials in mailings and client proposals. A CD can contain lengthy documents in PDF or Word formats, as well as extensive photographs, PowerPoint slide presentations, and even streaming video. Or, if you have high-quality video about a product or service, you can use a DVD to distribute a video brochure. It's basically an infomercial on a disc — instead of the harder-to-handle, old-fashioned VHS video format.

When is using the more extensive capabilities of a CD or DVD rather than, or in addition to, a traditional brochure more worthwhile? I recommend using a CD or DVD in either of these situations:

✔ If your "story" is complex and detailed, and prospective customers need and want to do extensive background research before buying

✔ If you want to make a good impression by using a new medium in a creative way

I use CDs for the first reason, because when I sell a complex service — like leadership training — I know that people want to see a lot of information, including examples of our instructors in action. And that kind of info is best done using new media rather than a traditional brochure.

If you have trouble visualizing how to set up a CD brochure, think about the design as a Web page. Why? Because you (or any competent Web design firm) can create Web-page style designs, just like any you see on the Web; the only difference is that you launch them off the CD. In fact, you should also put the digital brochure on your Web site and include the link in the cover letter for the CD and on the label of it, because some of your customers or prospects will prefer to view it that way instead of having to load a CD.

I don't have space to cover the how-tos in detail, but if you don't have the budget to hire someone who knows how, other useful references can help you, such as *Digital Video For Dummies* by Keith Underdahl, *Cutting Edge PowerPoint 2007 For Dummies* by Geetesh Bajaj, and *Web Design For Dummies* by Lisa Lopuck, all published by Wiley.

# Captivating Catalogs

If you think of a catalog as an elaborate brochure, you'll happily discover that you already know a great deal about how to design and print catalogs if you read the earlier part of this chapter. That's because everything I cover in those sections applies to catalogs as well. In fact, many simple catalogs are indistinguishable from brochures in their basic design, use of paper, and layout. The only difference is that a catalog focuses on describing a product or service line, which is what makes them catalogs instead of brochures.

More elaborate catalogs are made up of multiple pages stapled together. The most common catalog format uses sheets of tabloid (11-x-17-inch) paper, folded in half. When folded, each tabloid sheet gives you four 8$^1/_2$-x-11-inch pages to work with. When you use just one tabloid sheet, you have a front and a back page (these pages share one side of the sheet before you fold it) and two inside pages (which share the other side of the sheet).

Now imagine adding another tabloid sheet to this catalog design. This sheet nests inside the first sheet when folded, and both sheets are stapled together on the fold. With this two-sheet design, you have eight standard 8½-x-11-inch pages to play with — two for the front and back covers and six more on the inside of your catalog.

Add another sheet, and your page count goes up by 4 to 12 pages. Add another sheet, and your catalog has 16 pages you can work with. Bet you aren't surprised to find that most catalogs have page counts that are multiples of four! (If you plan to do frequent printings of such catalogs in small quantities, consider buying your own tabloid-sized laser printer. It's not hard to center-fold and staple a few dozen catalogs yourself, and you can buy an extra-long stapler that reaches the middle of a tabloid page. However, for larger runs, stick with commercial printers.)

## Design considerations

I go into considerable detail about the design of brochures in the section "Layout tips," earlier in this chapter, because I believe many marketers can and should roll up their sleeves and get involved in designing their own brochures. By getting involved, you don't feel intimidated by the project and can feel free to create and replace brochures whenever you have a need to.

The same is true for simple catalogs prepared in the same style as brochures. You can design one-sheet catalogs with one or more folds and have them printed at the local print shop or photocopied quite easily. But if you want to get into more elaborate, multipage catalogs, you may do better to work with a specialist.

Consider hiring a designer who specializes in catalogs. There's more to creating a catalog than the mechanics of design and layout, although those alone can become quite complex when you have many pages. The biggest challenge, however, is to sell your product effectively in the pages of a catalog. How you present each purchase option (in copy and art), what you choose to feature on the outside and inside covers (where you get the most impact), whether you include an index, what sort of look and feel you go for — all these decisions are really quite sophisticated and difficult, so I recommend spending the extra money for an expert's input.

Printing a multipage, four-color catalog can be costly (between $1 and $5 a copy depending on design, paper, quantity, length, and trim size). Mailing it adds up, too. You may as well invest enough in the design to give yourself good odds of getting a profitable return on that investment.

For a less expensive alternative, print a handsome brochure that highlights your best-selling products and directs the reader to your Web site. Design your Web site as if it's a high-quality catalog, with large or pop-up photos of your products, detailed supporting information, and an ecommerce store, as well as easy-access e-mail and telephone contact options for inquiries. An excellent example of this strategy is provided by Vermont Woods, which retails fine handmade furniture and gifts made by Vermont artisans, in its online catalog at www.vermontwoods.com.

For a very low-cost approach to do-it-yourself online catalogs, take a look at eBay (www.ebay.com), which supports vendors with templates and makes showcasing your products, accepting orders, or running auctions easy. Many vendors use an eBay store as their primary catalog and Web site, and run occasional auctions at low starting bids as a way to promote their store to eBay users.

## Benchmark catalogs for your reference

You can easily find good examples of multipage, full-color catalogs by examining your mail. Clothing retailers like J. Crew and Lands End usually have well-done catalogs that can serve as your benchmarks. Also look at glossy, sophisticated magazines on the newsstands for interesting approaches to graphic design that you may want to earmark for a catalog. Staples sends regular business-to-business (B2B) catalogs that are usually competently designed. I recommend keeping a folder of catalogs that appeal to you so that you can review their designs next time you need ideas.

Notice especially how good catalogs

- ✔ Use their front covers to feature special products or offers or to create appealing moods.

- ✔ Organize their contents in intuitive ways so that readers can quickly find sections of interest.

- ✔ Vary the page layouts so that each page doesn't look like the last and avoids monotony.

- ✔ Give readers plenty of ways to reach the company with questions or orders, including telephone and fax numbers (and perhaps a Web site) on each page, as well as a clear, flexible order form.

- ✔ Contain clear, accurate, sufficient information about products to support purchase decisions. (They answer all the customers' questions well.)

- ✔ Are positive in their emotional appeals, using smiling people, enthusiastic language, bright, warm colors, or all three to create an "up" mood in readers.

## Less is more

Here's an example of the power of white space. A company that sells office supplies wanted to liquidate a lot of inventory by publishing a special sale catalog. At first, the company's catalog had a cover design featuring a photo of a warehouse stacked so high and thick with all sorts of products that it looked like a maze. Across the photo, in big type, ran the title "Everything Must Go!" The design was overpowering, and it hurt the eye to look at this cover, so the company reconsidered.

Finally, the company published a catalog with a cover that was mostly white. This design showed an almost entirely empty, clean, white warehouse interior, cavernous in its emptiness except for one lone box far off in the corner with a man in a dark business suit standing there looking down at it. Across the top of this design ran the headline, "Everything Will Go." This new design was visually appealing and enticed curious shoppers into the interior of the catalog to find out more.

Notice how good catalogs break up space into smaller blocks by using a column or grid pattern to display multiple products on most of the pages. If you can tighten up the space used for each product without damaging the selling power of your coverage, you can generate more revenues per page. And because design, printing, and mailing costs vary with the number of pages, hardworking pages make for a more successful catalog.

Also notice that many of the most visually appealing and readable catalogs aren't too cluttered. They have that magic ingredient of great designs — white space. *White space* is the open space that you can see on the page where neither text nor images are. Amateur designers (that's most marketers, by the way) tend to cram too much onto a page, which makes focusing on any one item difficult. Open up your design with a little more white space than people usually use, and your catalog becomes more readable and attractive.

## *The list factor*

So who do you send your catalog or brochure to? A regional business-to-business marketer may be content to send a catalog to only a few thousand names. A national business-to-business catalog usually needs to go to at least 10,000 names, and sometimes four or five times that many. Consumer-oriented catalogs on specialty topics (like model railroading) may go to small numbers of names, but consumer catalogs usually need to go to hundreds of thousands of people to really be successful.

Set your circulation target based on the following factors:

- ✔ **How big the potential market is:** Try to reach at least half your potential market through your mailing. But if your catalog is new, test it on smaller samples first to make sure that it's profitable.

- ✔ **How much inventory or capacity you have:** Try not to send out so many catalogs that you risk being unable to fill your orders. Otherwise, customers will become upset and won't respond the next time.

- ✔ **How big your in-house list of past purchasers is:** You can, and should, try to supplement your in-house list. But don't let new names that you purchase dominate your mailing; getting a good response from them is just too hard. Build your list gradually until you have a substantial (for your market) in-house list rather than trying to supplement 1,000 past purchasers with 100,000 names from purchased lists.

- ✔ **How big your budget is:** In the real world, it doesn't matter that millions of people buy gardening supplies if you only have $3,000 to spend on launching a new catalog of specialty garden tools. Spend cautiously so that you can afford to recover and try another mailing, even if the first one is an abject failure. The path to success is paved with failures, so make sure that you can afford to survive a few low-response-rate mailings. Eventually, you'll discover a mailing design and strategy that really pays off for you — but only if you can afford to stay in the game long enough for luck to strike!

# Spectacular Spec Sheets

"Just the facts, ma'am." Too often marketers forget to communicate enough information or to communicate it clearly enough so that people can make informed purchase decisions. Marketing communications are often maddeningly vague to serious buyers, who want to know exactly what you do, how your equipment performs, what the specifications are, what the terms are, and so on. What, exactly, *are* the facts?

Enter the specification, or spec, sheet. A *spec sheet* is a simple, clear, one-page technical description of a product (or, rarely, a service). It contains all facts — or mostly facts; it may also have a testimonial or two and a nice photo or illustration. It often uses a tabular layout to provide consumers with detailed information that they need to make a purchase decision. Spec sheets serve this purpose well, providing the hard-core, informational backup to support more imaginative or persuasive marketing materials. I believe that everyone ought to prepare spec sheets for each product or service they sell. Not all prospects will want one, but those who do will really appreciate it.

Include a spec sheet in the sales collateral for a product if technical specifications are important to buyers or prospective buyers of that product. Include a spec sheet in the collateral materials for a video monitor, fire extinguisher, food processor, outboard motor, golf club, toaster, or remote-control toy car, for example, because buyers of these products may well want or need to know something about the product's specifications.

## Formatting your spec sheet

Spec sheets usually are $8\frac{1}{2}$-x-11-inch pieces of paper with printing on only one side. Include your company's name, logo, and contact information on the top or bottom of the sheet. Title it "Specifications for <product name/code>" at the top (or just beneath your company identification). Date it because specifications often change, and you may issue updated sheets in the future.

Use your company letterhead for a simple, quick spec sheet. You can use Word's table option and your office printer to create a simple but professional spec sheet on your letterhead.

Set up the spec sheet in two columns, with the left column listing a category of specifications (size, weight, voltage, pH, and so on) and the right column giving a specific measurement for each category. Use numbered footnotes to define any ambiguous or obscure terms or units. Avoid lengthy descriptions, and don't try to "sell" the product. Spec sheets give specifications; they don't promote. Hopefully, the product or service is good, and the specifications will do the selling for you!

Here's a simple template for spec sheets:

Specifications for <product>
Date/date/date

| Category | Data |
|---|---|
| Category | Data |
| Category | Data |
| Category | Data |
| Category | Data |
| Category | Data |

Company Name
Address
Phone/Fax
E-mail/Web page

## Ensuring that your spec sheet is up to snuff

Spec sheets should be *clear, readable* (don't use type smaller than 11 point, please!), *accurate,* and *sufficient.* Verify all the data you include on the spec sheet and include everything needed to describe the product.

To ensure that your specifications are sufficient, look at spec sheets of competing products. Also *ask customers or prospects what information they need.* If you're using units that aren't universal, provide conversions (for example, give the dimensions of a product in both inches and centimeters). And verify all specifications with product designers and producers. Ask them whether they're *sure* of the specifications. You don't want to be wrong. (If you're in one of those industries where regulations or legal liability are issues, also have a qualified lawyer review your spec sheet before printing it.)

If you hire a graphic designer or advertising agency to typeset your spec sheet, leave time to thoroughly check its accuracy after the design is finalized but before it's printed. The design process can introduce errors into spec sheets. Also, designers may want to "jazz up" your spec sheet. Discourage this urge. Keep spec sheets clean and simple and save the creativity for other marketing materials.

# Marketing with Booklets and Books

Consultants have long used the power of a book to promote their firm and its services. One of the reasons I write books is because they stimulate hundreds of thousands of dollars worth of business opportunities for my consulting and training business. A book can be a powerful demonstration of your expertise, allowing prospective customers to get to know you well enough to decide whether they want to work with you. Of course, the risk is that they decide you don't know what you're talking about, so be sure to approach books with caution. If you aren't a writer yourself, you can find ghostwriters and publicity firms that specialize in creating books for business clients.

If you aren't a consultant, do you still need a book? Well, anyone whose expertise is important to her customers, including doctors, lawyers, architects, accountants, heating and air-conditioning contractors, and so on, may benefit from having a book or booklet of her own. For example, one heating and air-conditioning contractor published a short but nicely done booklet titled *How to Increase the Comfort of Your Building* to promote his services. The booklet addressed upgrades and improvements to both residential and commercial structures, with short chapters explaining how and why to install different types of systems. The booklet had nice pictures and diagrams (provided by the suppliers whose equipment this company installed), plus minicases of successful projects. The three top people in the company wrote this booklet, and their photos and bios appeared on the back cover. Whenever company employees interacted with new or potential customers, they included this booklet as a handout, and it made a strong, positive impression that helped land the company many good jobs.

How expensive is it to make a book or booklet and use it for marketing? If you keep it short and sweet (64 pages or under, center stapled) and provide much of the content yourself, you won't need to pay a lot for ghostwriting. Writing your own material can save you quite a bit of money because the better ghostwriters charge anywhere from a few thousand dollars to a hundred thousand, depending on the project! (My firm charges between $5,000 to $10,000 to create one of these books for a client, for example.) When the time comes to produce the book or booklet, you can do it in-house using Word — if you're very brave — but I recommend working with a local print shop that has a Xerox Docutech machine or something comparable, along with perfectbinding machine equipment.

# On the CD

Check out the following items on the CD:

- ✔ Sample one-page B2B promotional flier (CD0701)
- ✔ Sample brochure with unusual layout (CD0702)
- ✔ Illustration of brochure from CD0702 when folded (CD0703)
- ✔ Product Offerings brochure template in Word (CD0704)
- ✔ Brochure template with photographic design elements (CD0705)
- ✔ Illustration of bitmapped versus vector line art options (CD0706)

# Chapter 8

# Planning Coupons and Other Sales Promotions

•••••••••••••••••••••••••••••••••••••••••••••••••

### In This Chapter

▶ Understanding the importance of profit

▶ Finding out how promotions affect sales

▶ Setting up coupon programs

▶ Using other sales promotions

•••••••••••••••••••••••••••••••••••••••••••••••••

**M**any marketing experts use the term *sales promotion* to describe the use of coupons, discounts, premium items (special gifts), and other incentives to boost sales. Coupons are probably the best known and most widely used sales promotions, but you can use plenty of other ways to give prospects an incentive to make the purchase. In this chapter, I look at a variety of options, explore some of the best ways (and worst ways) to use them, and end with an analytical approach that helps you figure out whether a specific incentive will prove profitable or not.

## The Importance of Profit

Making a sale is easy if you don't care about profits. Cut the price enough, and almost anything will sell. Witness the junk people buy at yard sales, flea markets, or dollar stores. But you're in business, so you don't want sales if they don't make you money. And sales promotions don't always make money.

In fact, some of the more common examples of sales promotions are hard to accept from a profit perspective. Take the periodic sale and clearance catalogs that London-based Victoria's Secret, a cataloger and retailer specializing in women's lingerie and clothing, distributes. The company usually prints a 7½-x-10-inch, full-color catalog with a cover featuring some of the new items.

But occasionally, the company sends out a clearance version using some of the items and photos from earlier catalogs, bound in a special sales-promotion-oriented version with a cover advertising all the special prices inside.

Here's an example of the offers featured (in bold, white print on a dark pink background) on one of its sale covers, a cover that actually had no photos or drawings of products, but simply contained text describing the special deals inside:

*"Sale: bras & panties 25% to 50% off!"*

*"Clearance: discontinued bras $9.99 to $12.99!"*

At the bottom of this cover, in smaller print, the company added more promotional offers:

*"Save up to an additional $75 on a qualifying sale purchase — and defer payment until September when you charge your order of $75 or more to the Victoria's Secret Credit Card. See page 2."*

Because the catalog shipped during the spring, deferring payment until September is a fairly appealing incentive. And, obviously, the idea of a quarter to a half off normal prices is an incentive to open up the catalog and do some serious shopping. Women who make occasional purchases from regular-priced catalogs tend to respond more to these sale catalogs and with larger orders.

But is this good marketing or not? The answer depends on what the mailing costs Victoria's Secret and what other objectives the company wants to accomplish. And, most of all, that answer depends on how people react to the special offers.

✔ **If Victoria's Secret customers get in the habit of waiting for the special sale catalog before ordering, the marketing won't be profitable.** This promotional practice might make full-price customers migrate to discount-price customers, training them to wait for a special offer. This migration often happens when companies experiment with price-based sales promotions. In fact, recently Victoria's Secret has done fewer sale catalogs in order to reduce this effect.

✔ **If Victoria's Secret customers are reminded of how much they like the company's product line by this sale catalog and not only buy from the catalog but look more closely at the next few mailings, then this marketing is a huge success.** Hopefully, customers will use the sales to stock up on some basics but still look forward to seeing new clothes in the next regular catalog. And if each season's new clothes are unique and appealing, many customers will want to purchase them in season and at full price rather than gambling that they'll end up in a sale catalog months later.

In reality, both reactions occur in any sales promotion. You do get customers who simply shop for deals and won't give you any business at full price. But you also may remind some customers that they like your products and recruit other customers for the first time, building a habit of shopping with you that carries over to future nonsale purchases. And that result is a great return from a sales promotion — one that makes even a break-even promotion worthwhile in terms of future sales and profits.

# How Promotions Affect Sales

How does a coupon, discount, or other form of sales promotion work? A sales promotion can basically have one or more of the following five effects on the market:

- **It takes your competitor's customers.** The promotion encourages the consumer to purchase a new brand or do business with a new vendor.

- **It attracts brand-new customers.** The promotion may draw in new users who've never bought products like yours.

- **It stimulates repeat purchases.** The consumer is more likely to keep buying the product or doing business with the vendor because of the promotion.

- **It stimulates bigger purchases.** The consumer buys sooner and/or in larger quantities as a result of the promotion. (Be careful, though; sometimes a corresponding decline in purchases occurs later on!)

- **It gives away profits to people who would have bought anyway.** This is the risk you run: What if all you do is cut prices to customers who would have bought at a higher price? Sometimes customers load up during a promotion and then don't buy at their normal rate afterward.

The first four scenarios are positive. They help generate more sales and grow your customer base. That's a good result for coupons or other sales promotions, and it's the reason marketers call these things *sales promotions*. Multiple paths can lead to those increased sales, and sometimes the increases are long term rather than short term. If you don't see a clear link from your coupon or discount program to increased sales, then forget it. You're wasting your time and your business's money.

# Planning Coupon Programs

*Boy, have I got a deal for you!*

These classic words (or offers to the same effect) are the bread and butter of many marketing initiatives. Offering a discount gives people a reason to buy. It attracts their attention. It converts vague intentions into immediate actions. However, it also costs you money, and that's not so good.

How much will a discount cost your company? Will the increased sales more than offset the cost? Don't know. Better find out. You need to do some careful thinking and forecasting before you offer any discounts or distribute any coupons.

If you print and distribute coupons, any number of things may happen:

- ✔ The prospects may ignore them.

- ✔ Some prospects may redeem the coupons and become loyal, profitable customers.

- ✔ Everyone may ignore the coupons except those people who constantly shop for deals — and these people won't become regular customers unless you *always* offer them a deal.

- ✔ Some stores may *misredeem* the coupons (apply the coupon to the wrong product), in which case you end up paying the coupons' face value but not winning new sales.

- ✔ Existing customers may use the coupons to buy just as much as they would have without the coupons, in which case you've just given away profits.

- ✔ New sales may flood in, making you very happy — until you realize that the costs of the coupon program are high enough that you've lost money in the process of winning that new business.

In other words, you can't really be sure what will happen, and a number of bad results may occur. Good things may result, too, but those aren't a certainty.

Enter *coupon profitability analysis.* If you do a careful analysis of several possible scenarios upfront and crunch the numbers on each scenario, you have a much better idea of the likely outcomes. Often, when people do a formal analysis, they're horrified at the results. They find that their initial ideas and assumptions have fatal flaws, and they realize that they were about to throw away some or all of their profit margin in exchange for very little new business. So I highly recommend doing a careful profitability analysis, which I describe in the next section.

Also, remember to experiment and gather data from your experiences. It takes time and experience to find those formulas that put you in your marketing zone (see Chapter 1). If you did some coupon programs in the past, running the numbers on them is a great idea to see how they worked out. Were they really profitable or not? The answer isn't obvious unless you do a proper analysis. And when you do, you can discover a great deal from these past efforts that can help you design more effective and profitable coupons in the future. Remember that creative experimentation — and learning from your experiments — is at the heart of all great marketing!

## The basics of coupon profitability analysis

So how do you perform a coupon profitability analysis? Basically, follow these steps:

1. **Identify all the fixed and variable costs of the coupon program.**

   *Fixed costs* are costs, such as design expenses, that don't change with quantity of coupons. *Variable costs* are costs that increase with the number of coupons printed and distributed.

2. **Figure out how much product you think you can sell directly to consumers because of the coupon redemption.**

3. **Figure out how much money you make by selling that product.**

4. **Subtract all those expenses from the profits you've earned to see whether the coupon program is profitable or not.**

This four-step method is perhaps not quite as simple as it seems, so take a look at an example for 1,000 coupons with a face value of $10 each. This example appears in the file CD0801. A $10 coupon is quite valuable, so the redemption rate should be high — in this example, it's estimated at 8 percent. When all costs are worked in, the net impact is estimated to be a gain of about $1,000 in profits. This coupon program ought to more than pay for itself — and if it attracts some new customers who then come back and buy again, it will have a good, long-term impact, too.

As you can see in Figure 8-1, the basic idea is to estimate all your costs, redemption rates, and other important statistics, and then to add an analysis of the impact on your sales and profits. (If you have trouble reading Figure 8-1, check out CD0801, which is a PDF of the figure.) To perform your profitability analysis, follow the step-by-step instructions I provide in the next section, which are based on an interactive spreadsheet template (CD0802).

## Coupon Profitability Analysis

WORKED EXAMPLE FOR YOUR REFERENCE

| | |
|---|---|
| Number of Coupons | 1000 |
| Face Value of Coupons | $10.00 |

**Fixed Costs:**
(Costs required to create and manage the promotion)

| | |
|---|---|
| Design and consultation fees (if any) | $500.00 |
| Setup costs for producing coupons | $250.00 |
| Other fixed costs (describe) | $50.00 |
| **Total Fixed Costs** | **$800.00** |

**Incremental Costs:**
(Costs varying with number of coupons)          *Incremental costs running total....*

| | | |
|---|---|---|
| Production costs per thousand coupons | $10.00 | $10.00 |
| Distribution costs per thousand coupons | $50.00 | $50.00 |
| Legitimate redemption rate | 8.0% | $800.00 |
| Misredemption rate | 1.0% | $100.00 |
| Processing costs per coupon redeemed | $0.10 | $9.00 |
| Other variable costs per coupon (describe) | 0 | $0.00 |
| **Total variable costs** | | **$969.00** |

**Total Costs:** . . . . . . . . . . . . . . . . . . . . . . . . .   **$1,769.00**

**Incremental Profit Contribution:**
(Number of incremental sales x profit margin on product)

| | |
|---|---|
| Number of sales directly from redemptions | 80 |
| Percentage that would have occurred anyway | 25.00% |
| **No. of incremental sales from redemptions** | **20** |
| Profit contribution per sale | $70.00 |
| **Total incremental profits resulting from coupon program** | **$1,400.00** |

**Bottom-line Impact of Coupon (Net Profit)**

| | |
|---|---|
| **Net Profit** (Incremental sales revenues minus total costs) | **$431.00** |

**Figure 8-1:**
Analyzing
a coupon
program
using the
spreadsheet
in CD0802.

# Coupon profitability analysis step by step

Please use the spreadsheet called CD0802 from your Marketing Kit CD. This form runs in Excel. To use it, make a working copy (so you don't accidentally mess up the master file's formulas) and then fill in the boxed cells with numbers representing your plans for a coupon program. The spreadsheet calculates everything else to figure out your costs and profits.

The general categories of costs are

✔ **Fixed costs:** Fixed costs are the costs of designing your coupon, printer's setup costs, and so on. Be sure to include all fixed costs that are necessary to create the coupon and program.

✔ **Variable costs:** These costs vary with the number of coupons. Note that many such costs are conventionally measured on a cost per 1,000 coupons rather than on a cost per individual coupon. When you get quotes from printers and the companies that handle coupon redemptions, those quotes will probably be in costs per 1,000 coupons. (If not, please convert.)

### Filling in the blanks

The following paragraphs go through the coupon profitability analysis line by line, and I show you how to enter appropriate variables so that you can see how a coupon program might work. You have to fill in 13 cells in order to complete an analysis of a future scenario or past program. Are you ready? Good. Here we go.

**Number of coupons:** _____

How many coupons do you plan to distribute? If you're planning on giving them out through a store or other public site, you may not be able to guess accurately how many coupons people will pick up. So just take your best guess, print a specific number, and then test several levels of distribution: Say *(a)* the entire print run, *(b)* $\frac{2}{3}$ of it, and *(c)* $\frac{1}{3}$ of it. If the program seems like it may be profitable at all these levels, then it's probably a good idea to try. Often, however, companies distribute an offer to a mailing list of a known number or to the subscribers of a publication. In these cases, you can use basic circulation or list data to determine how many coupons you'll be distributing.

**Face value of coupons: $**_____

What are you planning to offer the users of the coupon? Typically a coupon gives a discount on the purchase of a single product, so that's how I set up this spreadsheet. Enter a dollar value representing the amount the coupon is good for. For example, if you plan to offer a $20 discount off the next purchase of a carton of your special industrial cleaning fluid, then enter $20 in this cell.

Ah, but how much of a discount do you need to offer to get a good response? I was afraid you'd ask that! A good but vague rule is to offer just enough to get someone's attention. If you offer too much, well, you're just giving the product away. If you offer too little, nobody pays attention. So what discount should you offer? Regular coupon marketers run lots of experiments until they find some formulas that work. If you don't have any idea of what to offer, you need to run some experiments yourself. Start with a nice, safe number. "Safe" means from a bottom-line perspective, which means a number that's considerably less than your profit.

For example, say you make a cool new cat toy that you sell at wholesale to pet stores for $1.75, which they mark up to a retail price of $2.49. When you examine your costs, you find that it costs you approximately $1.20 to make and deliver each unit, so your profit is $0.55 on each cat toy you sell. Now, offering a $0.55 discount would be a costly experiment, wouldn't it? But a $0.25 discount you can readily afford. On the other hand, is that discount enough to get anyone's attention? Maybe not. The redemption rate may be pretty low. So perhaps a $0.35 coupon is better. This discount still leaves a little profit to cover (hopefully) the costs of the coupon program, but offers enough of a discount that it may get a reasonable response rate from cat owners. You may want to start there and see what happens.

**Design and consultation fees: $_____**

If you hire a graphic designer, marketing consultant, or ad agency to design your coupon, you're going to have to pay her. Enter the cost here.

**Setup costs for producing coupons: $_____**

If you're having a printer produce your coupons, you'll have some setup costs. Enter those costs here. If you're buying ad space in a newspaper or other publication for your coupons, then you probably don't have to pay setup costs, so just enter a zero.

**Other fixed costs: $_____**

If you expect to incur any other upfront or fixed costs, be sure to add them in here. Forgotten costs come back to bite!

**Production costs per 1,000 coupons: $_____**

If you're having a printer produce the coupons, your printer can give you this number (along with the setup costs, earlier in this list). Ask him what the costs are at several different volume levels because there may be a sliding scale based on quantity. If you're inserting your coupons into a publication, just enter zero in this blank. Then the next line item is the one for you!

**Distribution costs per 1,000 coupons: $_____**

What will the newspaper, trade magazine, or coupon booklet publisher charge you for inserting your coupon in its publication? What will stores charge you for placing your coupons at the point of purchase? What will some hot Web site charge you to put your discount offer in a banner ad? If you're using someone else's service to distribute your coupon offer to prospective customers, enter that service's cost per 1,000 coupons here.

**Legitimate redemption rate (Percent of coupons properly redeemed): ____%**

What percentage of those coupons will people actually use toward the purchase of your product? It may be 100 percent, but I doubt it. Usually, a small percentage of coupons are actually redeemed. For under-a-dollar discounts on consumer nondurables, often just a few percent of coupons are redeemed. For larger discounts and/or higher-cost items, the rates may be higher, even over 10 percent. But again, there's no substitute for experience, so if you've done similar coupon programs in the past, use them as your basis for estimating. If not, well, recognize that you're running an experiment and don't do anything on such a large scale that you'll regret the results later!

**Misredemption rate (Percent of coupons redeemed wrongly/for the wrong products): ___%**

Programs rarely work exactly as you hope. Sometimes the store clerks or order fulfillment staff apply the coupon to the wrong product. Sometimes somebody finds some way to scam you. If there are ways for things to go wrong, they will. So build a little error into your projections and make sure that it won't kill you.

The problem with misredemptions, obviously, is that you end up paying the face value of coupons but not getting a product sale in return. So the misredemptions come directly off the bottom line. Fortunately, misredemption rates are generally quite low.

**Processing costs per coupon redeemed: $_____**

If you're using a totally computerized system in which the coupon is scanned or the discount is applied to a customer code number, then you don't really have any appreciable processing costs. Your system (or some stores' systems) just processes the things automatically. But most coupons actually end up being handled by someone somewhere, and that handling costs you money, whether you use a redemption service or hire someone to do it. When you subcontract coupon processing, the costs are generally in the 5¢ to 15¢ per coupon range. If you plan to have someone do it by hand, estimate how many he can do per hour and work out what it costs per coupon. Enter your estimated processing cost per coupon in this blank.

**Other variable costs per coupon: $_____**

If other incremental costs exist that I didn't think to include, put them here. If not, just enter "0" on this line.

**Percentage of these sales that would have occurred anyway: ___%**

The spreadsheet calculates the number of sales from coupon redemptions. It does this calculation based on the number of coupons and the legitimate redemption rate you entered. If, for example, you plan to distribute 100 coupons and you anticipate a 5 percent redemption rate, the spreadsheet calculates that you will sell five units as a result of the coupon program. Now, many people just chalk up all five of those units as resulting from the coupons. In other words, they give the coupon full credit for all those sales in which customers redeemed a coupon. But is that fair? Maybe not. What if some regular customers would have bought anyway, but at full price rather than at the discount rate? Then your coupon isn't really bringing you their business.

So in this blank, you can account for those regular users who would have purchased anyway. You do so by estimating what percentage of all redemptions they'll make up. Make it a high percentage if you think that the distribution method that you're using will reach lots of regular, loyal customers. Make it a low percentage if you think that the distribution method will reach mostly new prospects — such as users of your competitor's products. Make it a zero if you're introducing a new product that doesn't have any regular users.

**Profit contribution per sale: $_____**

How much do you actually make in profits from each product that you sell? Calculate this number based only on the direct costs of making and selling one unit of the product. That number is the profit contribution per sale, and hopefully it's a positive contribution!

## The bottom line is . . .

That's it! When you fill in all those blanks, you get "the answer." In fact, you get a number of answers. The spreadsheet tells you what your fixed costs, variable costs, and total costs should be, assuming that your estimates are correct. The spreadsheet also figures out how many new sales you should get as a result of coupon redemptions. Finally, and most important, the program calculates the total *incremental profit* — that is, the amount of money that your coupon program makes or loses.

## Testing multiple scenarios

Because this spreadsheet has built-in formulas, you can and should test many different variables in order to get a feel for the range of possible outcomes. For example, I highly recommend that you test several different redemption rates. Build low-, medium-, and high-redemption-rate scenarios. Make sure that the coupon program appears profitable at all likely redemption rate levels before you run it, because you can never project redemption rates with complete accuracy.

## Learning from experience

When the coupon program is done and you have the actual numbers, compare each variable with your upfront forecast for it. Learn from your mistakes — yes, you will make mistakes. You can't forecast any coupon program with complete accuracy. In fact, unless you run very similar programs routinely, forecasting any program with even rough accuracy is hard to do! So the name of the game is to learn from your experiences.

Here are some great questions to use in debriefing yourself and preparing to design even better coupon programs the next time around:

- Did you do enough coupons to reach your market?

- Did your method of distribution get enough coupons to your target market?

- Did you offer enough of an incentive to attract new business (indicated by sufficiently high redemption rates)?

- Did you offer more of a discount than you needed to in order to attract new business (indicated by far higher redemption rates than expected)?

- Were your fixed costs higher than you expected — and, if so, how can you cut them next time?

- Were your variable costs higher than you expected — and, if so, how can you cut them next time?

- Were too many coupons misredeemed — and, if so, how can you reduce errors and/or cheating in the future?

- Did processing each coupon cost more than you expected — and, if so, how can you reduce this handling cost next time?

When you look at these specific questions, you're working on the key variables that drive the profitability of coupon programs. Learning more about each of these variables and how to control them gives you more control over the bottom-line profitability of your program. Like anything you do in marketing, experience helps you refine your formula.

## Ah, but did it work?

There's one more question you really need to ask after distributing a coupon or other sales promotion. This final question has little to do with the profitability of the coupon program. The question is "Did the coupon achieve my broader marketing objectives?" In other words, did your coupon do one or more of the following:

✔ Attract new customers, some of whom will become regular buyers

✔ Help ward off competition

✔ Boost sales for the period

✔ Introduce customers to a new or improved product or service

✔ Support or enhance other advertising or sales initiatives

✔ Help cushion a price increase

✔ Help cross-sell another product to existing customers

✔ Help motivate the sales force by giving them a new sales incentive or tool

✔ Make your distributors, retailers, or other intermediaries happy and more willing to push your product or service

✔ Help you gain access to greater distribution

✔ Help you migrate customers to direct or Web-based purchasing

✔ Increase repeat purchase rates

✔ Maintain or increase your market share

✔ Attract frequent switchers — those customers who are always looking for a deal

✔ Attract a specific, attractive segment (or group) of customers with an offer designed for and distributed to them

✔ Make a profit

As this lengthy list demonstrates, many reasons exist for distributing coupons or offering special deals. Sometimes marketers are willing to run a coupon program at or below break-even costs in order to accomplish their marketing objectives. The most important objective may not be to make a profit; it may be to give your salespeople an incentive or tool for boosting distribution. In this case, you may be happy to lose money on the coupon as long as you get greater distribution because you figure it's so valuable that it's worth investing in. But even so, make sure that you know how much you're going to lose and keep the program under control.

# Some Alternative Approaches to Sales Promotions

What if you want to offer some incentive to prospects, but you don't want it to be price based and cost you directly on your profit margin? The following sections describe some alternatives that usually build sales or loyalty without costing you as much of your profit margin.

## Offer free food

Face it: People love to eat, at least if the food is good, the location is pleasant, and the company is tolerable. So put some marketing imagination into ways of using free food as an incentive.

One insurance company in California recruited its agents by offering a free seminar at the most luxurious hotels and restaurants, complete with a free meal of the agents' choice. The company promoted the offer with postcard mailings to purchased lists of agents. Then it followed up with a phone call from its call center. Its turnouts were best when the company held the event at the best possible restaurants. And when the dust settled, giving away a free meal in exchange for the chance to build long-term business relationships was really quite economical. This is a good example of business-to-business marketing, where the target is an intermediary, an insurance agent. Sign up agents, and they, in turn, will sign up end customers, giving you a potentially huge return on your investment in free food!

Another good example — this one retail oriented — is JCPenney's occasional practice of giving out chocolate bars at the door. Each is wrapped in a coupon, and the discount offered in these coupons varies, so customers may get lucky and win the rare 50-percent-off coupon.

## Give gifts

Plenty of other alternatives exist for your sales promotions. Only your imagination limits your options in this area, as it does in everything you do in marketing. I recommend collecting examples of clever sales promotions from other marketers — especially marketers who aren't in your industry and don't compete with you. When you look around at all the ideas people try in the world of marketing, you can often find something that adapts well to your business and industry.

Maybe you can try making better use of premium items. Many businesses do. Rocks Communications, a marketing agency that I have worked with in the past, recommends using "lumpy envelopes" with interesting, even funny, gifts inside them. The contents can be simple and useful or simple and zany — it's up to you. If your envelopes are three-dimensional, people open them, and almost 100 percent of them get read — which is way above average for direct mail. Spending between 50¢ and $5 to make an envelope interesting and memorable often pays off well.

I know one executive of a regional moving company who had a bunch of high-quality canvas tote bags embroidered with her company's logo and phone number. She gives these bags out to good customers and prospects, and she reports that the bags are very popular. Also, they tie in nicely with her service, reminding people that her business can help them carry things from one place to another. She has probably gotten more repeat business and referrals from this simple gift item than she would have gotten new business from a series of print ads offering 5 percent discounts on her services. And the premium item is obviously a lot more profitable.

## Offer rewards for repeat business

I highly recommend looking at loyalty rewards and programs. Many businesses are exploring this concept. A program can be something as simple as the coffee card that collects stamps each time you fill up until you earn a free coffee. Or, a loyalty program can be something as complex as an airline's frequent-flier club, with all its rules and benefits and tie-ins to other companies' sales promotions, too. Or maybe you can find a unique formula of your own.

## On the CD

Check out the following file on the CD-ROM:

- Coupon Profitability Analysis example (CD0801)
- Excel spreadsheet for doing your own Coupon Profitability Analysis (CD0802)

# Chapter 9

# Spreading the Word with Newsletters

*N*ewsletters are a great vehicle to deliver information about your field in general, or to bring people up-to-date about your company, product, or organization. Depending on the content, you can publish them monthly, quarterly, or yearly. (I like the idea of sending out a newsletter at the holiday season, even if you don't do one any other time of year.) Like brochures, letterheads, envelopes, and business cards, newsletters reflect your company's personality and should be consistent with the look and feel you have reflected in your other publications. In this chapter, I not only share enough technical information to help you create great newsletters, but I also do my best to convince you to treat newsletters as a very powerful and important marketing medium.

## Why You Need a Newsletter

I really like newsletters as a marketing medium, and if you don't currently have a newsletter, I strongly suggest that you consider creating one. (If you do have one, see whether you can make it even better.)

Why do you need a newsletter? Here are just a few reasons. Newsletters are

- ✔ Relatively cheap to produce (but that's just the beginning of why I like them)

- ✔ A great engagement device that gets people involved and interested

- ✔ One of the best ways to express your personality and values, as well as your offerings

- ✔ Remarkably flexible — you can use them to convey information, promote your own offerings, share customer testimonials, provide interesting or amusing content, share a funny cartoon, and so on

- ✔ A relationship builder that helps retain good customers, as well as attract good prospects

Best of all, most of your competitors don't know how powerful a well-done newsletter can be. So you have a chance to outflank them on this one!

You have both knowledge and news that may be of interest to customers and prospective customers. Use a newsletter to make sure that they find out what you have to share with them. Think of newsletters as a great way to "spread the word" about your business, products, and people, as the old expression puts it. Also, keep in mind that *publicity* — editorial coverage about your business in the media — is usually very effective at raising awareness of what you do and building a positive reputation. When you write and distribute a newsletter, you're in essence creating your own editorial content. The publicity is in your control. It's a good way to strengthen your publicity program.

You can also use a newsletter to make connections with people. Let the newsletter share some of your (or your company's) warmth and enthusiasm, along with the facts. You may often hear people talk about *relationship marketing* — a buzzword that generally means building a more genuine, meaningful, lasting business relationship with your customer. In my mind, a newsletter fits in wonderfully with this strategy. A newsletter gives you many opportunities to explain yourself and present the readers with useful information, entertainment, and other "gifts" on the printed page or via e-mail, CD, or Web site.

I write a lot of educational booklets and other training materials, and to gain greater control over their marketing, I started an educational publishing company some time ago. My business partner, Stephanie Sousbies, believes in relationship building, and one day she pointed out to me that I had written more than 30 books, but that I had not written a newsletter for our customers. "We need one," she said. "Every business does!" Okay, I agreed, but I didn't want to write it. I write too much already. A month later, the first issue went out, and I hadn't written a single word. She did the whole thing herself, even though I'm officially the writer in our partnership. CD0901 is a sample page from one of the issues showing how she makes good use of short articles, color, columns, and graphics to draw the reader in. She sends them out regularly and has experimented lately with HTML and PDF versions via e-mail to supplement the traditional printed version. Each time she sends out a new issue, we get calls and orders — even though the newsletter carefully avoids a hard-sell approach. I think that the numerous educational and interesting short articles help readers get to know and trust us so that they come to us when they need to buy publications.

When you first think about publishing a newsletter, it's easy to fall into the trap of committing to something that is too ambitious. You don't need to publish every month. In fact, once a quarter or irregularly (meaning only a few times a year or less) can be effective and easier to accomplish. Be careful in planning the frequency of your newsletter and never commit to more than you can produce. Start out with a comfortable schedule, maybe quarterly or bimonthly, and work up to a monthly publication when you have the resources and content to put it together. Give yourself enough time to write a good newsletter — and also to continue doing your other marketing tasks.

# Examining the Elements of a Newsletter

The following sections describe the most important parts of a newsletter. Electronic newsletters don't always have these elements, but in my view, they should because these elements help attract and hold reader attention.

## Masthead and nameplate

The *masthead* is the area that appears at the top of the newsletter. Its most important element is the *nameplate,* which is a full-width display of the newsletter's name, issue number, and date. Sometimes the masthead is made up only of the nameplate, but in more complex designs, a company logo, *teasers* (small boxes of text describing stories inside), or even a teaser photo may be added to the masthead. The design of the masthead should remain consistent throughout all your newsletters, changing only the date and volume/issue numbers. Consistency in the masthead brings identification to the publication. If you change the masthead, people won't recognize your newsletter each time they receive it.

Mastheads usually contain a nameplate with the following:

- ✔ The name of the newsletter — usually done in a headline typeface — that reflects the nature of its contents
- ✔ The name of the person or organization that publishes the newsletter
- ✔ Date of issue, as well as issue and volume numbers (if you're committed to making the newsletter regular; otherwise, this information can be omitted)

In addition, give some thought to the headlines and any teasers that advertise your stories. They should be designed to integrate into the look of your nameplate but also to attract enough attention to entice the reader into each specific story. Figure 9-1 shows and names the elements of a well-designed newsletter. As shown in Figure 9-1, your nameplate is usually the boldest design element, with the main story headline taking second place to it, followed by other headlines and illustrations. Readers can only look at one thing at a time, so as you write and design a newsletter, have a plan for the order in which you want readers to look at each element. The masthead is the boldest element, so it will be seen first. Make it pop out through bold design elements: large size, big type, and contrasting or bold graphics.

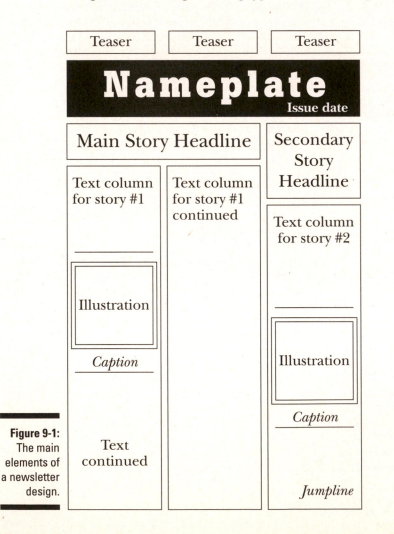

**Figure 9-1:**
The main elements of a newsletter design.

The masthead area of your newsletter is important because it announces your intentions and sets a tone for the entire newsletter. Pick a title that draws attention and defines or brands the newsletter effectively and keep it short enough that it can be set in large, bold type in the nameplate. Figure 9-2 shows an example of a striking nameplate and effective newsletter name. (The newsletter shown in Figure 9-2 is a Microsoft Word template that appears as CD0905. You can adapt it to your own use by replacing the title with one of your own. I cover its use in the section "Templates for Desktop Publishing," later in this chapter.)

**Figure 9-2:**
A strong
nameplate
design
draws
reader
attention.

## Modules

Newsletters, like newspapers, Web pages, and blogs, are usually laid out using *modular design.* Modular design divides the available space into rectangular modules, creating a grid into which the masthead elements, the articles, and the illustrations must fit. Thinking about your newsletter's modules will help you organize your newsletter visually. The rule is simple: As long as you keep each section in its own rectangle, you can combine a wide range of elements. A vertical rectangle may include a headline, columns of body copy, and an illustration with caption, for example. CD0902 shows how modular design works if you'd like a visual explanation of it.

## Articles

The most important article in each issue is called the *lead story*. Give your lead story the most visible headline and more space than any other story — between a third and two-thirds of the space on the front page. The lead story should be either extremely useful to the reader or extremely interesting. A useful lead story tells readers how to do something — solve a problem or accomplish a goal. An interesting lead story shares news or gossip about people and events that are especially interesting to the readers. Other articles should also be useful how-to tips or interesting news.

When you decide what articles to include in your newsletter, make sure that you cover a *variety* of topics. You want to have something of interest to everyone. And make them good journalism, not just disguised sales pitches.

### Keeping it short and sweet

Make sure that your stories contain solid nuggets of useable information, such as when and where events take place, what happened (news is always of interest), what *will* happen (forecasts are always of interest), and how to perform tasks successfully (how-to tips and lists are great). Also, make sure that you *tell stories*. Tell who did what, when, and why they did it, how they did it, and what happened. Insert a photo of the person the story is about, if possible. People read the news for stories, and the same is true with newsletters. Include case histories, interviews with people who are telling their stories, or simple news stories describing an event or happening.

Write short, to-the-point, simple articles using any or all of the formats mentioned in the previous paragraph. By short, I mean 100 to 300 words. That is very short, as you'll soon discover when you start writing. Choose Tools⇨Word Count in your Microsoft Word program to count words and cut text if you're over your word limit. Short articles don't have to be brilliantly written because they allow the reader to get the key information quickly, so just bang out three to ten short articles and call it a wrap!

Articles can be digests of interesting tips, facts, or examples you glean from other sources — but if you rely on sources, be sure to give them credit. For example, you can say, "According to a recent Gallup survey, 55% of . . ." or "A Feb. 2009 article in *Industrial Engineering* magazine included these three tips for safer workplaces. . . ." Also, try to assemble three or more sources, even for the shortest of articles, so that you're truly adding your expert value, not just revising someone else's article.

If you're a poor writer, you need to hire a writer to do the newsletter for you. But the problem is, most writers don't know enough about your business to write a really smart, useful newsletter. Consider writing poorly written but functional articles yourself and then hire someone to edit them. Or, work with a writer or publicist who knows your industry. I've sometimes worked

on newsletter projects for clients. (I design them and find the right researchers and writers to do a batch of issues in advance.) My feeling is that you
need to manage the writing aggressively to keep it interesting and useful.
Otherwise, the newsletter just becomes another throwaway.

### Grabbing and holding the readers' attention

Design is as important as writing in making an appealing newsletter and
building a following for it. Lay out articles in such a way that they capture
the readers' attention and invite them to read further. Break them up with
new paragraphs at least once every two or three column inches. Interrupt
long flows of text with headers, tables, bullet points, or an illustration. Add
a *sidebar* (a very short story or how-to tip that relates to the main article) to
increase the appeal for readers.

Try to use interesting sentences, especially at the beginning of each paragraph or section. If the first sentence grabs the reader, you'll probably keep
her attention for the rest of the paragraph. How can you ensure that each
paragraph and each major section of a newsletter article has an engaging and
attention-grabbing introductory sentence?

The best way to be sure opening sentences are catchy is to go back and write
(or rewrite) them *after* you've written the article. Take a half hour or more
just to craft good lead sentences that queue up the content of the paragraph
or section. Sentences that stimulate the imagination by asking an interesting question or challenge a common assumption are also good. Imagine that
you're editing an article for a company newsletter that has the following paragraph in it:

> *The Divisional Quality Improvement Team leaders got together last week
> for a leadership training event that included classroom study, a self-assess-
> ment of their leadership styles, and two hours of "experiential training" on
> a high ropes course. The training was sponsored by Corporate Headquarters
> and lasted for six hours. It took place at Sleepy Hollow Retreat Center in
> Headlesston, Indiana.*

The preceding paragraph is an example of the kind of writing that consigns
most corporate newsletters to the recycle bin. If you have time, get some
quotes from people about how scary the high ropes course was and how it
really taught them what true teamwork is all about. Maybe someone over-
came a fear of falling that you could include a personal story about. Content
can always be improved when you put on your storyteller's hat. But even if
you don't have time to perfect this article, you can do a great deal by simply
adding good introductory sentences. For example, you might amend that
boring article as follows:

> *What lengths — and especially heights — will our volunteer team leaders
> go to in order to improve their own performance? The Divisional Quality*

*Improvement Team leaders got together last week for a leadership training event that included classroom study, a self-assessment of their leadership styles, and two hours of training on a high ropes course. The training . . . (and so on).*

By adding a catchy opener, you greatly increase the rate of readership for that article. If you can work a few quotes in from participants or witnesses, you make it even more interesting. Add a photo, and it's a really engaging story!

## Headers (like this one)

*Headers* (also called headlines of headings) should be set in a larger and bolder type than the body of the article. A header should not be too wordy, but it must contain enough description to invite the viewer to read on. Instead of my going on at length about how a header should be written, just read a bunch of mine throughout this book, and you can at least see the type of headers I prefer. You can also read a well-designed newspaper to see how it uses headlines to draw readers in. *USA Today* is a good model for headline writers, and its articles are often well written and appealing, too.

You can use special headline types for your headers or use bold type from the same family of type used in the body of the article. Figure 9-3 illustrates some of the headline type styles. Your printer will have numerous choices, and you probably have some good options in your Word library of fonts, too.

This book uses Georgia for its headers — a bold, italic version of Georgia. Bold versions of fonts often work well for headers, so keep that option in mind. The last example in Figure 9-3 is a bold version of the body copy you're reading right now, Times New Roman.

**Arial Black**

**Charcoal CY**

**Copperplate Gothic Bold**

**Delta Jaeger Bold**

**Helvetica Neue Black Condensed**

**Figure 9-3:** **Impact**
Headline
type styles. **Optima ExtraBlack**

**Times New Roman Bold**

You don't want to use too many type styles in a single publication. As a rule, I recommend sticking to one type style for most or all of your copy. But headers are the exception. You can try a contrasting style for the headers because it sometimes adds an appealing contrast to the design. You may also want to use a separate font for captions. (This book uses Times New Roman for body copy, Georgia bold italic for headers, and Arial for captions, for example.) Sometimes it looks good to set sidebars in a separate style, too.

Figure 9-4 shows a header added to a paragraph. The header is set in Helvetica Bold and the body copy is in Times New Roman to illustrate the impact of contrasting styles and sizes.

Use plenty of headers. When in doubt, break up a story with more subheads. People have short attention spans, especially if the writing isn't the greatest in the world. So give them many smaller chunks to read, each wrapped up nicely in a good header. (See Chapter 13 if you need more help and ideas for your writing.)

### Team leaders on the ropes

What lengths–and especially heights–will our volunteer team leaders go to in order to improve their own performance? The Divisional Quality Improvement Team leaders got together last week for a leadership training event which included classroom study, a self-assessment of their leadership styles, and two hours of "experimental training" on a high ropes course. . . .

**Figure 9-4:** Header and body copy.

# Type

The body of an article should use a clean, conservative type set large enough so that you can read it easily — usually 10, 11, or 12 points. (If readers are middle-aged or older, 12 point is your minimum.) A serif font style is more readable than a sans serif style. *Serif fonts* have the little decorations at the ends of the lines of font, as you can see in the serif font this text is written in. Times New Roman (this book's type-font) and Palatino are popular and attractive serif fonts. *Sans serif fonts* have clean edges. Save these fonts for headers unless you want a clean, modern look for your text. Helvetica is the most popular sans serif font. Personally, I like Arial. Figure 9-5 illustrates the difference between serif and sans serif letters.

If the type is too hard to read, you'll lose your readers' attention.

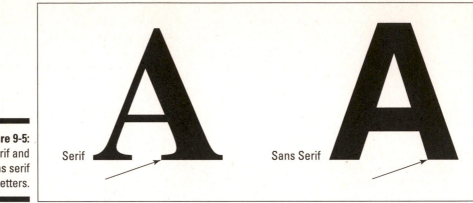

**Figure 9-5:**
Serif and
sans serif
letters.

Serif      Sans Serif

If you're designing in Word (which can produce two-column, neat-looking newsletters at low cost and also has lots of creative brochure templates — just choose File⇨Project Gallery⇨Newsletter), avoid using Times. The Times font is designed for viewing on-screen, not for printing, and it's often the default font. Switch to Times New Roman, which is optimized for the printed page rather than the screen. (This paragraph is set in Times New Roman 10 pt.; it reads well, doesn't it?)

Never select a font because it has a cool name. Stone is a neat-sounding font, but I don't recommend it for most uses. Apple Chancery looks and sounds interesting, and preteens like to use it for school papers, but avoid it for business uses because it's hard to read. Also, avoid all fonts designed to look like handwriting, comic book scripts, or old typewriters, unless you have a really, really good reason to use them. You have hundreds of fonts to choose from, but most of them are inferior to the classics I mention earlier in this section.

## Columns

Use columns whenever you have a large amount of type. The eye may waver and jump from line to line when it has to follow lines of type that go across an 8½-inch-wide sheet. If you break up the same article into two or three columns, the line is shorter, so the eye has to stay focused for a shorter amount of time and doesn't get sidetracked.

## Leading and kerning

*Leading* refers to the space between the lines of type. Layout programs have an automatic setting for adjusting the leading, but you can also adjust it manually. Adjusting the leading manually comes in handy when you're trying to get just one more line to fit in a particular article. By adjusting the leading to a smaller size, you can scrunch up the lines and allow that extra line to fit in. Type size and leading are usually written in this form: 10/12. The type size appears on top of the slash, and the leading size appears on the bottom. Figure 9-6 shows you the type of spacing that leading and kerning control.

Try to be fairly consistent with leading and type size throughout the publication because irregular type and leading sizes look out of place.

**Figure 9-6:**
Leading
and kerning
control the
spacing of
your type.

Leading → The quick brown fox jumped over the lazy dog. Then the lazy black cat crawled under the fence.

The quick
Kerning

*Kerning,* also known as *character spacing,* refers to the space between characters (letters). Like leading, layout programs adjust the kerning between letters automatically, but you can manually override this command, too. Sometimes you need to tighten the kerning in order to fit a story into the available space.

After you write and lay out your newsletter, check for *widows* and *orphans.* These are words or sections of words (when they're hyphenated) that are awkward to the eye at the end or beginning of a line. You want to make sure that the reader's eye can flow naturally and easily from line to line. Redesign as necessary to eliminate any rough spots where the reader may get hung up or confused. For example, if a line ends on the word "a," you may want to manually insert a *soft carriage return;* in Word, a soft carriage return breaks the line without inserting a paragraph-separating break. Eliminating such disorienting strays takes only a few minutes. (Note that these rules of good layout apply for all marketing copy, including printed and Web ads.)

## *Flow and readability*

Make sure that your newsletter flows (see Figure 9-7). If you have to continue articles on another page, don't make finding the continuation difficult for readers. If possible, keep articles together to make reading less frustrating. (And remember to keep articles short. If they're short, you won't need to break up many of them.)

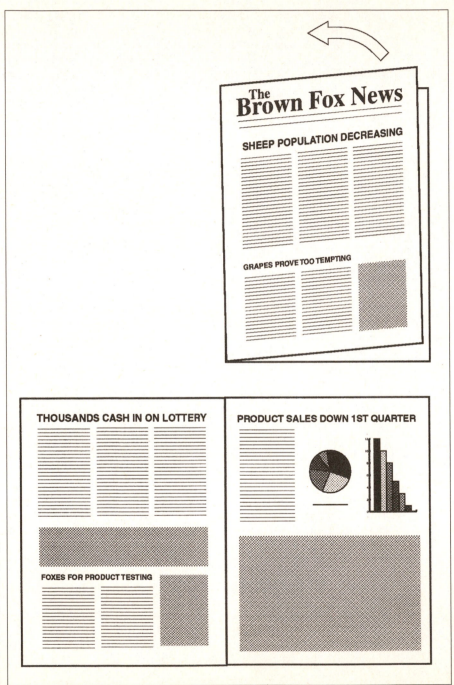

**Figure 9-7:**
Make sure that the layout supports a natural, easy flow through the pages.

If you publish your newsletter on a tabloid-size sheet (11 x 17 inches), lay out the articles to keep page-turning from becoming a problem. Specifically, don't make readers have to flip over the document because the next articles are upside down. Also, minimize the amount of flipping back and forth between pages. You lose readers when you make the reading path too challenging.

## Size

You can publish newsletters on virtually any size paper. The main determining factor is the amount of content you have (think smaller if you have a limited budget!). Newsletters can range from both sides of an $8\frac{1}{2}$-x-11-inch sheet to a 11-x-17-inch sheet that's printed on both sides and folded in half. Or you can add more sheets and staple at the fold to make lengthier newsletters. You can also apply the formats and designs for brochures that I cover in Chapter 7 to printed newsletters, which gives you lots of interesting options.

Figure 9-8 shows the two most common and easiest formats for newsletters. Plan to use one of these paper sizes and layout styles unless you have a very good reason (and extra money in your budget) to deviate from them.

**Figure 9-8:** The two most practical formats for newsletters.

LETTER SIZE (8.5" X 11") NEWSLETTER

TABLOID SIZE (11" X 17") NEWSLETTER

## Photos and artwork

I cover the use of visuals in many places in this book, especially in my discussions of print ads and brochures (see Chapters 5 and 7). As with brochures, you can use photos and artwork to make a newsletter article more interesting and to create an appropriate mood or feeling. *Text wrap* — when text wraps around a box containing artwork rather than stopping above the box and continuing below it — can also be an effective strategy in a newsletter.

For technical information about how to handle artwork, what your choices in photocopying and printing are, what screens are, how to handle color, and so on, turn to Chapter 7. I cover these details in my discussion of how to design brochures, and you can directly apply this knowledge to newsletter design and production, too.

If you're desktop publishing a newsletter in small quantities, the main consideration for art is your printer. Do you have a good quality color printer? If so, then you can make quite crisp, full-color pages with high-quality photos and other graphics. Just drop photographs into your master document (which you can design in Word). Make sure that your photos are high enough resolution (at least 300 dpi) to print clearly. If you aren't sure about an image, try printing it. If it looks fine, then it is fine. The proof's in the pudding, as they say!

# Templates for Desktop Publishing

As with brochures, you have a wide range of options, from hiring experts and offset printing (expensive but easy and good for high quantities), to doing everything yourself. Many of my readers are do-it-yourselfers — they realize that it's important to communicate often with customers and prospects, even if you don't have a big marketing budget. So, how can you write, design, and produce your newsletter without spending any money? Good question! I'm glad you asked.

The first thing I want to say is, why make it complicated? Start with a one-page newsletter. Yes, just one page. If you find after a few issues that you're getting the hang of it and want to write more than that, expand to the back page. After another couple issues, maybe you can switch to printing on tabloid paper and folding it down the middle so that you have four pages. But start with one page if you've never written or produced a newsletter before.

Also, why commit to monthly production? Many newsletters are monthly, but that schedule means you have to start writing the next issue at the same time you're printing and mailing the current one. If you have a business to run, creating newsletters will take too much of your time. I recommend starting quarterly. A seasonal theme is easy and gives you a break between issues.

Figure 9-9 shows the top third of a simple but eye-catching, one-page, seasonal newsletter template. You can access the template in CD0903, which is a Word document set up for three brief stories. It uses blue, green, and yellow and looks quite summery. All you need to do is drop your text, company name, and address into the template and print! (This newsletter uses two columns, one of them wider than the other, and the nameplate sits above the wider column. This innovation breaks the rule of making the nameplate go all the way across the front page. Rules can be broken in design — but only after you think about the exception and make sure that your unusual design really works.)

Date can be put here

# SUMMER
## *newsletter*

Your Company Name

Short, pithy tag line can be added right here!

**Main Story Headline**

Main story body copy. Main story body copy. Main story body copy. Main story body copy. Main story body copy. Main story body copy. Main etc.

**Small Story Headline**

Small story body copy. Small story body copy. Small story body copy.

**Figure 9-9:** The banner of a simple seasonal newsletter template (see CD0903).

What if it's not summer? Then you'll have to shop for a seasonally appropriate graphic and shift the color palate to something better suited for your first season of printing: orange maple leaves and brown headlines for autumn, a green fir tree for winter, pink or purple tulips for spring. I found the blue butterfly and green leaves in the free symbols libraries in Adobe Illustrator and combined them with a circle I filled with yellow to create a nice summery graphic for this issue. The same symbol library offers orange maple leaves, and you can also find lots of symbols and clip art in other programs or free on the Web, so just be creative and come up with something artful for each issue. You'd be surprised at how a good seasonal design or photograph will attract reader interest.

Plan to print your simple one-page seasonal newsletter on a color inkjet or laser printer, or if you want to make more than your printer can handle, shop around for a copy shop or print shop with a digital laser printer.

The trick with contracting out for digital color printing at low quantities (under 500 copies) is to shop for price. Many copy shops charge a dollar a page for good quality color copies or prints, and that won't do. You ought to be able to get the price down to a third or quarter of that. If you can't, consider buying a color laser printer with rapid *through-put* (which means it was designed for quantity printing) and make your own. You'll pay for the new printer in the first issue or two if you have a copy shop print a several-hundred-copy run at a dollar a page.

For your reference, CD0904 shows the template from CD0903 in PDF, which isn't editable unless you have Acrobat Professional (as opposed to Acrobat Reader, which is a free program that you probably do already have on your computer). I'm including a PDF version because sometimes text boxes and art jump around in different versions of Word. Use the PDF to check that your template in CD0902 is still formatted the way it was on my computer. If not, just select and drag any elements that got out of place.

If you want to get more ambitious and desktop publish a four-page newsletter, see the editable Word template in CD0905 (a PDF version of it appears in CD0906 for your reference). This is the same newsletter whose masthead I share with you in Figure 9-2. I titled the newsletter *What's New in . . .* (fill in your own industry or area of interest). My goal was to create a template that really was applicable to any business, and the What's New title achieves that goal. It attracts interest because everyone wants to know what's new in their industry.

The front page of the What's New newsletter template in CD0905 is set up for two columns of body copy, which gives sufficient visual interest when combined with the bold masthead design. However, the second and third pages are set up in three columns, which makes for an interesting change when you open the newsletter. There are generic photos in these interior pages which you should replace with something appropriate to your stories.

I recommend you read the text in the template in CD0905 because I have inserted a variety of tips and suggestions for how to write a good newsletter. Of course you'll replace my writing with your own in the version you create for your customers, but I thought it would be fun and helpful for me to provide some additional advice within the template.

Before you produce (print) your four-page newsletter from the template in CD0905, first, please proofread your writing carefully! It's amazing how many errors and typos get past your eye the first few times. Read your newsletter over repeatedly and get someone else to proofread it too. Once all the typos and corrections are taken care of, then you're ready to check formatting one more time. Is everything lined up neatly and in place? Are any of the stories too big for their text boxes? If they are, the endings will disappear, so you'll need to either click and drag the bottom edge of the text box to expand it, or better yet, cut some of the words out of your story.

Once you're sure everything is just right, you have three basic choices for desktop printing. You can print the sheets one at a time, just the way the template cues them up, and then staple them. Or to save paper and make the newsletter look more professional, you can print two-sided. In some versions of Word and some printer interfaces, you can automatically print two-sided. The simple way, however, is to just print the odd numbered pages first and then turn them over and feed them through your printer a second time, printing only the even numbered pages.

To set up for printing on tabloid ($8^{1}/_{2}$-x-11-inch) paper, you first need a printer than can accommodate this size. We have one in our office, so we often print our newsletters this way, which requires that we create a new file in which we select Tabloid under File⇨Page Setup and also select landscape (horizontal). Each horizontal tabloid page will hold two vertical $8^{1}/_{2}$-x-11-inch pages. For a four-page newsletter, the first tabloid sheet has the fourth page on its left side and the first page on its right side. When folded, they form the back and front covers. The second horizontal tabloid page holds the two inside pages of the newsletter: the third page on its left, and the fourth on its right side.

To create the tabloid master pages for printing it yourself, you need to move everything from the $8^{1}/_{2}$-x-11-inch template pages to the new, larger tabloid pages. One way to do this is to select and group each and every object (text box, graphic element, and so on) and copy and paste them into the new file. Yikes! Lots of opportunities for error. A better way is to finalize each page in the regular template file and then print each page as a separate PDF. Then you can insert each of the four PDFs of your pages (high resolution JPEGS will do, too) in the new file. This approach is what I recommend if you want to do it yourself. And you may find that your local printer asks for PDFs, too. To create a PDF of your Word newsletter page, access the Print menu, select the PDF button, and then select Save as PDF. (If your Word commands don't seem to match my instructions perfectly, don't panic. Microsoft seems to believe in variety in each version, but trust that the options are there somewhere. Consult your Help menu for specifics.)

Ninety-five percent of offices do not have color laser printers that can handle tabloid paper. That means you may have to contract out for printing your tabloid newsletter. Take it to your favorite local print shop and get a quote for the job (if it has the right equipment — if not, consult your Yellow Pages or local Web directories for other options). While you're at it, you can have the printer you select lay out your newsletter for their printer. The setup charges should be quite small as it's not a lot of work for them, and they're used to doing it.

If you want to produce a longer newsletter, simply add more pages that are copied exactly from pages two or three of the template in CD0905. These are the interior pages, so they should be consistent in style. If you're printing on regular $8^{1}/_{2}$-x-11-inch sheets, you can add one or more at will. If you're printing on tabloid sheets, remember that you have to work in multiples of four, so you need to write enough new stories to support an eight pager. That quantity may be difficult, but it's not impossible! Consider asking experts to write columns for you or look for interesting recent articles and blogs on the

Web and ask the authors for (written) permission to reproduce their stories in your newsletter. Give them credit, and they may be tickled to be included.

# Measuring Your Success

You'll know that your newsletter is a good one if you get positive feedback from readers and requests for copies or subscriptions. The most popular newsletters have good design plus good writing. To be more specific, the design should be visually interesting with plenty of features to avoid long, boring-looking columns of text. Color also helps. Short articles with good how-to tips, interesting facts, and exciting stories also help your newsletter achieve popular appeal. If you have an article that seems to lack excitement, look for a short paragraph that can stand on its own as a sidebar (for example, an interesting fact from a survey). Create a small box with its own headline and put the paragraph there. Also look for illustrations that complement the article.

Even though most marketing-oriented newsletters are sent out for free, you can and should build a mailing or e-mailing list for your newsletter. Communicate with your list occasionally to check that recipients are enjoying their complimentary copies of the newsletter and ask them whether they'd like to request any special topics or have any stories for you to include. (Interviews with customers are a great way to built interest!) Also ask them whether they'd like you to send the newsletter to any of their colleagues. Positive feedback from current readers and a growing mailing list are both good signs of a successful newsletter.

I'll put more examples and tips for newsletter design on the Web site that supports my *For Dummies* books, www.insightsformarketing.com.

# Saving a Tree: Electronic Newsletters

We live in a computerized world, meaning that interesting variations to traditional printed products are extremely popular. In this section, I discuss a few of the most common variations.

For details on how to create electronic newsletters, contact a media designer with marketing experience. If you're interested in a referral, you can find links at my Web site, www.insightsformarketing.com. You can also check out the growing list of *For Dummies* books about Web page design; I'll keep the latest editions ready on the Web site for your convenience.

## E-mailing a Portable Document Format (PDF) attachment

Many organizations have switched their newsletters from print mailings to e-mail documents, which isn't a bad method if your target readers check their e-mails routinely and like to receive news this way. Write and design the newsletter as if it were for one or more $8\frac{1}{2}$-x-11-inch printed pages. Then convert it to a PDF file and attach it to an e-mail addressed to your subscription list. The e-mail subject line simply needs to announce the newest issue of the newsletter so that recipients know it isn't spam and don't delete the attachment before opening and reading it.

By designing it for a standard sheet of paper, you allow recipients to print it themselves if they wish (and many people will if the content is good because it's nice to have a hard copy for easy reference).

## E-mailing an HTML page

Another option is to design a simple, half-page-size newsletter in HTML as if it were for a Web page. Then insert it directly into an e-mail so that it appears on-screen for the recipient. With this method, you get the content in front of your recipients without having to depend on their opening an attachment.

Some people don't like receiving big, visual e-mails — they think you're hijacking their computers — so you have to decide whether or not your audience will object to this approach. Also, many e-mail systems automatically screen out e-mails with HTML embedded in them, so if you use this method, consider offering it as a downloadable PDF as a backup option.

## Sending hybrid e-mails

*Hybrid e-mails* basically display what looks like a banner ad from a Web page or, even more simply, a one-line link. When the reader clicks the link, her Web browser opens, and she's taken directly to a Web page.

Of course, now you can deliver your newsletter content on a Web page, which opens up the options for design. For example, in addition to conventional articles, you can include high-quality color photos, animation, and even streaming video. You may find it hard to make a text-oriented description of a routine event interesting, but imagine how much more appealing your coverage will be if you show a video of the event on your Web site with a short caption underneath.

A very simple way to make your newsletter available online is to post a notice about the latest issue on your Web site with a one-click option for downloading the PDF version of the newsletter. And you can archive past issues and have them available for download, too.

## Blogs instead of newsletters?

Quick now, what's the difference between a newsletter and a blog? Um, hold on, let me see. . . . Well, the blog has opinions and editorial content you've gathered and written in your own words, and the newsletter — oops, so does the newsletter. Well, how about this for a difference: The newsletter is updated periodically, but the blog . . . now, wait, so is the blog. Okay, I give up. What *is* the difference?

Well, actually, I'm not sure either. In practice, blogs are often more editorial and personal than newsletters, but there's no reason you can't use a blog as your electronic newsletter if you want to simplify (and cut the costs of) your design and production. Why not do a really modern newsletter that uses a blogging template instead of bothering with traditional printed paper at all? And to publicize it, you can send e-mails (or hybrid e-mails) with the link each time you do an update.

A nice thing about blogs is that you can keep adding the new content above the old because there's endless room on the Web. So a new reader can have access to all your past writing, not just your current news.

I have not seen very many businesses adopt the blog as a newsletter, but why not? Maybe you can pioneer this new marketing medium. Do a Google search for the latest offerings in blog services or check out these links for places where you can create and publish a blog instead of a newsletter:

- ✔ **TypePad** (www.typepad.com) is my first suggestion because it's easy and offers clean, business-like design templates. Martha Stewart uses this host for her blog. Check it out at http://blogs1.martha stewart.com.

- ✔ **Windows Live** (http://www.service.spaces.live.com) is Microsoft's easy-to-use site for publishing simple blog-like content. It's specifically for people with MSN Hotmail, MSN Messenger, or Passport accounts, so it won't necessarily be right for everyone.

- ✔ **Terapad** (www.terapad.com) has good tools for building blogs, as well as for attaching Web sites, stores, and other products to them. This Web site gives some interesting examples that are more business-like than Windows Live Spaces.

✔ **WordPress** (www.wordpress.com) seems to be an easy-to-use and popular blog-hosting site. Most of the blogs are personal, but I think you can use this platform to create a good business newsletter if you wanted to. Bump up the capabilities for a more sophisticated blog at www.wordpress.org. (And while this platform can sometimes be challenging to use, there happens to be *WordPress For Dummies* [Wiley] by Lisa Sabin-Wilson to help you if you run into trouble.)

✔ **Squarespace** (www.squarespace.com) is an interesting option with lots of modules you can use to build sophisticated, professional blogs and Web sites. Have a look — you'll get excited about the ease with which you can add forms, browsable photo galleries, search capabilities, forums, and many other features that a normal newsletter doesn't have.

Other services also help you find readers for your blog, such as FeedBlitz (www.feedblitz.com), which also helps you publish what it calls an e-mail newsletter. Its product is not all that different in practice from the blogs I describe in the preceding list, except it has more of an emphasis on building an e-mail subscriber base, which is not a bad idea if you want to target prospects and customers regularly. Otherwise, you'll have to send your own e-mail notifications about new content.

## Mailing a CD

Although it's not as exciting as blogging, burning a newsletter to a CD and sending it by mail is another practical and easy option. This tool makes sense when you have a lot of rich content that might make for too expensive of a printed newsletter, and you have old-fashioned mailing addresses for your customers instead of e-mail addresses. But don't bother sending a CD to people who won't recognize your name. They need to trust you before they'll dare put a CD into their computer, for fear of computer viruses.

The CD can contain your newsletter, either in printable form (as a PDF or Word file) or in color designed for on-screen display. Your CD can also contain supporting information and materials — almost anything that you can imagine — because a CD has so much more capacity than a printed newsletter. Use the CD to provide more and better photos to illustrate the newsletter. Or put the latest copy of your full catalog and price sheet on the CD in folders that readers can open when they need this information.

# A Few Thoughts on Logos

I touch on the subject of logos and how to design them in Chapter 6, when I talk about branding. I thought I'd add to that advice by addressing logo design here, in the context of newsletters. Why? Because designers and writers often are asked to create a dynamic, exciting-looking newsletter for a client whose logo is dull and boring. Oops. Fundamental problem. What can be done?

In my opinion, the newsletter is a good place to experiment with bumping up your visual branding. You can give the newsletter itself an exciting logo and name, and you can also consider displaying an exciting new version of your company's brand name in the masthead. I kind of prefer the latter option because the most important marketing goal is to bring fame and fortune to your company, not to your newsletter. However, I did try to create some exciting masthead designs you can use in the templates for this chapter.

If you tried your own hand at masthead designs, you may have found that finding symbols and shapes and combining them into dynamic logo designs is easier than it seems at first. If so, why stop there? Maybe you should revisit your corporate logo or product logo, too. If it's dull, see what you can do.

CD0907 is a PDF showing four very different logo concepts I designed recently. What they have in common is that they're built up from readily available sources (symbols, shapes, and fonts), and they're more dynamic and interesting in appearance than the average logo. A dynamic look should be your goal whenever you design anything that has the potential to contribute to your brand's appearance.

The simplest way to create a visually appealing branded look for the nameplate of your newsletter is to turn the name itself into your design. Set the name in an interesting font, for example. Or — and this is a trick I've used several times with success — make the first letter of the newsletter's name much larger and turn it into a design element. Figure 9-10 shows a branded newsletter name that was created simply by setting the first letter of the name (the Q in Quality Logistics) much larger than the rest of the name. To design a name with a much larger first letter, you have to float the first letter separately from the rest of the name (for example, in Word, put the first letter in its own text box). Then experiment with size and positioning until you get a nice looking, artistic (balanced, attractive) design that is still readable but doesn't look like an ordinary title any more.

In CD0908, I share a more exciting and elaborate masthead design that uses the same trick of designing the title with an especially large first letter. In this example, for Tile and Flooring News, I reversed the type (white on dark field) and used a variety of textures to create boxes that look like tiles. The overall design is very distinctive, giving the newsletter a strong brand identity. However, it actually only took me five minutes to build this nameplate design, and I did it entirely in Word, using text boxes and rectangles from the drawing toolbar and filling the rectangles with assorted textures. I wanted to leave you with this example of a well-branded newsletter nameplate that took almost no time and absolutely no money to design. It's true that a good graphic designer can do much that the desktop publisher can't do, but if you haven't got a budget for design, don't despair! A little ingenuity is all it takes to create an exciting, well-branded newsletter that will draw customers to you and build your reputation.

**Figure 9-10:**
A branded
newsletter
title using
a large
initial letter
for visual
appeal.

# On the CD

Check out the following items on the CD-ROM:

- ✔ A sample of a well-designed newsletter (CD0901)
- ✔ A newsletter marked to show how modular design was used (CD0902)
- ✔ Seasonal newsletter Word template (CD0903)
- ✔ Seasonal newsletter PDF file (CD0904)
- ✔ What's New four-page Word newsletter template (CD0905)
- ✔ What's New PDF file (CD0906)
- ✔ Newsletter logo examples and notes (CD0907)
- ✔ Tile & Flooring News nameplate (CD0908)

# Chapter 10

# Taking Advantage of Publicity

*In This Chapter*

▶ Understanding the value of publicity

▶ Generating great publicity

▶ Creating a media kit, press release, and mailing list

▶ Using Web publicity services to boost your media hits

*T*his chapter is probably the one that you, as a small or medium-size business owner, feel most like skipping over because creating newsworthy stories about your business may seem out of your reach. Don't feel discouraged! Publicity is a very real part of your marketing plan, and it's one that *is achievable* for you. Besides, understanding what publicity can do for your company can save you a bundle in advertising costs.

## Understanding and Using Publicity

Publicity is a special, powerful tool. But it doesn't have to be complicated. When you understand what it can (and can't) do you can add publicity to your marketing toolbox. A little publicity goes a long way toward boosting brand visibility and generating sales leads.

Imagine that you own a midsize tooling company that caters to the furniture market in North Carolina (which is often called the furniture capital of the world). Growing your business has two components:

✔ Producing the best quality products available (satisfied customers keep coming back and refer other customers)

✔ Getting name recognition to attract a whole new customer base

Suppose that you place a story in the business section of the largest newspaper (by circulation size) in the region. (I discuss how to place a story in the section "Pitching Your Release to the Media," later in this chapter.) The story is about the fact that your company just received the most sophisticated machine in the world today to produce the kind of tools needed by the furniture industry.

The first result of this positive publicity is that new customers will call you to find out more about what you can do for them. In addition, your existing customers gain more confidence in your products because the newspaper or magazine article validates the fact that your company is progressive. Another positive result is that potential employees and current employees become aware of your cutting-edge capabilities and consider you a good company to work for, and employees naturally want to work for the best.

So, with one carefully placed article, you've increased your company's name recognition, reinforced that your company is the best, and highlighted the fact that your company is a great place to work because of the cutting-edge technology it possesses. Not bad, huh?

Another valuable way you can use this article is to post it on your Web site and send a copy of the article (with a cover letter and a product information sheet) to new and potential clients. (Note that you'll need permission from the publication to make copies of the article — but permission is routinely granted to you if the article is about you.) You may even do something as simple as placing a reprint of the article in the envelopes that hold your employees' paychecks or your customers' invoices.

*Publicity* tells the story of a business, executive, or employee within the business. A good publicity campaign results in a positive public image and attracts new customers and makes you a more desirable employer, too.

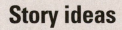

## Story ideas

Your publicity program is a powerful image builder. Not sure what story to tell the world, though? Here are some ideas you can use in a story:

✔ Your cutting-edge technology

✔ Your quality product or service

✔ The many ways your company gives back to the community

✔ What you're doing to conserve energy and recycle

✔ The awards your company has won

✔ That your company is growing — renovating, relocating, and updating

✔ How you're helping high school students by offering summer internships

✔ How your CEO has kept the company healthy through difficult economic cycles

✔ That your company has started a new advertising campaign

In short, editorial coverage creates a publicity-marketing umbrella that other forms of marketing can't compete with. Just think about it: Are you more likely to hear two businesspeople saying, "Hey, did you see DeHart Tooling's new direct-mail piece?" or "Hey, did you see that article in *The Charlotte Observer* about DeHart Tooling getting that new machine?"

## Publicity versus advertising

I find that people often don't understand the difference between publicity and advertising. Consider advertising that you pay for, such as posters, brochures, newsletters, billboards, direct mail, and advertisements: You write a check to produce them and place them in front of an audience. Advertising involves *paid placement of marketing messages.* Not so for publicity.

Publicity is *not* advertising. You don't pay for an interview on a radio or TV program or for the space a newspaper or magazine uses to write about your company. If a local business program interviews you or a TV station comes to your company and videotapes a special event for the evening news, it doesn't send you a bill. Publicity falls into the editorial side of any media company's business, not the advertising side. This means that not only is publicity free for your company, it's also inherently more interesting and credible than space or time that you pay for.

## Publicity versus public relations

Publicity is not public relations, either. Publicity is a tool of the public relations umbrella. *Public relations,* as a function, generally includes all sorts of other stuff, such as how you relate to your community — which may or may not generate profitable publicity for you. I'm going to focus on getting you publicity, because that's what you need to promote your business.

Publicity, in short, is obtaining free editorial coverage based on factual, interesting, breakthrough, and newsworthy information about your company, product, or service. Now, the question is, how do you get publicity?

## When to hire a pro

Many companies hire a professional public relations firm to help them obtain publicity. In many cases, hiring a good public relations firm is a much better investment of your marketing dollars than advertising is, but keep in mind that you'll need to pay several thousand a month for a major publicity campaign. If that doesn't seem necessary or affordable right now, consider doing a simpler campaign yourself. The rest of this chapter covers the essentials of do-it-yourself publicity.

## Be newsworthy

To generate publicity, you have to find something about your story that lends itself to generating news coverage. How do you know whether your business is newsworthy? Here are some criteria to determine whether your company's story is newsworthy:

- ✔ **Show of progress:** One way to determine whether your company is a good candidate for publicity is to determine, through a focus of your marketing program, whether the information you can share about your company, product, or service shows progress. Progress is always newsworthy.

- ✔ **Local angle:** The closer the story is to a reader's home or business, the more important it is to them. In many cases today, so much generic global information is available through the Internet and syndicated wire services like the Associated Press that the real gem to a reporter is a real person at a real company telling a real story with a real local angle.

  But, to give you the best chance of making it in a paper (or in a magazine or on the radio or on TV), you need to do your homework before you approach the media. Specifically, you need to prepare some thoughts and information, and you need to package your contributions to the media in one or more of the forms that they're used to working with. (The following sections look at what forms the media like their information in and how you should prepare them.)

- ✔ **Unusual:** Your company's story is different — not the same old story recycled over and over again.

- ✔ **Timely:** Of course, you want your story to make sense considering the business conditions or the time of year.

  By the way, *timely* means that your company is doing something before anyone else. If you're the third company to send a press release about new ideas for holiday gifts, the media is a lot less likely to pick up your story than if you had been the first one to do it.

- ✔ **Needed and important:** Your company provides a needed service or is doing something significant for the local or regional area that's *important right now.*

## But isn't much of what we do newsworthy?

The way to generate publicity is to let journalists know about anything that you can point to as having news value because it represents significant progress, has a local angle, is unusual, is timely, and/or is important right now.

Sounds easy, doesn't it? I know what you're thinking:

- ✔ My company is doing lots of great things that are newsworthy.

- ✔ But no one from the media calls the company to ask about it. Why not?

- ✔ How the heck is the media going to know what's important to me and my customers about my business, product, or service?

Well, nobody in the media is going to cover your business unless they know what's newsworthy about it. Media professionals don't read minds, you know. So you simply have to tell them.

## It's not newsworthy until journalists know about it

The idea of you calling a business reporter at the largest paper in your region and telling him about a new product or service you offer or about a sales record your company has achieved or about the expansion your company is making within the state isn't so far-fetched. But most — really almost all — business people never pick up the phone and call a journalist or editor to share their information. When have you ever initiated such a call? What, *never?* Those editors must be getting the idea that you don't like them. They may think that you don't *want* news coverage.

Any media professional needs information, and most of them need and want some help gathering that information. The days of the reporter with a steno pad, trench coat, and hat, seeking out a great story, are gone for good. Sure, reporters still have beats, but their beats are probably the largest companies in the area. No business reporter today can do his job effectively without the help of others to keep him informed. And under the "others" category are professional publicists who work at public relations firms, seasoned public relations professionals who work internally at companies, and *you.*

By becoming a liaison with the media, you can help your company accomplish one or more of the following:

- ✔ Inform people about how to choose, buy, and use your product or service

- ✔ Persuade consumers to buy your product or service

- ✔ Counteract misconceptions about your product or cause

- ✔ Get customers in your store or on your Web site

- Get information to the public on issues your organization is concerned about
- Bring people to an event or a series of events
- Recruit highly qualified employees
- Attract investors

Because reporters need help gathering information that isn't readily available — such as a breaking story about your company — the chances of your company getting coverage for what it's doing is pretty likely. Finding good stories is always a problem for journalists. And their problem is your opportunity.

Take a look at CD1001, which is a copy of a press release sent by one of the leading U.S. furniture makers to a national list of editors and reporters. (I show you how to write a good press release in the section "The Press Release That's Going To Get You Publicity," later in this chapter.) This release tells a simple but compelling story: Century Furniture joins forces with a famous designer, Oscar de la Renta, to create patio and garden furniture inspired by the antique outdoor furniture from the estate of the Duchess of Devonshire. The company timed the release to come out just before the industry's biggest annual trade show in High Point, North Carolina, and it attracted interest from a wide variety of media, including Sunday supplements of major newspapers, which often run seasonal stories on landscape design.

# Developing a Media Kit

It's important to have a sense of what your story is — the hook that's going to get you noticed by writers and editors after it's sent to them in a good press release. However, before you write and send your first press release, you have to do some homework. You need to create a media kit to support your press releases. (Some newspaper people and many publicists still call this a "press kit.")

A *media kit* usually consists of a folder (with two inside pockets) that includes one or several news releases about your company, photographs that relate to the information in the releases, a background sheet with an overview of interesting facts about your company (such as its history or milestones), bios and photos of your management team, and any other information that compiles a complete overview of your company as it stands today.

The media kit serves as the basis of your publicity program because media professionals can always refer to it at a moment's notice for factual information about your company. The primary purpose of a media kit is to help news people report your story as thoroughly as possible. It saves the reporter's time and shows that you and your company are competent and serious about providing accurate, up-to-date information.

## Assembling your kit

To assemble your kit, you can start by purchasing shiny duotang (two-pocket) folders at your local office-supply store or major office-supply store chain. These folders are available in many colors and usually come 25 to a box. You can insert all your information inside the folder and interchange the information as needed. Some companies even print stickers for the cover (with the company name and address on the sticker) because it's a low-cost alternative to printing directly onto a folder. (Center the sticker on the front cover.)

But why be cheap? First impressions are the most important, right? I recommend investing a little money in this part of your publicity program and getting two-pocket folders with your company name and logo printed on them.

If you anticipate a move or a new area code coming to your city, you may want to print a smaller quantity or leave off your address and phone number and focus on putting your name and logo or a picture on the cover.

You'll find many additional uses for this printed media kit folder. When you're not using it for publicity, it makes a great folder to give customers. You can use it to interchange price sheets and information easily. You can also use it as your employee handbook to hold information that employees need. You may even find yourself bringing one to the bank when you visit your loan officer or passing them out at the pressroom at a trade show. Consider the many uses a media kit folder can serve and design it flexibly. (For example, don't print "media kit" on it!)

## What about using your Web page as a media kit?

Sometimes a company's Web page includes its media kit. (Put it under a tab called "For the Media" along with an archive of your press releases.) Some journalists will be happy to visit your site to pull off the background information that they need. But I still recommend producing a written copy of a media kit because even in our wired world, reporters for both electronic and print may want the convenience of a kit that they can refer to, throw in their briefcase, or put in a file.

## What's the hook?

Now for some bad news. Did you know that most media kits never get more than a passing glance from journalists? In general, media kits don't generate publicity. Not on their own. Not without a *hook* — that is, a current, interesting story to provide a focus for the media's coverage. So your media kit is just a foundation for generating publicity. You still have more to do.

The hook is the newsworthy information in your most current press release. How will you create that press release? By figuring out what is really exciting about your executives, staff, products, services, earnings, special event, or milestone. I discuss press releases in detail in the next section.

# The Press Release That's Going to Get You Publicity

The best way to decide what the story should be is to ask yourself what's new at your company. So, ask yourself now: Have you launched a new product? Did you add new employees? Did you have outstanding earnings for this quarter? Are you expanding in the region? Will you be merging with a new company? Is it your anniversary? Do some of your employees run in marathons or volunteer for a local charity? Does your business support a youth soccer team or league?

Whatever your story is, whether you received a new contract with a major client or you just received an award, you want to put it on paper in the form of a press release.

Because space and time equal money, keep your press release brief, breakthrough, and newsworthy. How? Imagine that you're writing a short article for the front page of your local paper.

## Getting a reporter to take notice

Try putting yourself in the reporter's seat for a moment. A reporter receives many press releases each week. She may have only an hour to read them, so she has to make quick judgments and scan a paragraph or two of each one. Keep in mind that she also gets e-mails and voice mails every day, too. Your release has to rise to the top of this weighty pile of communications. And the pile is far bigger at larger newspapers, where you may be most eager to get coverage.

Make your press release as professional as possible so that a reporter places yours in her credible pile. Make it stand out! Here are some of the tricks. Your press release needs to

✔ Consist of news that's really news, not just promotional material. (*Newsworthy* means something that represents significant progress, has a local angle, is unusual, is timely, and/or is important right now.)

✔ Contain the name, address, phone number, and Web site of your company in the upper-left corner of the first page. Also, give the name, phone number, and e-mail address of the person to contact (probably you) for further information.

✔ Be short. Yes, short! (No more than two pages.)

✔ Be word-processed and printed on your company's letterhead on a laser printer. If it's more than one page, use a matching second page and staple your pages together.

✔ Be spell-checked and read over by several different people for accuracy and typos.

I'm serious about checking your release for accuracy and professional appearance. In many cases, you're sending it to editors and writers. They will *know* whether or not it's well written and professionally laid out and printed. Have several people at different levels in your company read over your press release. You'll be surprised by what different people may see. The third reader often finds a mistake that the first two missed or adds some insight that nobody else thought of.

---

# Good versus bad press releases

A good press release is professionally typed and printed on original letterhead. It includes the name of the contact person, his phone number and e-mail, the date, and the words *For Immediate Release*. It also

✔ Has a great headline

✔ Is double-spaced

✔ Is clearly interesting

A bad press release — one that will end up in the garbage can — is

✔ Too long

✔ Missing a much-needed visual, such as a photograph, which can help tell the story

✔ Not newsworthy

✔ Too soft or self-promotional

✔ Poorly written with obvious mistakes

✔ Lacking valuable information that makes the story more interesting

✔ Lacking in attention to details

✔ Late or off-season

If your release must go to a second page, try to end the first page with a completed paragraph or, at least, a completed sentence. Type **-More-** across the bottom of the first page. Then start the second page with a brief heading in the upper-left corner that includes the name of your company and page two.

Mark the end of your release with the digits **-30-** or the number sign, **###**, repeated several times across the page. These symbols are two versions of journalese for "that's all there is for now."

Many media outlets now post instructions for how to submit releases to them. Look for instructions on your local newspaper's Web site (and anywhere else you plan to send your release). Adjust your format, length, and style to meet their requirements.

## Making sure your release is "news ready"

A good press release reads like a news story, which is exactly the point. A good release sounds as if it's ready to be inserted in a paper. Here's how to write one that meets this important criterion.

- ✔ **A good release starts with a *headline*.** A short title at the top tells the media what your hook is. "Local business agrees to support youth soccer programs for five years." "Tooling company adds cutting-edge equipment." "Author explains the secrets of generating publicity." Whatever your hook, start right off with it so that they "get it" right away.

- ✔ **Next, a good release has a *lead paragraph* that covers the who, what, when, where, and why of the interesting subject that you're sharing with the media.** Then, subsequent paragraphs clearly and cleanly elaborate upon that story with details and interesting tidbits.

  Who, what, when, where, and why: That's the journalist's mantra. Let it be yours when you write a release; otherwise, they don't have a story fit for print (or air) until they've answered those questions. In a way, you can think of that opening paragraph as providing the *bait* for your hook. And that bait is the who, what, when, where, and why that provides a journalist with all the essentials needed to turn a hook into actual editorial content.

- ✔ **Finally, a good release needs to follow through on the promise of the header and lead paragraph with a few more paragraphs of *supporting text and images*.** Make sure that this supporting text is truly relevant and to the point, not boringly repetitive. Provide some interesting or important background information. Throw in a quote or two from a company representative, if you like. Give some evidence to support your contention that you've actually done something important or unusual or timely. And if at all appropriate, provide a photo or other visual to illustrate the story.

# Pitching Your Release to the Media

When you have your press release (probably about two double-spaced pages) and media kit ready, you need to make a *media pitch*. In other words, you have to sell your story.

Make your first media pitch by selecting one reporter and trying the process once. Select the main paper in your region and choose the reporter who covers the beat most affiliated with what your company does.

For example, if your company is an art gallery and is opening a new exhibit, you'd obviously contact the art editor at your local paper. If your company just bought a huge piece of land to develop over the next two years, find the reporter who covers construction and development.

You may also call the section of the paper that best relates to your company and ask who writes about your specific topic. You'll usually find that someone is happy to point you to the correct contact.

Here's a list of some typical specialty areas at a large metropolitan daily:

| | | |
|---|---|---|
| Art | Movies | Books |
| Music | Business | News |
| Real Estate | Editorial | Science |
| Education | Society | Entertainment (Criticism) |
| Sports | Entertainment (News) | Sunday Editor |
| Events Calendar | Television | Fashion |
| Technology | Features | Theater |
| Food | Travel | Foreign Affairs |
| Women's Page | Home and Garden | Local |

Lots of choices, aren't there?

Before you approach the most appropriate person, confirm the reporter's name, business address, and phone number via phone. You have to be sure you know who you want to talk to and how to contact him.

## Including a cover letter

Finally, you're prepared to generate some publicity. Well, almost. Your next step is to put together a short, clear cover letter that tells the reporter why you think he should write about your company. It can go something like this example:

> Dear Doug Smith:
>
> I enjoy your feature article every week as you overview construction and development in western North Carolina. I particularly enjoyed your article dated June 1, 20XX, regarding the proposed new highway. I think your readers will enjoy hearing about the land my company is purchasing for development. The attached press release specifically outlines our plans.
>
> I have also enclosed a media kit, which gives you background information on our company and a visual rendering of the proposed project. Digital versions of these illustrations can be e-mailed to you, or they can be obtained in the pressroom on our Web site. I will follow up with you shortly.
>
> Best Regards,
>
> John Builder

Now you're actually ready to make the contact. Put your cover letter, press release, and kit into an envelope (don't fold them!) and send them via first-class mail.

## Don't forget to follow up!

You absolutely must make a follow-up call. If you want to be successful with publicity, never send anything that you don't follow up with. Four or five days after you send your package, make a follow-up call and talk to the media person about your potential story. You may get voice mail, or you may actually get a live person on the phone. In case you do talk with the reporter on the phone, be sure to have the media kit and press release right in front of you so that you can quickly discuss key points.

If you get voice mail, which is most common, make sure that you've practiced a solid voice mail message that goes something like this one:

> "Hi, Doug. This is John Builder. You may not recognize my name, but I'm the Director of Marketing at Build Right Construction Services. I read your articles all the time in the Gotham City Observer and sent you a press release that I think is something you can use and is something that your readers will be interested in. As you know, my company has just purchased a tract of land, and the package I sent to you reveals our plans for the land. You can reach me at 555-6666. I look forward to talking to you soon."

I can't emphasize enough the importance of calling a reporter. Don't be shy and don't think you shouldn't call because you'll be bothering her. If you don't bother reporters just a little bit, they probably won't notice you or your story.

Making that follow-up call is far easier when you have something in mind that's worth saying — and that you know the reporter will find worth listening to. A clever strategy is to offer some significant detail that wasn't covered in your press release (either on purpose or because it wasn't confirmed yet). Then you can feel good about calling because you have another piece of valuable information to share with the reporter. For example, you can amend the earlier call script to include this additional sentence: "We've just gotten approval last night from the zoning board for our plans, so I thought you'd like to know that we'll be beginning construction next week." Now the story is timely, and you will probably get a prompt response.

By the way, monthly magazine and Sunday newspaper supplement writers are more likely to respond to you in a hurry if you reach them just before the end of their writing cycle when they have to hand in enough stories to fill the next edition. Next time you talk to anyone at a publication, ask when the deadline for each issue falls in the weekly or monthly cycle. Once you know this information, you can make a short reminder call about your release the day before the deadline in case a reporter is desperately looking for one more story to fill the next issue.

## Dealing with rejection

When you pitch a story, you're selling your hook to journalists. (See "What's the hook?" earlier in this chapter.) It may not seem like "real" selling because you aren't asking for money, but it's still sales in that you need to select a target, make an approach, find a way to present your information, and ask them to do something that's beneficial for you.

And sometimes they do. But often, the media ignores you and declines to cover your story, in which case, you need to deal with rejection, just as you do in personal selling. (See Chapter 15 for helpful advice.) Now, remember that rejection means nothing to journalists and should mean nothing to you, either. Maybe they just don't need your story right now. Or they just don't think the hook is very sharp. Or they don't think the story is very relevant to their area or focus. But because you presented yourself professionally and politely, they're still happy — in fact, more than happy — to see your next release or hear your next voice mail follow-up on a mailing. So rejection doesn't preclude later coverage.

In fact, a journalist who has rejected you in the past is more likely to cover your company than someone who has never heard of you. Even though a journalist declines to cover a specific story, she generally makes a mental note of the source and puts you in a physical, or at least a mental, "possible sources"

file. Your well-prepared, professional letter, press release, and media kit earned you the right to be a source of news in the future. So don't let rejection worry you. You're still closer to coverage than you were before you made the contact.

# Creating Your Mailing Lists

Start by targeting one reporter at the largest paper in your area. Pick someone who has written stories like yours in the past and develop a relationship with him or her. This person can probably do more for your company's exposure than all your marketing efforts combined. Then build relationships with additional reporters, until you have a good in-house list.

As you build your list you will find it makes sense to break it down into multiple categories or even into separate lists. You'll have occasions when you want to make a mailing to a specific type of medium — large metropolitan dailies, smaller daily papers, weekly newspapers, trade magazines, local television, or radio. It's a good idea to begin by keeping them in separate lists so that you can easily extract them for a particular use. Also, if your geographic areas become larger, you can easily expand these more specific lists.

You may need only one or two lists of a very limited nature to begin, but planning for future lists at this time as well pays off. You'll get a good understanding of what your growth potential is, and you'll establish a workable pattern for your lists: how you keep them, the type of information you collect — that sort of thing. As you prepare more and more lists, you can shuffle and combine them for temporary or immediate goals, eliminating the need to build a new list each time you send out a mailing.

The lists you may eventually be building may include

- Company "hometown" media
- Branch offices' "hometown" media
- Wire services that have a bureau where your company is based
- Daily newspapers (A list: big papers)
- Daily newspapers (B list: smaller papers)
- Weekly newspapers (C list)
- Television and radio stations (those that have business shows that may cover your company; you'll find the appropriate producers in the stations' news production department)
- Trade, professional, and technical journals and blogs
- Consumer publications (usually national; look for a reporter who covers your subject and thinks you're unique)

# Finding the names for your list

Deciding what sorts of lists you want to compile is one thing, but actually creating those lists is quite another. Where are you going to find the names of the appropriate editors, writers, and other journalists?

One suggestion is to go to a local newspaper stand in your city and buy all the publications that someone who would use your products or services would read. (You probably read many of them anyway.) You can find out who's writing about your subject, and you can literally start a print database that way.

If you make business-to-business sales, you also want to compile a list of contacts at trade and industry publications. You can always find at least a few publications read by purchasers in any industry. Put those publications on your list. If you aren't sure what your customers read and what professional associations they belong to, ask them!

For radio and television programs that may offer opportunities for exposure, you can simply go through a television-programming guide published by your local paper. If you see that Channel 10 in your area offers a business-focused program every Sunday morning, you know that the producer of that program should appear on your media list.

What? You were thinking Oprah, Peter Jennings, Dan Rather, Tom Brokaw, or the front page of *The Wall Street Journal?* Your company may produce products or services that warrant exposure nationally, but for learning the process of publicity, I recommend starting by focusing locally. You can use the experience you gain and the techniques you master on a local basis for regional and national publicity. It's far easier to go to the local media first to gain experience and confidence. And, in truth, most publicity is local and regional. Over the long run, this media is where most businesses get the ongoing exposure they need.

# Opting to buy a list instead

A second option is simply to order a list from one of the media list-management companies in the country, such as Bacon's Information in Chicago, which is now distributed by Cision. (Visit www.cision.com or, in the U.S., call 866-639-5087 for details.) This company publishes an extensive media list. The company can also pull a list for you based on your criteria and then charges you only for the records that it pulls for you. You can obtain the records on disk along with a printout.

For example, suppose that your company offers services to banks in the southeastern United States. As a starting point, you'd ask the researcher at Bacon's to pull a list of all the banking reporters in the Southeast at every daily and weekly newspaper and every business-industry trade magazine that has a banking reporter. After you have that list, you literally can get to know every editor on that list by sending them your press release and media kit. These media contacts are perfect for your company because they fit the criteria of being in the right region and being specialists in the field of banking. To pay a list company to pull the list for you is probably a good starting point and probably worth what it charges.

Remember to check your list for changes each time you use it. No matter how your list originates or how you decide to update it, check your list frequently.

Don't oversend to your lists. Make each and every contact with the media count, just as you'd want every contact with your customers to count.

# Going Online: Web Publicity Tools

There is still no substitute for studying your market (whether a local area, region, or industry) and digging up good editorial contacts for personalized calling and mailing. However, taking advantage of the power of the Web to supplement these traditional PR activities is also helpful. Two key strategies are to send your press release to an e-mail list and to post your press release on Web newswires, where editors often check for story ideas.

## Sending releases to your e-mail list

You may want to use two kinds of e-mail lists. The first is the personal list of editors and writers who have given you their e-mails and will recognize your name when you e-mail them. This list comes from your research and contacts and builds gradually over time. By the time you've done your tenth press release, your prospecting and follow-up calls should have generated enough personal contacts to give you a decent e-mail list.

Use your e-mail list judiciously by writing personal e-mails only — do not blast generic sounding e-mails to your personal media contacts, or they won't want to accept your next e-mail or phone call.

The second kind of e-mail list is an impersonal list of editors and writers that you don't know — yet. However, if you send a short, interesting release to them, a few of them might take an interest in your story and e-mail or call to find out more. This approach is a good way to expand your reach and pick up new contacts for your core media list.

As with mailing lists, you can find commercial sources for e-mail lists, and you can hire a firm to do a bulk e-mailing to editors. But be careful: A lot of vendors offer thousands of e-mail addresses for a very cheap price, but they don't sort and check their names very well. Pick a vendor who specializes in business names by title or job and won't send your press release to a generic e-mail list. Also, keep your e-mail press release short and simple and ask the recipients whether they're interested in future releases and, if so, to reply to you. This way, editors and writers with an interest in your business news can add their names to your in-house list, and the rest won't be bothered by you again.

## Using Web press release services

A variety of companies will, for a modest fee, blast your press release to thousands of journalists. If you have news that may be of broad interest (and do try to make sure that every release fits this description!), then a press release service is worth a try. At the time of writing, I see that e-releases (`www.ereleases.com`) is offering a special price of $399 on a distribution of your release via the PR Newswire, which it says reaches approximately 70,000 journalists. Not bad. Specifically, the PR Newswire service is used by tens of thousands of individual journalists. Plus, thousands of newspapers, radio and TV stations, and online news services also subscribe, so you definitely put your news in front of a lot of media people for the price.

However, keep in mind that most journalists aren't going to be covering stories such as yours; finding an interested journalist is something of a needle-in-the-haystack problem, so getting wide exposure for your press release is important.

Also, keep your release brief and newsworthy, emphasizing information that perfect strangers may take an interest in. Go to PR Newswire (`www.prnews wire.com`) or a similar service to read current news releases from other marketers. Which of them are most compelling to you? Use those releases as models when you write your own. Another good way to use PR Newswire and similar services for planning your release is to type in a key term related to your story and read whatever releases pop up. How can you differentiate your story from these stories? Make sure that you add a new twist or some fresh news so that your release stands out.

Here are several press release services you can check out:

- ✔ **PR Newswire** (`www.prnewswire.com`)
- ✔ **Send2Press** (`www.send2press.com`)
- ✔ **PRLog** (`www.prlog.com`)

(The above list is specifically aimed at U.S. media, so if you are in a different country, search for similar services that target media closer to where you operate.) You have lots of options, many of them quite affordable. Even if your main release is by mail, you certainly should do an electronic release as well, just to see whether you can pick up a few extra hits.

## Multimedia e-releases

PR Newswire is leading the way (and other services are quickly following) in offering you the option of attaching streaming video to your electronic press release. This is a great idea! For example, if you promoted your new pizza parlor by entering a regional or national pizza-making contest and won an award, you could prepare a short written news release, plus a several-minute video showing highlights of the event. Your electronic news release can include the video, and your written releases (both snail mail and electronic versions) can mention the video and give a YouTube (www.youtube.com) address where people can see the video.

Press releases used to be printed, because most news was printed. But now people take in more news on television, radio, and the Web than by reading newspapers and magazines. So think multimedia. Get hold of a digital video recorder or get a friend who is good at it to document any interesting events or goings-on. Then make the video available — after all, seeing is believing.

### Talking it to the street

I hesitate to mention it, but there is another great way to get out there and generate some great visibility for yourself and your business without buying ads or even creating a media kit and press release. That is to simply be a public speaker at events that attract people who may become customers or may lead you to customers. When you speak at a local business club or group, a convention, or a conference, you're taking your content directly to interested people rather than relying on the media to distribute it for you.

Many organizations seek out speakers including local chambers of commerce, continuing education programs, and large corporations. Don't be afraid to ask to put on a seminar. Be the first to suggest and produce a seminar to pave the way to additional opportunities. Don't forget to tape your presentations. You can place video and audio files on your Web site or integrate them into your e-mail newsletter to secure future speaker engagements. And often, when you know you have a speaking event on the calendar, you can use it as a source of publicity by creating a press release and notifying an appropriate media list that you're making a presentation. Tell them what you'll be speaking about, why it's a new or important approach, and who the sponsor and audience are. Send out your press release a couple of weeks ahead of the event, but not too far ahead; otherwise, the media will forget about it by the time it occurs.

CD1002 is a screen shot of a PR Newswire story from Omni Hotels, timed to be picked up in stories about summer travel plans. It includes a streaming video, along with instructions for accessing a higher resolution version of the video in case an editor wants to make it available on her site.

Also, make sure that you provide good quality (well-lit, colorful, and clear) photographs for the media to use if the e-release service you use allows it and post a print-quality (300 dpi or better) version of the photo with the release itself. If not, include at least a thumbnail, along with a link to your Web site or an online photo service where journalists can download the images at high resolution, such as photobucket (www.photobucket.com). Make telling your story in words, pictures, video, and sound easy, and you'll get more hits.

## Keep e-releases short and sweet

Journalists and editors are even more impatient online than when reading traditional releases. Give them the story in as short a version as possible. If you can keep it to less than a hundred words, do.

A good example of a simple, clear, brief electronic news release is provided in CD1003, which describes a new line of teen clothing with a Japanese flavor.

## On the CD

Check out the following files on the CD-ROM:

- ✔ A well-done press release announcing a new product line (CD1001)
- ✔ A screen shot of a PR Newswire release that includes streaming video (CD1002)
- ✔ An example of an effective, brief, electronic news release (CD1003)

# Part IV
# Honing Your Marketing Skills

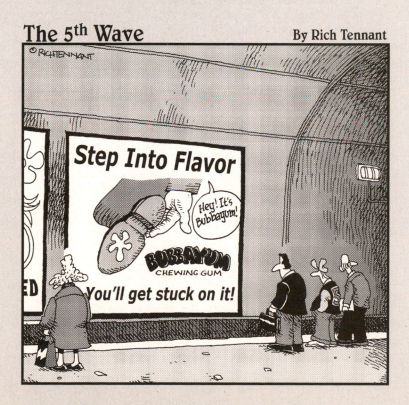

The 5th Wave                                    By Rich Tennant

Step Into Flavor

Hey! It's Bubbayum!

BUBBAYUM
CHEWING GUM

You'll get stuck on it!

## In this part . . .

Sales and marketing always benefit from the dramatic boost that creativity can give your appeal, so in this part, you find lots of tips and techniques for harnessing the power of creative marketing. Writing is also essential to almost everything in marketing, from the lowly sales letter to the modern Web site, so I include a hands-on chapter on how you can make those marketing words and phrases ring out and draw in customers.

Because I'm a big believer in understanding and empathizing with your customers, I start this part with a chapter on what I think of as real-world research: practical, affordable ways to find out what's happening in your industry and ways to stay ahead of the trends. If you want to be a leader in your market, you always need to be sniffing the wind!

# Chapter 11

# The Customer Research Workshop

*In This Chapter*

▶ Getting to know your customers

▶ Making sure service is winning you converts

▶ Experimenting to find out what turns customers on

The concept behind market research is simple: Knowledge about people's needs, preferences, and habits may be useful to you as you seek ways to boost sales. Professional market researchers tend to use highly complex sampling and statistical analysis methods to look for subtle refinements to their advertising and marketing plans. However, those techniques are worse than useless for the average marketer. Fortunately, simple insights that help grow your sales *are* of value, and this chapter helps you seek and find them.

In this chapter, I cover the best ways to conduct customer research: interviews, customer service audits, and experimentation. I also point you to places on the CD that help you with these methods.

## Talking to Your Customers

Industrial chemicals maker Cabot Corporation developed an informal marketing research technique that involved the use of in-depth customer interviews. The corporation designed the interviews to identify customer concerns and suggestions and to help Cabot find out how it was viewed in the marketplace. And here's the most original part of the project: Cabot's salespeople or distributors conducted all the interviews. No expensive survey research firms. No statistical analysis or boring bar charts. Just talking with customers.

Cabot implemented its plan as follows: People who normally made sales calls took a few days off from selling and spent the time conducting informational interviews with key customers instead.

## Poison ivy marketing

Scientists at Duke University have published studies of poison ivy that show how this weed grows more vigorously when carbon dioxide is at high levels and the weather is hot. Some federal grant paid for this laborious study, but anyone can cash in on the results. It happens that the climate in the United States (where poison ivy is native) is getting hotter, and $CO_2$ levels are rising as a consequence of urban air pollution and the global warming trend. So you can forecast healthy times ahead for poison ivy — and lots of rashes and problems for anyone who tries to garden where it grows. Entrepreneurs are jumping on this emerging opportunity by offering poison ivy eradication services. (For example, `www.poisonivy horticulturalist.com` offers eradication in the Philadelphia, Pennsylvania, area.)

How do you advertise a poison ivy eradication business? If P&G owned it, it would conduct focus group studies in which homeowners would be asked about their experiences with the rash-causing weed. However, you can gain insight into consumer behavior without that costly step. Common sense tells you that people are concerned about poison ivy in spring and summer — so it will be a seasonal business and advertising in the winter will be a waste of money. Also, people who are active gardeners, who have pets (which carry the itch-causing oils into the house), and/or who have children who play in the back yard are especially likely to be concerned. Probably a bad case of poison

ivy will also precipitate a strong desire to eradicate the weed. Add these insights up, and you have some good clues as to who you need to talk to and when.

These insights can help you design a good marketing program. Putting brochures on the counter of local garden-supply stores would reach active backyard gardeners, for example. And a spring press release to lifestyles editors of local newspapers could focus on how to protect children from poison ivy. Perhaps those brochures on eradicating the weed could also be dropped off at local medical clinics, where people with bad cases of poison ivy are bound to turn up after the first hot weekend of the season.

I went through this example to show you how asking simple but powerful questions about market trends and consumer behavior patterns can help you find your marketing zone more easily. But you're probably not in the poison ivy eradication business. Whatever you do, you may be able to gain some insights that help you to increase sales, reduce customer turnover, raise prices, and increase profits. If you're doing marketing for an ongoing business, asking for customer feedback is your single-most powerful technique for planning or improving your marketing activities. Somewhere in customers' heads or hearts lies the answer to every question, including how to grow your company tenfold in the next three years. You just have to get that information out of them in order to profit from it.

To make sure that their salespeople and distributors knew how to conduct polite, research-oriented interviews, Cabot first ran them through a short training course. In the course, they received a printed guide with step-by-step instructions and questions to ask. The training also taught them *how to ask* by having them practice role-playing exercises. The main point that a training session like this one needs to convey is that the interviews are informational only and can't be turned into disguised sales pitches. Customers will be angry if they feel deceived about the purpose of the meeting or phone call. (I've conducted some training in similar informal, qualitative survey techniques and can tell you that it takes a little practice to become a good listener and a nonjudgmental interviewer.)

The reason Cabot Corporation trained its people before letting them do customer interviews is because it really needed them to change their behavior to get good results. They couldn't act like an interested party. They needed to play the role of researchers if they wanted customers to play the role of "researchees."

Just remember when you're doing research, no matter what your customers say, don't argue with them. Got that? I don't care if their views are based on incorrect information or a false interpretation. You're doing research, not debating. For customer interviews to work, you need to avoid defensive reactions. Act like a dispassionate third party who just wants to clarify exactly what the customer thinks. Then study their reactions later and decide what to say in your next ad campaign, brochure, blog, or sales pitch.

Try calling a few customers and asking them whether they're willing to participate in an informational interview to help you with your research into how to improve your product and/or service. I think you'll be pleasantly surprised at how many of them are willing, and even eager, to provide their input after they see that you're sincerely open to constructive criticism. Most customers feel like their opinions aren't wanted, and they're thrilled to find someone who cares.

Keep in mind that your customers probably don't know what they know, so the research process isn't as easy as just asking them what to do. You need a system, a method, and the willingness to sift through a lot of junk information for a few pearls of wisdom or a single startling insight. But doing customer research is definitely worth the effort.

If you don't have the staff to do customer interviews, advertise at a local college and hire college interns for the work. Just make sure that you train them and then conduct a mock interview with them to see how well they perform. If they aren't professional and pleasant throughout the mock interview, send them back to college and hire someone more competent.

To ensure that you, your salespeople, or your interns conduct successful customer interviews, try using the Customer Debriefing Form on the CD (filename CD1101), which you can adapt to your specific needs and print multiple copies for use in interviews. My firm has used this form when training salespeople in *active research,* which basically means any simple, hands-on ways to gather insights from your customers or others in your market. (My associate Charles Schewe calls it "walking the dog research" and suggests asking exploratory questions in casual, natural interactions with customers.)

REAL WORLD

## All you have to do is ask

Whenever you have questions, concerns, or a desire to boost performance, the first action you need to take is to talk to your customers. Customers usually know how to talk, after all, and getting them talking about your product or service isn't too hard. Often, they're flattered that you value their opinions.

Here's an example from my own business of how willing customers are to answer questions. I recently went to a conference in Las Vegas (no, I didn't gamble wildly . . . just a little) where I gave a talk on how to train managers to be more effective leaders in the workplace. A lot of experts on employee training — who also happen to be my prospective customers — were in the audience. These people often spend their companies' money on course materials and books for their employees — and I write and sell that sort of product. So I brought along

copies of a draft of the new book I was working on called *The Starfish Files,* which I wanted to sell to companies as a handout for their managers to teach them about leadership. At the end of my talk, I held up a copy of the draft version of the book and asked audience members to give me their business cards if they were willing to read and review the book and send me feedback about how to make it better. I wasn't sure what kind of reaction I'd get, so I was amazed when almost everyone in the audience volunteered to review the new product for me. And they did: I received a lot of great suggestions and reactions via e-mail, and I used these ideas to improve the product before launching it.

Note that my research was done entirely for free. I didn't pay them, nor did I hire an expensive firm to do formal research. I just asked for help, and people gladly gave it.

The customer debriefing is a particularly good tool for doing action research, and it's one that I've used many times for my own business as well as for clients. Try it. I guarantee you'll discover at least one new and useful thing about your own business when you ask customers to open up and give you honest feedback.

# Auditing Your Customer Service

Whether you market a service or a product, every marketer should take a close look at the quality of their service. For example, a company that makes and sells products wholesale, for others to sell retail, may seem to be strictly a product-based company. However, as soon as you start asking buyers at stores about their suppliers, you discover that they care a lot about service. When they need to reorder, can they easily reach someone? If a defect exists, can they get help, a refund, or a replacement in a hurry? Service matters, even if you think you're in a product-oriented business.

How good is *your* service? A good way to find out is to ask customers for an overall rating of it. Surveys like the 7 x 7 survey in Figure 11-1 (and on your CD as CD1102) give you an idea of whether customers think that your company is good, fair, or poor to do business with.

---

**Customer Satisfaction Survey**

Please answer these questions while thinking about your customer service from

**Dave Lane Home Improvement**

*Scale: 1 = Strongly Disagree to 7 = Strongly Agree*

1 2 3 4 5 6 7  I am highly satisfied with all aspects of customer service.

1 2 3 4 5 6 7  I definitely will make more purchases from this company in the future.

1 2 3 4 5 6 7  I commonly reccommend this company to my friends.

1 2 3 4 5 6 7  This comapny is highly responsive to customer needs.

1 2 3 4 5 6 7  This company's service is faster than typical of the industry.

1 2 3 4 5 6 7  This company's employees are helpful and cooperative.

1 2 3 4 5 6 7  This company is good at solving my problems.

*Thank you for your input!*

---

**Figure 11-1:**
An example of an effective customer satisfaction survey.

Surveys like the template I provide in CD1102 allow you to "take the temperature" of customer service quickly and easily. If the answers aren't near the top of the scale, you know your patient is ill.

But then what? What if customers don't like you as much as you'd like them to? How do you know what to actually *do* about it? The file in CD1102 includes suggestions for interpreting your score on the customer satisfaction survey by examining each of the seven questions. If you collect a few dozen or more surveys and then average the scores for each question, you'll have enough information to compare the scores on each question. A difference of two or more is probably significant. Look at your lowest scoring question and focus on correcting your marketing and service based on the following suggestions:

✔ Question 1 is a general customer service question. If your score is 3 or less on question 1, look for the reasons in low scores on any of the other, more specific, questions.

✔ Question 2 measures customer's future purchase intentions. If your score is low, focus on delivering a quality experience and product and follow up after the sale to make sure that users are happy with their purchase.

✔ Question 3 measures customer willingness to make referrals. If low, focus on boosting positive word-of-mouth by raising overall quality and, in particular, by making sure that you notice any problems or critical incidents and resolve each one positively.

✔ Question 4 measures your responsiveness to customers. If low, make sure that you recognize and react to customer requests, complaints, or problems quickly and visibly. Also train service employees to demonstrate more empathy (sympathetic listening skills).

✔ Question 5 measures service speed. If low, work on handling customer orders and needs more quickly and reliably.

✔ Question 6 measures your overall helpfulness to customers. If low, work on providing supportive services characterized by being accessible and available to customers and eager to meet their specific needs.

✔ Question 7 measures how well you resolve customer problems. If low, make sure that you have appropriate processes for identifying and resolving complaints or customer concerns, including ways of compensating customers for service interruptions.

The customer satisfaction survey asks questions about six specific components of customer happiness. Any one of them can sabotage your customer relationships and cause customers to complain and, eventually, to leave you. The survey helps you identify what specific problem is bothering your customers. I can't tell you what to fix — only your customers can. Your customers have specific expectations about you that you need to explore and understand.

I did a survey for a large trucking company and discovered that their customers care more about reliability than speed. They wanted to be certain about when to expect a shipment. Before this survey, the trucking company had been focusing on how fast it could move freight across the country. After the survey, we switched the focus and made the service a little slower but much more reliable. Customers were a lot happier and sales grew.

The customer satisfaction survey in Figure 11-1 and on CD1102 is powerful and may be all you need. However, if it doesn't clarify what you need to do, or if you suspect there may be multiple problems with customer service, I recommend you use an even more sophisticated tool, the Customer Service Audit. It's a much more powerful tool than the 7 x 7 survey and can reveal information you didn't even know that you didn't know. (Got that?)

Review the sample survey on your CD (CD1103) and consider printing and handing out copies to a few dozen customers. You may need to offer them an incentive to complete it, such as a special gift or a discount on their next order, but it's often well worth the cost to find out what problems they see in your service.

UPS, like other trucking companies, traditionally assumed that speedy delivery was the key to success. Competitors competed on speed, and customers always said they valued speed and were upset when packages came late. So UPS understandably focused on speed. Their drivers raced in and out of offices and up and down front porches trying to beat the clock. Then UPS talked to some customers who said they thought the drivers were in too much of a hurry to be friendly or helpful. Customers said they wanted drivers to stop long enough to answer questions and give advice. This response revealed an entirely different dimension of customer service that the company had ignored in its quest for speed. When the company bigwigs realized that the drivers' friendliness and helpfulness were important to customers, they changed the company's approach. The company gave new instructions to its drivers and gave them permission and training to provide more in-the-field customer relations and advice. Customers were much happier when the drivers took time to talk with them, and customer loyalty increased.

## Performing a customer service review

Probably a quarter or more of your customers aren't too happy with your product or service. And you won't know most of their concerns unless you look for them because less than 5 percent of unhappy customers complain. The other 95 percent of them are like the sunken part of an iceberg: They're a serious hazard to navigation, but nobody can see them — except maybe other customers. People are about five times more likely to tell others about bad experiences than about good ones. So those hidden grumblers are spreading the bad word without your knowledge. Time to find out what's troubling them.

How are you going to get to the bottom of hidden, complex customer attitudes toward your service? An audit is the best approach. A *customer service audit* uses a survey to explore the specifics of what customers want and how well they think you deliver what they want.

Here's a five-step process for performing your audit:

1. **Identify specific attributes of customer service, such as speed, friendliness, convenience, availability, or quick response times on complaints.**

    In other words, break down customer service into as many components as possible so that you can get specific in managing them.

2. **Ask customers how important each specific attribute of service really is.**

   Some aspects of service are more important than others. And when you know what your customers value most, you know where to put your efforts so that you can do the most good.

3. **Ask customers how well your service performs on each of those specific attributes.**

   Do they think your company is doing well or not?

4. **Think about the responses.**

   Specifically, look for gaps between customer priorities and your product/company's performance. If you're performing less than wonderfully on your customers' top-priority service attributes, you better work on those areas right now. If you're doing wonderfully on issues that they rank as low priority, you can slack off a bit in those areas, which can give you room to improve on their higher priorities. So think about what changes you can make to better match your service performance to your customers' service priorities.

5. **Make changes.**

   Often, surveys and analyses like this one end with a nice report or to-do list. To make your audit pay off, you actually have to *make some changes* in how you deliver your customer service. So make an action plan and then remind yourself to check on your execution next week, next month, and so on until you see real, lasting improvements in high-priority service specifics.

## *Using the audit template*

Figuring out what to ask customers is the hardest part of doing a good customer service audit. This task seems easy, but don't be deceived. If you just ask customers about the obvious issues, you may miss something important! So take plenty of time to brainstorm a long list of specific aspects of customer service. Then ask a few customers whether you've covered everything and add any ideas that they suggest.

 A good, detailed list of what customer service consists of is the start of every great customer service audit. (And when you have yours ready, post it where everyone who interacts with customers can see it routinely! Also, put it in your next marketing plan along with action steps on how to improve on all the items on the list.)

Here are some candidates, taken from a variety of businesses and industries, to get you started:

- Answering the phone quickly
- Apologizing for delays
- Being available when needed
- Being consistent and predictable
- Being creative at problem solving
- Being reliable
- Billing accurately
- Friendliness of personnel
- Getting a job done right the first time
- Helping to solve problems
- Honoring frequent-user offers fairly without tricky small print
- Informing customers quickly and fully about problems
- Keeping things neat and clean
- Making up for mistakes or delays with offers of real value
- Matching competitors' capabilities
- Matching competitors' prices
- Not arguing over who's responsible
- Not pestering with irritating sales pitches
- Not stuffing bills with junk-mail advertisements
- Not using rude letters to collect bills
- Not using rude phone calls to collect bills
- Performing only the necessary work
- Performing only the requested work
- Politeness of personnel
- Product/service ready when promised
- Product/service made convenient for customer
- Prompt warranty work
- Providing frequent-user benefits
- Providing loaner equipment when your customer's is being repaired
- Providing useful information
- Reminding customers when their products need maintenance

✔ Reminding customers when they need supplies

✔ Responding fairly to complaints

✔ Responding quickly to complaints

You can copy this list (CD1103) or make up your own. Then ask a few customers to look at your list and tell you whether it describes the issues they care about. Encourage reviewers to point out any issues that may be missing; using their feedback is a good way to get the most complete list possible.

After you have a good, long list, you can prepare a survey and systematically ask as many customers as possible to respond to it. The survey should basically look like Table 11-1, whether you plan to fill it in yourself or have your customers do it.

| Table 11-1 | Customer Service Survey | |
| --- | --- | --- |
| *Customer Service Element* | *How Important Is It?* | *How Do We Do on It?* |
| Politeness of personnel | __not important<br>__slightly important<br>__important<br>__very important | __poor<br>__fair<br>__good<br>__excellent |
| Getting job done right the first time | __not important<br>__slightly important<br>__important<br>__very important | __poor<br>__fair<br>__good<br>__excellent |
| Apologizing for delays | __not important<br>__slightly important<br>__important<br>__very important | __poor<br>__fair<br>__good<br>__excellent |
| Prompt warranty work | __not important<br>__slightly important<br>__important<br>__very important | __poor<br>__fair<br>__good<br>__excellent |
| Not arguing over who's responsible | __not important<br>__slightly important<br>__important<br>__very important | __poor<br>__fair<br>__good<br>__excellent |
| Things ready when promised | __not important<br>__slightly important<br>__important<br>__very important | __poor<br>__fair<br>__good<br>__excellent |

## Surveying successfully

The key to performing the survey successfully is to ask a bunch of customers. The best methodology lets you talk to your customers as easily and quickly as possible. If customers are willing to fill in a written survey and return it, then let them do it. (And your response rate will improve if you offer a gift, such as a coupon, pen set, or something relevant to your business, as a reward.) Sometimes, though, customers don't pay much attention to such requests, in which case, you'll need to ask them in person, by e-mail, or over the phone to answer some questions for you. Face-to-face interviews in which you explain that you're auditing your customer service and then ask customers to rate each statement while you fill in the form get reasonably high participation rates. (If you're too busy to do face-to-face interviews, consider recruiting college interns.) Telephone requests in which you ask the same questions have somewhat lower response rates than face-to-face interviews. E-mail requests (if personal) get moderate response rates. Mail requests get the lowest response rates, but because these surveys are the least trouble for you, receiving only 5 or 10 percent of mailed surveys back may not matter.

If you aren't sure which method works best or whether a particular method of administering the survey may be biased in some way, try two or three different methods. Collecting a bunch of responses is key. And be polite, always explaining who you (really) are and why you need the information (to improve your company's service), and always get permission to ask them some questions. Then at least you don't make any enemies, even if they decline to participate.

What's a "bunch of responses"? How many do you really need? Well, statistically, survey research firms often want to get several hundred or more responses. But then, they want to do fancy statistics in which they chop up the responses into little subsets by cross-tabulating one response against another, so they need big starting numbers. You probably don't. A dozen responses tell you something useful. Two or three dozen responses give you more certainty that the results accurately represent your customers. Don't be obsessive about getting responses; just get as many as you can in a few weeks of effort, at most.

## Analyzing the results

When analyzing the results of a customer service audit, look for discrepancies between the first and second ratings: The first rating is the importance to the customer, and the second rating is how good your company is. Here are a few key points to remember:

✔ If your company is doing well on an important service attribute, you can leave well enough alone.

✔ If your company is doing poorly on an important service attribute, you need to improve your performance on it right away.

✔ If your company's doing well on an unimportant attribute, consider putting less effort and resources into it so that you can emphasize a more important attribute instead.

Often, you find that you're putting lots of energy into something that isn't too important to your customers and not putting enough energy into something else that really matters to them. For example, in the case I describe in the preceding section, UPS had been focusing only on speed, not on helpfulness and friendliness. The sample results in Table 11-2 indicate the same results as well.

| Table 11-2 | Sample Results and Display Format | |
|---|---|---|
| *Customer Service Element* | *Average Importance* | *Average Performance* |
| Politeness | 3 | 4 |
| Right the first time | 4 | 2 |
| Apologizing for delays | 3 | 4 |
| Prompt warranty work | 2 | 4 |
| Not arguing | 4 | 3 |
| Average Scores | 3.2 | 3.4 |

This table illustrates the common problem of overperforming on some elements of customer service and underperforming on others. Note that I give each rating a number from one to four using the following conversions.

1 = not important  1 = poor
2 = slightly  2 = fair
3 = important  3 = good
4 = very important  4 = excellent

That way, comparing the results on each item is easier. If your performance rating is equal to or above the importance rating, well, you don't have any trouble on that element. But if your performance rating number is below the importance rating, this result suggests that you need to make the item a higher priority.

Using numbers also permits you to average each customer response and compare your overall performance rating with an overall importance rating for all the elements you tested. This mathematical exercise is helpful, but don't let it blind you to item-by-item problems and opportunities to improve. In the example in Table 11-2, you can see that averages can be deceptive. Performance averages higher than importance. Does this high-performance rating mean everything's fine? Not at all! The higher average performance rating suggests that the firm is putting too much effort into some items. It's overperforming in areas where performance isn't very important to customers.

If you get a high average performance rating combined with overperformance on the most important service elements, then you're in a position to celebrate. But as long as you see underperformance on any important elements, you know you have an opportunity to improve your service.

# Using Experimentation as a Research Technique

You don't always have to do a survey or ask customers for input in order to do good research. Sometimes all you have to do is carefully track what you do and what happens. This is the scientific method applied to marketing. For example, companies like Lands End or Staples that send catalogs to people on their mailing lists are always testing different designs and methods. Is putting the color-printed catalog in a brown paper mailing sleeve or letting the color cover show better? I don't know, but if you send some catalogs one way and some the other and then compare the response rates, you'll find out in a hurry.

The first step in using a scientific approach is to identify your marketing variables. *Marketing variables* are any aspects of your product, service, or marketing communication that you can control and change and that may affect results. Variables for a mailing include the size of the envelope, whether it has a customized (personal) cover letter, and whether it has a special time-sensitive discount offer.

After you determine your marketing variables, start varying them and tracking the results to see what works best. I do this variation in my own businesses. For example, on our Web sites, www.insightsfortraining.com and www. insightsformarketing.com, I discovered through experimentation that we get a lot more orders when we do two things:

✔ When we buy key-term listings through the Google and Yahoo! search engines, they drive lots of traffic to our sites. (If you want to do the same thing, check out their Web sites, www.google.com and www.yahoo.com, for information on advertisers.)

✔ When we have a special offer on our home page that entices people to make a purchase right away, our orders also increase. For example, we often offer a 15 percent discount on all purchases received by a specific date.

These two variables — key-term bids and special offers with a time limit — combine to stimulate immediate credit-card purchases over our Web sites. Without these variables, the rate of Web orders falls significantly. When we figured this out, we began using these variables to boost sales strategically whenever we needed more sales volume or wanted to attract attention to a new product.

I don't know exactly what your marketing variables are or what combination and approach will boost your sales most effectively, but I know that you can find out, if you take a scientific approach and are willing to experiment. Every business has its own successful marketing formulas, but each business has a different and unique set of formulas. You're responsible for doing the research and experimentation necessary to find your formulas. If you always take an inquisitive approach, you'll find and polish your own winning formulas.

# On the CD

Check out the following items on the CD:

✔ Customer Debriefing Form (template) (CD1101)

✔ 7 x 7 Customer Satisfaction Survey (CD1102)

✔ Customer Service Audit (template) (CD1103)

# Chapter 12

# The Creativity Workshop

You can't succeed without the new, no matter how much you're in the marketing zone (see Chapter 1). This is where creativity comes in. Whether it's just a new, fresh set of mailers, advertisements, or blogs to keep attention high or a more major rethinking of your product line or distribution and pricing methods, you certainly need to be doing something new. Every good marketer's mantra needs to be, "What's next?"

In this chapter, I clue you in on just how important creativity is to marketing success, and I show you how to spur your creativity when you're stumped for more ideas. I also give you advice on how to manage a creative team or project. You may at first think that managing a creative team is "not you," but in truth, almost all marketing efforts are team efforts. Even the smallest business usually draws in a team to work on marketing — graphic designer, Web programmer, distributor, radio ad producer, consultant, and so on. And these informal teams almost always have a creative element to their work. So to be a good marketer, you need (among many other skills) to be an expert at running a creative team.

## Creativity's Impact on the Five Ps

A good way to think about your marketing activities is to create a T table in which the left-hand column is labeled Old and the right-hand column is labeled New. In the Old column, list everything that you can keep doing the same way. Hopefully, a number of things you do work well enough that you don't have to change them right now. In fact, if you're in your marketing zone (see Chapter 1), quite a few things should be working well and don't need to be thrown out. Highlight the good items in the Old column — and cross out the ones that are outdated, so you can shift resources to something new and better.

Now take a creative look at the New column in your T table of old and new marketing activities. You need to list some things in the New column, and that's where creativity enters the picture. When you want to benefit from creative thinking, it's helpful to frame the project using the Five Ps (see Chapter 1). In fact, sometimes I run a marketing brainstorm session for my clients in which we take that New versus Old T approach and break it out with five rows crossing the New and Old columns — one row, of course, for each of the Five Ps: product, price, placement, promotion, and people.

I tell you lots of stories about creativity in this section because getting inspiration from others is often the easiest way to get your own creative juices flowing. It's a good idea to collect your own examples of creativity, too.

## Product innovations

Products often come to life as a result of creativity. Someone innovates to improve a product or invent a new one, and the market changes forever. To see the power of creativity, all you have to do is think about the products that you use every day. Look around you right now and ask yourself how many of these products existed ten years ago. Spotting dozens of new ideas with just a quick glance around is easy to do.

New products and clever variations on old products are the bread and butter of marketing. Some are made possible by new technical breakthroughs, but many product innovations have nothing to do with technology. Sometimes the innovations are fresh combinations or forms of traditional products and services. For example, leasing used to be offered only for big companies that ran fleets of trucks or cars. Then someone had the bright idea to offer leases to car buyers, and he created a new kind of product — a car lease.

Yes, I agree, the example of leasing automobiles involves some innovation in how to price the product — in fact, this example used a new form of pricing to change the product. So this innovation uses a hybrid idea because it affects two of the Five Ps in combination. Creativity often defies categories, and that's okay. Why do you think they call it "out-of-the-box thinking?" People were thinking way out of the box when they invented products like the iPod, PostIt Notes, or the online auction.

You may not manufacture any products yourself. Many of my readers own businesses that resell products. If this is the case for you, then the way to be creative about products is to shop out of the box. Find a new, exciting supplier who is making something unusual. Be the first to introduce a new product line.

# Pricing innovations

Price-oriented creativity is at the heart of thousands of discounts, coupons, and other special offers.

The other day, I came across two little boys on the sidewalk who were raising money for their school's track team. How? They sold me a book of coupons along with a card and an ID number for a Web site, where I can go to cash in more discounts. A portion of the proceeds goes to the school, and the rest goes to the company that organizes the coupon booklet and runs the Web site. Now, getting me to hand over a $20 bill to elementary school students on the sidewalk may normally be a hard thing to do, but this official-looking package of coupons made parting with that money easy for me.

Sometimes you can make creative changes in when or how people pay rather than in how much they pay.

For example, the arm of my business that sends trainers to companies to lead workshops under contract has a problem that many such service businesses have: A client may call to book a several-day, expensive event, and we work hard to prepare for it. Then, at the last minute, the client cancels. Of course, if the client has an unexpected problem or priority and simply can't pull employees out of work for three days to do the workshop, then it has every right to cancel. But what about us? We may have told other clients that we couldn't work for them that week because we were booked. Not to mention that we also spent time and money preparing for the event that now we won't get reimbursed for.

A few years ago, one of our associates suggested that we ask for half the fee in advance in order to hold a date and that we also add a clause to our contract stating that if the client cancels on short notice, we won't refund that portion of the fee. This strategy is a simple, creative way to avoid getting hit financially by clients who change their minds at the last minute; it's also allowed us to reduce the risks associated with scheduling expensive client events needing upfront investment and preparation. The alternative was to raise our rates to cover the risk of unpaid events because of last-minute cancellations. But higher rates seemed unfair because they extracted the cost of disorganization from our more organized clients, so the advance-payment approach solved the problem in a fairer way.

Here's another example from the Norton Museum of Art in West Palm Beach, Florida, that may inspire you. Museums can't live on ticket sales alone; they depend on people buying more expensive annual memberships. So when the Norton Museum has an especially big crowd of visitors on a busy weekend, the marketing manager sometimes hands out special coupons to visitors, offering a refund of the cost of the ticket they just bought if they apply it toward buying an annual membership. Usually, some of them do, and the museum wins new members this way. Can you use a similar strategy to upgrade customers to more expensive or long-term purchases? I recommend spending a half hour brainstorming at least 20 ideas for how to achieve this goal in your business. Then take the best one and see what happens when you implement it.

## Placement innovations

One of my associates stayed at the W Hotel in Los Angeles and was impressed by the decor: tasteful furniture, lamps, and even trash cans; luxurious linens and pillows; and the finest soaps and shampoos. You'd expect the finest at an upscale hotel, but the innovation she discovered was an elegantly designed catalog from which you can order any of the items in your room. Now that's a clever new way to sell bed and bath products!

I live in a college town, and we have a lot of pizza restaurants. Some are on the main street and highly visible, but one is in a mini-mall set back from a side street. New students in town might not notice it, if the owner did not stick a "DETOUR" sign in the ground out on the nearest main street. The sign catches your eye because it looks semi-official, but then you see that the next line says "To Athena's Pizza." Rather than bring the restaurant to the main street, this marketer uses a sign to bring the main street to the restaurant. And when you get there, you see the advantage of being off the main street: Plenty of convenient parking right in front. Some people may view the location as a disadvantage; however, the owner makes the most of it and manages to do a thriving business.

I'm very visually oriented, as a lot of marketers are. In fact, as a side business, I show my photographs and paintings in art galleries. However, I don't give it anything like my full time or attention because I'm busy with my day job. So, how can I make sure that art buyers are aware of my work? I have my own Web site, which helps. However, I also participate in a Web site called www.newyorkartists.net, which shows dozens of artists' work. This site brings me the most inquiries because of its larger scale.

If you're a relatively small-scale marketer, look for ways to take advantage of group Web sites. They're the malls of the Internet, bringing you into contact with many more prospective customers than you could afford to attract all by yourself.

What's the future of distribution in your business? Can you think of some ways to take costs out or reach more customers more conveniently? Creative placement is often behind the best business plans and the biggest profits.

# Promotion innovations

What you name a product and what you say about it can make or break your business plan. Promotional creativity is the most important and attention-getting form of creativity in business. Turn on any TV, and every time a show breaks for commercials, you can see dozens of examples of efforts to make promotions creative. You may not have the budget to do creative television advertising, but apply the same kind of creative thinking to whatever you can afford to do.

For example, take the simple brochure, something almost every marketer uses. Does your brochure cover stand out and catch the eye? If not, apply your creative thinking to the challenge of making it more notable. A strong new photograph, a catchy headline, or an interesting shape or size can set it apart. (See Chapter 7 for details on how to design a good brochure.)

What about your ads, business cards, and signs? Are they creative? Hmmm. Signs are an interesting challenge because if they get too creative, they can put people off and be hard to read. Your brand image needs to constrain your creativity. Match the creative concept to the business so that it's a good look and not a mismatch. For example, a tax accountant should not use a bright orange hot air balloon full of clowns who are about to pop it as his new logo. Something more cautious and conservative would be better — how about a firm-jawed seas captain, his hand steady on the wheel of his ship?

Also, look for creative ways to get your message in front of people. Take, for example, an agency in New York City that's renting forehead space for logos (so now you see a company logo on people's foreheads as they walk around town). A bit crazy? Yes, but many good ideas seem that way, at least at first. Or how about the strategy of renting spaces for a new car model in front of the finest restaurants in order to get it in front of prospective drivers? Maybe these ideas won't work for you, but see whether they inspire you to try something new that *does* fit your business. For example, if you've never tried them, consider having some nice refrigerator magnets made up as giveaways. People use them, and it would be nice to have your business name and contact information in people's kitchens.

Or how about T-shirts? If your customers wear them, try giving away an appealing design that has a subtle, attractive brand image or marketing message on it. People will wear your marketing message if you make it attractive enough. If you aren't sure how to make a T-shirt design that is appealing and fashionable, ask your daughter or any junior high or middle school girl who cares about fashion. My daughter is a font of wisdom about current fashion, and I wouldn't print any clothing design without running it by her first. I'm not alone; many large companies use panels of teenagers to help them find out what's hot and what's not. (See *Marketing For Dummies* for lots of ideas and information about creative ways to use signs, banners, flags, T-shirts, and other silk-screened products, such as tote bags.)

## People innovations

Here's a wild and crazy idea: How about taking turns answering the phone live, and not allowing it to go to a computerized answering system? In this age of computerized phone systems, having real, live, knowledgeable, friendly people answer customer calls is a radical idea. So few companies offer this service today that it could give you a real competitive advantage.

Another way to innovate is to think of times and places where you can meet customers and prospects in person. Is there an event or conference you could attend that would expose you personally to good prospects? Could you have some kind of party that would draw in customers and prospects?

Also give some thought to finding new people to help you sell. Personal selling can be very effective, but finding the right sort of salesperson is tricky. Someone who has been in your customers' shoes is probably better than someone who is a professional salesperson but who doesn't know your industry inside and out. Being able to identify with and talk shop with prospective customers is probably the key to good salesmanship. It works better than high-pressure sales techniques, in most cases.

When, where, and how you have people interact with customers is a very important part of your marketing. You can do it innovatively and well, or you can do it poorly. The difference between a bad server and a good one determines whether or not you go back to the restaurant a second time. At Pike's Place Fish Market in Seattle, the staff is encouraged to joke and clown around in front of customers, and this innovation has made the store a major tourist attraction and a multimillion-dollar success.

People can be your most important and valuable asset — but only if you can find ways to connect them meaningfully with your customers. Spend time thinking about how you and others can make more and better human contact with existing and future customers. Throw a party. Go to a convention. Make a sales call in person. Ask a happy customer for a referral. Put your staff in fresh new uniforms. There are many creative ways to harness the power of people in your marketing.

# Being Creative but Also Practical

In business, I find that creativity needs to be a cyclical activity, not a continuous one. After you come up with and introduce a creative idea, you often want to repeat and perfect it, milking it for profits before doing the next creative thing. In marketing, perfecting an idea may mean testing several new creative magazine ads, discovering that one of them seems to *pull* (generate leads or sales) especially well, and then repeating the ad for the rest of the year or until consumers finally grow tired of it and stop responding well.

Being creative takes effort and money. A new idea for an ad or brochure requires someone to design it and print it, which involves time, effort, and usually money as well. So focusing your creativity where it can do the most good is important. Creativity helps you find your marketing zone. Then once you've proved the concept works, keep doing it with only minor variations for as long as it continues to be successful.

## Harnessing your creativity for profit

The pure artistic approach to creativity is just to be as creative as you can for the pure joy of it. In marketing, you usually have some practical objectives — although creativity should also be fun, because you can't come up with winning creative ideas unless you're in a good mood and are relaxed enough to free your imagination. A good way to keep creativity fun but also profitable is to decide what your creative goals are; then, be creative within the discipline of your business goals.

For example, I sometimes lead brainstorming sessions for client companies. But I never do a completely unstructured session; I always start with a clear strategic goal, such as

- Thinking of ways to freshen up an aging product
- Coming up with attention-getting ideas for a new promotional event
- Improving the company's Web site or printed brochures
- Designing a fun and effective new trade show booth
- Thinking of a better new logo and tag line to use on the company's letterhead and in advertising

Each of these topics can provide the focus and purpose to a wild and crazy brainstorming session. I've run sessions on each of these topics many times. Usually, I set a goal for the session, such as 100 new ideas for modernizing or renewing a product. Quantity is a better goal than quality for creative idea sessions; if you tell everyone that the goal is one really good idea, they'll self-censor their ideas and not be freely creative. But if you say that the goal is 100 ideas — any ideas, it doesn't matter how dumb or crazy — you'll probably get 200 ideas. And ideas tend to build on each other, so as the group generates more and more, the quality begins to take care of itself, and you usually get at least a handful of really promising ideas out of the crop of hundreds.

## Not getting carried away

My editors asked me to put this topic in. Editors often have to rein us creative writers in and keep us focused and disciplined. You may have to play editor with creative ideas in your marketing. An editor seeks the best and cuts the rest. Use this strategy with your creativity.

Sometimes a wonderfully entertaining, creative ad comes on TV, and everyone talks about it. But here's the interesting thing: Half the time, people remember the ad vividly but aren't sure what product or company the ad is for. That creativity isn't useful because it doesn't connect the impression the ad makes with what the ad is selling.

To make sure that you aren't getting carried away, stop for a moment and ask yourself whether the creative ad, brochure, Web page, event, or whatever it is is in danger of becoming its own product instead of selling yours. Try to avoid the trap of "creativity for its own sake." Entertaining or amazing an audience without making any sales is expensive. You aren't doing creativity just for the fun of it in marketing!

# Generating Creative Concepts

I use the term *marketing imagination* throughout this book, and this concept is probably the most important factor in marketing success or failure. Your ability to imagine new approaches is vital to your success as a marketer. The salesperson who invents an opener or comes up with a strategy for generating leads is the one who sells the most product. The distributor who finds creative new ways to serve customers over the Web gains on its competition. The small business that seeks new ways to promote its products or services makes a bigger impact at lower cost. And the advertiser who creates an imaginative message captures consumer attention and makes more sales.

In contrast, any marketer who fails to be creative or who tries to just use last year's formula or borrow directly from others is destined for failure. Marketing demands more creativity than any other business activity. So it seems only fair for me to help you be more creative in your approach to marketing. In this section, I give you techniques to help you engage your creative imagination and come up with breakthrough sales and marketing ideas.

The creativity methods I discuss here are drawn from my work in corporate and government training. My firm puts on creativity trainings and also facilitates creative problem-solving retreats. In addition, we develop and publish a variety of resources for trainers and managers in the area of creativity. (See my book, *The Manager's Pocket Guide to Creativity,* available from Trainer's Spectrum at `www.tspectrum.com`, for a larger collection of creative techniques.) I want to share the best of these many resources with you. I don't want you to feel stuck and unable to come up with fresh ideas. If you ever get to that point (most people do fairly often), dip into this section and reignite your marketing imagination!

## Revel in the irreverent

Seek out and enjoy unconventional and crazy approaches. Any examples of how people can flaunt the rules of convention are inspirational. Even if they have nothing to do with marketing, irreverent attitudes can inspire your marketing imagination. For example, today's wild teenage fashions will end up in tomorrow's high-end clothing lines because most of these designers' new ideas are inspired by teenagers who are trying to break conventions, not make them.

When I get stuck on a marketing communication and can't seem to come up with a fresh idea, I like to watch a few scenes of the movie *Crazy People.* The movie is a comedy about an advertising copywriter who goes over the edge and gets sent to a mental hospital, where he and his fellow patients create such crazy and wonderful ads that his agency ends up begging them for more. The story is silly, and it makes me laugh. After 15 minutes of that silliness, my mind is much freer, and I'm able to think more creatively about my own ads or other marketing communications.

I recommend any comedy, whether it has something to do with business or not. Humor is based on unusual viewpoints, and it helps you loosen up and find your own creative perspectives.

I also recommend keeping an eye out for crackpots and others who do things strangely on the fringes of your industry. For every successful business, a dozen marginal ones operate outside the normal rules and rarely amount to anything. But sometimes these businesses have the weirdest ideas, and when you combine those weird ideas with a sound understanding of how the industry works, they may just lead to breakthrough insights. So don't forget to pay attention to the crazy people in your own industry. Sometimes they're better at inspiring your marketing imagination than more successful but conventional role models are.

# Force yourself to develop alternatives

The quest for new and better alternatives is the essence of creativity. The marketing imagination is never content — it's always seeking new approaches. I remember one two-day product development session that I helped facilitate for Kellogg's, the breakfast-cereal company. Leaders of the company hoped to come up with one good new product as a result of the session. But which idea would be the winning idea? Hard to know. Best to make sure that you have plenty of alternatives. So the group and I generated more than 900 new product concepts during our retreat.

Was coming up with so many good ideas hard? Yes and no. Generating the first five ideas was pretty easy, but in hindsight, they weren't worth a second look. Coming up with the next 20 ideas was much harder, but that list had hints of inspiration. But still nothing to write home about. We had to keep going.

After we got past the first 100, we were on a roll and could've kept inventing new concepts forever, if we'd had the time. In the long run, the few new product concepts that made it to the test market were in the high hundreds — so we'd already come up with hundreds of ideas before them. That means we may not have come up with *any* useable concepts unless we'd been as persistent as we were.

Perhaps this result also means that we could've come up with even better ideas if we'd developed twice as many. . . . Oh well.

# Don't overplan

Most experts tell you to write a careful plan. Marketing plans and business plans in general can help you anticipate the future and make sure that you're ready for it. But they can also destroy creativity. Plans hurt creativity in two main ways:

✔ **If you have to write everything down upfront, you won't have the opportunity to come up with creative approaches later.** The weight of the planning exercise deadens creativity. To decide all the year's marketing activities in just one week of planning is pretty hard. And it's certainly not fun. People who have to do that task aren't going to spend much time being creative. They're going to approach marketing in a mechanical way, looking up costs and writing them down one after the other until they've fulfilled their obligations.

✔ **If you have to follow a detailed plan, then the plan does the thinking for you, and you miss the opportunity to learn, experiment, and invent as you go.** Rigid plans and microplanning that structure every decision and action are the enemies of creativity. They keep people from reacting and creating.

To make planning creative, leave room in your plan for improvisation. Sure, you face budget limits, and you need to follow broad strategies that you expect to work. But also leave room for modifying the plan. I like to revisit my plans every month or two, and, if I get a better idea, I simply rewrite my plan around it. Your plan is only paper. Throw it out if it's getting in your way and write a new one!

Also, make sure that your plans aren't too detailed. For example, specifying that you're budgeting so much for publicity, most of which should focus on generating press about your business activities, is one thing. That example is fine because it leaves you plenty of room to invent clever ways of getting publicity. But planning exactly how you're going to spend that publicity budget is quite another thing. For example, if you specify one press release a month to the in-house press list of 250 names, you've just guaranteed that nothing imaginative will happen all year. Don't overplan!

## Identify your personal barriers and enablers

A *creativity barrier* is anything that gets in the way of your creativity. And plenty of things can do just that. Being more aware of those barriers helps you learn how to avoid them or minimize their impacts. Here are some of the most common barriers:

✔ **Pressure to conform:** Thinking and behaving differently from others is taboo in many organizations and industries. This approach means that people are more conservative than they need to be.

✔ **Perfectionism:** If you worry too much about how well you perform, you'll be afraid to try anything really new. Sometimes I remind myself that when it comes to creative innovations, "If it's worth doing, it's worth doing poorly!"

✔ **Overconfidence:** It's easy to assume that you're doing the right thing without stopping to question yourself. Overconfidence keeps you from examining your assumptions or developing and considering alternatives.

When you know that a creativity barrier affects you, you can guard against it. Awareness is the key.

*Creativity enablers* are factors that help you be more creative. They work in the opposite direction of barriers, helping you overcome barriers and leading you to creative insights. Here are some of the more common enablers:

- ✔ **Open-mindedness:** An open, accepting approach to other ideas and methods is a great enabler. If you're open-minded, you often receive inspiration from others that you may otherwise miss.

- ✔ **Role models:** Creative innovators are great enablers. Try to find and spend time with such people. They can get your creative motor running in no time!

- ✔ **Persistence:** Perhaps the most powerful enabler of all, persistence keeps you trying even when your initial efforts at creativity fail. Often, the only major difference between highly creative people and those people who aren't creative is that the creative people don't give up as quickly. Do you?

A lot of creativity trainings use this barriers/enablers model to help people identify factors that they need to focus on in order to boost their personal creativity. If you want to find out more about this topic, see my *Personal Creativity Assessment* booklet (published by HRD Press) for details and a self-assessment test. I put information about it on this book's Web site, www. insightsformarketing.com.

## Incubate

*Incubation* is just what the term suggests. You sit on a problem or idea, keeping it warm, until it hatches a solution. But first, you have to lay that egg. In other words, start by focusing hard and furiously on your subject of concern. Research it thoroughly and bang your head against it over and over all week long. Wear yourself out. Then relax. Time to sit on the egg that you just laid. Take a little time off. Or work on something else. Just stop to have a quick look at the problem or to turn it over in your mind every now and then.

After you've let your problem or idea incubate for a while, you may begin to hear from it. It starts to call your attention back to it as new ideas and approaches come to mind. Then, and only then, is your idea ready to hatch. When you revisit it and give it your undivided attention again, you may find that you have more and better ideas than you had before.

 Because incubation works so well, try scheduling your marketing development efforts to permit incubation. For example, rather than planning to spend three consecutive days writing a new brochure, why not schedule two days to study it and begin work on it, take three days off the project for incubation, and then one final day to complete your work? The result will be more imaginative and better because of the incubation period, yet you won't have spent any more of your work time on the project.

# Break it down

When I get stumped on a project, I use a strategy called breakdown brainstorming, and I've used it to good effect on many difficult tasks. The idea behind *breakdown brainstorming* is to put some creative effort into thinking about the task itself rather than moving directly to formulating solutions. (You can find more information on this strategy in my book, *The Manager's Pocket Guide to Creativity,* published by HRD Press.)

For example, say that you're working on a Web page, and you want to do something creative and special. But what? You're stuck. So break down the task into as many subproblems or subtasks as you can imagine. Your list may include issues such as "attract people to our site," "make our site more entertaining," "create an opening page for the site that really wows people," and "find a game people can play on our site." Now you've broken the broad problem of designing a good Web site into many smaller problems, some of which may fire your imagination more easily than the broader definition of the problem did.

# Compete

You're more likely to come up with a creative breakthrough when you have two or more individuals or groups working on the same creative task at the same time. So why not create a contest for yourself and a few other associates or friends? Pick a good reward — sometimes a joke reward is best. Give each person or group the same amount of time and the same starting information. Then compete to see who comes up with the best ideas!

# Record more of your own ideas

You often have ideas that you discard or forget. If you get in the habit of recording more of your ideas, you may find that some of them are more valuable than you thought. Also, your marketing imagination becomes more active when it gets attention. By simply making notes or recordings of your ideas, you stimulate their production and soon generate many more.

I record ideas in several ways. I keep a large daily planning book, with room to write down not only my appointments but also my ideas. When I'm stuck, I flip back through the pages and pick out a good idea to follow through on. I also keep idea boxes where I can toss my notes or interesting articles that I clip out to stimulate my thinking. I have an idea box for each of my major projects. In addition, I keep a miniature tape recorder in my briefcase and often dictate ideas into it. Then I get the tapes transcribed so that I can read them later.

Come up with your own system for recording ideas. Whatever works best for you is the right one, so try several. Or you can enlist others in your quest for ideas. You may want to provide everyone in your company with an idea journal and reward the best ideas in your monthly journal awards!

## Look hard at your assumptions

Many smaller businesses assume that TV advertising is too expensive for them. That's a silly assumption. You can buy local television advertising very cheaply in most markets, and you can even find relatively inexpensive national cable ad slots. I'm not saying that all businesses ought to advertise on TV, but some businesses could and don't realize it because of their assumptions.

All marketers make assumptions, and, in general, most of them are questionable. For example, assuming that your business isn't newsworthy is a common assumption, so your business never explores the potential of publicity. And many people assume that they can't manage word of mouth, so they do nothing to try to build referrals. Watch out for such assumptions! They keep you from considering many creative alternatives. You can create breaking news by sponsoring a benefit concert for a charity. You can encourage positive word of mouth referrals by offering a prize to the customer who brings you the most new customers. You can . . . wait, it's your turn to come up with an idea now!

## Talk to ten successful people

I recently ran into a friend who's an artist. She complained that she needed to reach a broader market with her work but didn't know how to do it. She asked me whether any of my books held the solution. I hate to pass up a chance to make a sale, but I had to tell her no. The specific solution to marketing her work isn't found in *any* book. It has to come from her. It has to be something unique and creative. So where can she find the ideas she needs?

I suggested that she contact ten other artists and ask them how they market their work. Each one probably has a slightly different approach. By listening to each of their stories, she may begin seeing more possibilities than she does right now.

It's a wonderful discipline to go out and interview ten people and ask them how they do their sales and marketing. Put on your journalist's hat, take along a pad and pencil, and collect information about how other people do it. You're sure to come across something new and different that gives you a good idea for your own business. Some business owners have set up round-tables at local coffee shops or through their local Chamber of Commerce in order to have a group of like-minded people to discuss marketing and other business challenges.

# Managing Creative Projects and Teams

When you have a group of people trying to be creative together, all sorts of complications arise. The first issue to watch out for is overly critical feed-back. If one person tells another that an idea is stupid or won't work, the other person is going to hesitate to present more ideas. So try to instill an open-minded, positive attitude in your group of creative marketers. Praise creativity, even if it isn't practical. The more you recognize and reward cre-ative behavior, the more creative ideas you'll have to choose from.

Next, recognize that different people are creative in different ways — and some people are more creative than others. The classic creative personal-ity is very inquisitive, open-minded, and artistic, but not very organized or focused. Do you have someone in your office or on your marketing team who has great ideas and lots of imagination, is interested in all sorts of odd topics, but can't keep his or her desk clean? If so, this person is a great one to put in charge of looking for new product ideas or coming up with better headlines for new ads.

But don't ask this person to make sure that you meet all the deadlines for submitting ads to magazines on time. Obviously, for this part of the creative process, someone with a more organized personality and a clear focus is a better choice.

If you can, build creative teams out of people with contrasting personalities so that the team has all the complementary strengths needed to take a project from idea stage to execution. In marketing, you have to turn creative ideas into practical projects and complete them on time and within budget. This task requires a challenging balance of different kinds of personalities, skills, and roles. Some people can do all these things themselves, but most can't. Working with at least two or three other people whose creative profiles are different from your own is wise. Doing so makes passing the baton and filling all the roles needed to bring great ideas to practical fruition easier.

I include a great tool for managing creative groups or building creative marketing teams on the CD. It's called *Creative Roles Analysis,* and it's an assessment booklet that my firm uses in creativity trainings and retreats with clients. (You can find it on CD1201.) Normally, you'd have to buy the booklet from my firm, but you can print as many copies as you need for each member of your staff or team so that they can take the assessment and discuss who's best suited to play which roles on creative marketing projects. So if you want to really dig into the topic and discover more about your own and the rest of your team's creativity, print this assessment and make sure that each member completes it. (I also include instructions for interpreting and using the results on CD1201.)

# On the CD

> ✔ Creative Roles Analysis (CD1201)

# Chapter 13

# Writing Well for Marketing and Sales

**S**ometimes marketing seems as if it's all about writing. I can't recall an ad in any medium that didn't have some writing in it, and many ads are dominated by writing. Similarly, coupons, contests, memberships, and other special promotions need clear writing to communicate their benefits and rules to customers. And sales materials rely on writing, too. Many people do sales approaches or follow-up proposals to businesses in writing instead of verbally, and sales materials always take written form. So, you can see why writing is an essential core skill for all marketers.

How do you go about the process of conceiving and writing great ads, direct-mail letters, brochures, Web sites, signs, or other marketing communications? Every good marketing communication starts with ideas that make it persuasive and effective. Marketing is all about communicating your offer in a compelling manner — a manner that gets attention and shapes opinions and behaviors. And that's a tall order!

We ask a lot of our marketing communications, whether they're ads, mailers, Web pages, catalogs, brochures, or other forms of communication with our customers and prospects. So you need to do quite a bit of thinking in order to come up with ideas that really work. In this chapter, I share some techniques that can help you differentiate your communications from the pack.

# Avoiding Power Words and Phrases

If you search for help with marketing and sales writing on the Web, you'll be inundated by expert advice and products that have one common theme — write using stock phrases and words that are guaranteed to sell. Often called *power words* or *power phrases,* these overused, exaggerated words are supposed to make your communications effective. More often than not, they have the opposite effect — they make you sound like a huckster or con man who has nothing substantive to say.

Self-styled experts will tell you that you should use power words and power phrases that "guarantee success," "boost sales dramatically," and so on. Yeah. Right! The trouble is, consumers aren't actually idiots, so marketers can't afford to be, either. If your writing is full of stock catch-phrases, it'll look like it was cut and pasted from old ads or sales letters. Don't make the mistake of trying to punch up your writing by filling it with exaggerated claims and generic power phrases.

Table 13-1 lists examples of words and phrases that you'll probably be told to use. Please don't! You can use these sorts of words and phrases if you want to sound like a million other hucksters, or you can craft a simple, clear communication that says what it means and means what it says. You don't have to sound like a marketer to make a sale. In fact, it's better not to sound like a stereotyped sales copywriter. Much better!

For example, if I want to write copy for a Web site describing a business service, I could fill up the screen with trite power phrases, such as, "Unbelievable! You have to try this to believe it! A remarkable breakthrough that will save you untold time and trouble! Enjoy the ultimate in complete business support on the Internet by taking advantage of this unique limited time offer, for preferred customers only. Act now and . . ." But what am I selling? What are its real benefits? Nobody really knows. All that I make clear with this kind of writing is that I don't have a fresh phrase or thought in my head.

| Table 13-1 | Power Words and Phrases to Avoid |
|---|---|
| *Overused Power Words* | *Overused Power Phrases* |
| Daring | What you should know |
| Blockbuster | Proven steps to . . . |
| Revolutionary | Act now! |
| Astounding | Unlock the hidden . . . |

| Overused Power Words | Overused Power Phrases |
|---|---|
| Dazzling | The shocking truth about . . . |
| Mammoth | Limited Edition |
| Powerful | For preferred customers only |
| Remarkable | Enjoy the ultimate . . . |
| Electrifying | A breakthrough! |
| Vital | Once in a lifetime opportunity |
| Incredible | Let me show you how to . . . |

Here's a straightforward approach to describing the Internet-based business services that the preceding copy failed to sell effectively: "You can upload your financial, accounting, sales, and marketing information easily, no matter what business software programs you use. As soon as you log onto our site, you will start getting integrated reports, error flags, expert suggestions, and other services to help you run your business better in less time, effort, and expense." This copy works because it describes the user's experience and benefits, and nothing else.

Try to write marketing copy as clear and simple as that. If any power words or phrases or other stock elements of traditional marketing-speak slip into your writing, cut them. Marketing communications are like any other communications in that less is more.

And another thing! (I'm up in arms now about bad copywriting, so bear with me.) Never say "Trust us" or "Trust me." If you have to tell the prospect to trust you, then you or your offer must seem untrustworthy. Fix the underlying problem instead. Deals should not sound too good to be true. Nor should they be packaged in superlatives and overexcited prose. Keep your writing calm, professional, concise, and factual. Let the facts do the convincing. If your offer or claim is unconvincing, then dig up facts or testimonials to make it believable. Don't ever tell people to "Trust you." That's what con men say.

When writing for a Web site, follow the rule of sticking to the core benefits, just as if you were writing for print. However, keep it much shorter. Most of your paragraphs should be one or two sentences when you write for a Web site. If you need to give more detail, provide links to supporting pages or PDF documents. Also, before you start writing for a Web page, make a list of a half-dozen key terms that will help interested buyers find your page on search engines. Then make sure that you work these key terms in naturally as you write.

# Writing Persuasively

As a marketer, you need to create effective writing for ads, sales letters, Web sites, press releases, catalogs, and many other applications. Whether you do most of this writing yourself or use others to help draft it, you need to make sure that it's *good* writing. Your writing has to be clear, interesting, professional (no obvious errors, please!), and — most important — persuasive.

## If you don't want to write yourself

Are you a good writer? I know that's a personal question, but you need to be honest about your writing talent. In ad agencies, specialists called *copywriters* do the writing — and they're excellent writers. But most people aren't. If you enjoy writing and are at least moderately good at drafting and editing clear, interesting copy, then by all means, read this chapter and write your own marketing materials, sales letters, and ads. I'm a writer (okay, I guess that's obvious), so I often draft catalog copy, ads, and letters for my own company, as well as help my clients put marketing magic into their writing. But I know lots of great marketers and businesspeople who don't write well and probably never will.

So, what can you do if writing isn't one of your strengths? Here are a few ideas:

✏ **Take advantage of templates.** Published books of business letters can provide a good starting point, allowing you to customize and refine a letter rather than having to start one from scratch. If you suffer from writer's block, a starting draft — even a poor one — may break the logjam and get you writing. And for a little more money you can also purchase templates that open in Microsoft Word (for example, see WriteExpress at www.writeexpress.com).

✏ **Make friends with writers.** Some people love writing and editing and enjoy the challenge of improving your copy. These eager volunteers can exercise their talents when they volunteer to help you write. Return the favor by doing something you're good at, and they aren't; then everybody's happy.

✏ **Hire a writer.** Most writers are underpaid, so you can probably afford one. But don't assume that all writers can produce good marketing copy. A novelist writes 300-page stories, not short direct-response ads. Look at writers' portfolios and select the person whose portfolio includes the kind of writing that you need. Also, check samples of their writing. If the style doesn't fit your taste, keep shopping.

- ✔ **Hire an ad agency.** This strategy is the expensive approach, but sometimes turning the work over to the pros is a good idea. However, still insist on checking the portfolio of the copywriter assigned to your work and refuse to sign a contract until you have a writer who obviously can do just what you need.

- ✔ **Copy good writing . . . sort of.** Sometimes I clip a great ad or file a good brochure to use as inspiration the next time I need to do some marketing writing. However, I don't copy the writing directly; I only use it as a general model to inspire my own creative work. Copyright laws apply to any marketing materials or ads that you collect, which means you can't use the writing. Not even one paragraph of it. Remember in school how teachers taught you how to use source materials to write a paper but warned you not to plagiarize? Same rule applies here, except now you can go to court instead of the principal's office. So be careful when using other marketers' work for inspiration.

These strategies are for marketers who find writing painfully difficult. If you don't mind sharpening your pencil and crafting a careful paragraph or two, the rest of this chapter can help you make your marketing copy more effective. Oh, and even if you don't do the writing yourself, as a marketer, your job is to make sure that it's engaging and persuasive, so maybe you'd better read this chapter anyway! Someone has to manage the writing project and approve the final copy, and that someone should be you.

## Engaging and persuading your audience

Basically, you can engage and persuade people in one of two ways:

- ✔ By appealing to them with a compelling, logical argument
- ✔ By appealing to them with an engaging story

Or you can use a combination of these strategies. But the point is, these two strategies are always options when you're communicating. And thinking about which option you might use is a wonderful source of inspiration whenever you need to create strong marketing communications.

In this section, I show you how to write incredibly effective *copy* (the words or story behind any ad or other marketing communication) that you can use for a print ad, a direct-mail piece, a brochure or catalog, a Web page, a broadcast fax, a radio or TV commercial, or whatever. The basic strategy applies to anything, even to a personal sales presentation. And the strategy's based on using these two very different ways of making a point when you communicate.

## Dusting off your writing skills

Remember back in your old high school writing class when you explored the many ways of making a point through writing? Perhaps you had an assignment where you had to show how a character in a story feels when something bad happens to her. Well, you might just describe her feelings:

"She was hollow. Empty inside. She felt cheated and alone. In fact, she'd never been so down in her life."

Or you might create an imaginary scene that portrays her feelings:

"She slumped against the railing of the bridge, tears streaking her cheeks, tempted by the cold waters far below."

Both approaches communicate your point that the character is having a really bad day, but they do it in very different ways.

Which way is best? The approach you take depends on what you're trying to accomplish, the context, and the reader. It depends, in part, on your taste and style as well. There isn't necessarily one best way to make a point, but when you recognize and experiment with alternative approaches, you're more likely to find a good solution in any situation.

## *Straight facts or a little drama*

Thinking about whether you want to make a factual argument in your ad or dramatize your point with some sort of story is always helpful.

In fact, every marketing communication has a factual and a fictional version that's just waiting for discovery. So which approach should you use? Or should you try something that's a combination of the two forms — part fact and part fiction? Simply posing this question opens up many possibilities to you as you develop your ad or other marketing communication.

Let me illustrate the difference between factual and fictional versions of a marketing communication. Imagine that you're designing a letter that you want to send to prospects of a training firm to introduce a new training program that teaches employees how to handle customer complaints effectively. I'll call this program Handling Angry Customers, or H.A.C., for short. And I'll assume that it's a really great program and companies that use it to train their employees have happier, more loyal customers and make lots more money as a result. But how do you convince managers and training directors that H.A.C. is a good service? What should the introductory letter say to catch their ears and get them interested in the training? You have a couple of options.

### Just the facts, ma'am

First, I suggest that you rough out a factual letter. A *factual letter* makes a logical argument, such as the following:

> *Dear Manager:*
>
> *Everyone knows that it costs ten times as much to win a new customer as it does to do business with an existing customer. Yet companies routinely lose their good customers because of errors or slip-ups that anger those good customers and open the door for defection. What can you do to keep your customers from leaving you? What can you do to make sure that they buy more next year instead of less? What, in short, is the secret of high customer loyalty?*
>
> *People. It comes down to people in 99.9 percent of the cases, according to our extensive research. We studied the companies with the most loyal customers in a dozen different industries, and, in every case, these winning companies have more sensitive, better trained employees. Employees who know what to do when customers are upset or angry. Employees who know how to convert each problem into an opportunity to build loyalty instead of losing business.*
>
> *That's why we designed Handling Angry Customers (H.A.C.), the radical new customer-service training program that has a measurable impact on your customer retention rates — or you get your money back.*

Now, that argument is pretty powerful. It makes the case for the H.A.C. service quite forcefully. And most people who want to describe a new service for business-to-business sales probably would choose a factual approach based on argument, just like this copy employs.

### A flair for the dramatic

But remember what your ninth-grade teacher told you about all the different ways of making your point? You should also be able to present the H.A.C. training program in a completely different manner using the tools of the dramatist and telling a story (or stories) instead of arguing the facts. For example, you could draft some copy for that direct-mail piece that goes like this:

> *Dear Manager:*
>
> *I want to share a story that I think you will find interesting.*
>
> *Rick, the purchasing manager for SysTech, was a man of action. He hated to waste even a minute of his company's precious time. Yet today, he was doing something uncharacteristic. He was doing nothing. He had been doing nothing for four and a half minutes already, and it was obviously wearing on him.*

*Rick was on hold. On hold with your company, to be specific. He was on hold because he had called to complain about a minor problem with the last order and been put on hold by one of your employees who didn't know how to handle the call.*

*In contrast, your employee was quite busy. She was busy asking anyone she could find what to do. She had no idea how to solve Rick's problem. But she sensed the urgency in his voice, and she, too, was well aware of the ticking of the clock. Finally, after searching fruitlessly for the appropriate paperwork and getting a wide variety of unhelpful advice from her associates, your employee came back on the line. Five minutes and sixteen seconds had passed since she had put Rick on hold. You don't want to know what Rick said in reply when her first words to him were, "I'm sorry, sir, but I can't find any record of that order. Are you sure you really sent it in?"*

*Accidents happen, as the old saying goes. But whether you recover from them gracefully or lose a customer for life depends on how you handle those accidents. If that employee had only received Handling Angry Customers (H.A.C.) training, she would have known not to put poor Rick on hold even for one minute. That violates the Adding-Insult-to-Injury principle, which says that you must handle all unhappy customers with a high degree of consideration and support. And never, ever, put them on hold or question their word when they are upset!*

*But Rick doesn't care any more. He's already busy placing his order with one of your competitors. A competitor who has recently trained all its employees in the H.A.C. program and is not likely to lose a customer over a minor problem. You may as well throw Rick's business card away. You're not likely to do business with SysTech again!*

This example uses a dramatic approach to make a point. It creates a plausible scenario that catches your reader's attention and draws her forward. It makes her wonder whether such dramas are playing out right now somewhere in her own business. And if so, well, she's certainly likely to question her staff's ability to handle angry customers and wonder if a little training may not be a wise investment. . . .

If you switch on your TV, you're bound to see a number of examples of both styles of advertising within a short period of time. Some TV spots make rational arguments, presenting facts and attempting to make you believe their product claims. Others present dramas, tell stories, and try to affect your attitudes toward their products by making their stories compelling.

### Considering which option is better

Which works better, an argument-based communication or a dramatic one? There is no hard and fast rule. Sometimes one approach works better, and sometimes the other one does. So consider both options as you develop and test ads using different styles. You may find that for what you're selling, a factual ad works best — but you won't know until you try both. Think of a company that wants to send a letter to training managers and executives to introduce the new Handling Angry Customers training program. Rather than simply writing the standard argument-based, factual letter, I drafted copy for two kinds of letters in the preceding sections — one with a fact-based approach and one with a fiction-based approach. One letter will work to the extent that its arguments are persuasive. The other will work to the extent that its dramatic scenario is compelling.

With both approaches in hand, I can test two very different types of letters. I can simply divide my mailing list in half, send out the two different letters, and wait to see which one more training managers respond to. Odds are, one letter or the other will pull significantly better. And if I hadn't written both versions, I never would've had a chance to find out which approach was best in this specific situation.

Always think "test" when you're working on a marketing communication. You can run one ad one week and another ad the next. You can mail or e-mail multiple letters by randomly dividing your list into sections. You can try different brochures on different customers or prospects. You can always find a way to experiment and compare multiple options. And when you do, you can discover far more than most of your competitors ever will, because most people aren't thoughtful enough to design even the simplest of experiments. This is one of the reasons why most people market in the dark.

## Hybrid ads: Have your cake and eat it, too

Here's another way you can take advantage of the fact that ads can take either a factual or dramatic approach. Why not incorporate both approaches into one ad? Using this strategy, you may create a hybrid that works better than either form does on its own. At least it's worth a try. Why not test these three versions of any sales-oriented communication letters?

- ✔ A straight, rational, persuasive argument based on facts
- ✔ A dramatic ad that's based almost entirely on a story or scenario
- ✔ A combination of fact-based argument and a brief story to dramatize your point

After you create a factual and a dramatic version, developing the hybrid of the two is no big deal. Then you have three options of your sales communication to test, and testing them is easy because you can measure the response rates.

I prefer communications that combine argument and storytelling. I find the hybrid approach often makes the most effective ad or direct-mail letter. You can even use this approach on the Internet.

For example, you can include storytelling on a Web page or in an electronic newsletter. Whenever you have the opportunity to engage the reader long enough to communicate any details, a combination of argument and storytelling can work wonders. You can do it in a broadcast fax. You can use a picture that tells a story in a print ad, combined with written arguments. You can combine personal testimonials from happy customers with a factual description of the benefits of your product in a brochure. You have no limits when you're incorporating elements of both argument and narrative into a single marketing piece.

You can even incorporate both styles in personal selling by weaving some case histories or testimonials into a sales presentation. I'm always amazed at how seldom people actually use any form of storytelling in sales, yet it's an extremely powerful tool. In fact, I noticed over the years that the most successful salespeople tend to weave three or four stories into each sales presentation. They often use stories about other customers to illustrate a point. Similarly, some of the most effective sales collateral — brochures, catalog sheets, audiovisuals, and other materials that the presentation refers to — are full of stories. They may include actual case histories, customer testimonials, or generic stories written to illustrate how the product or service works. Never underestimate the power of storytelling when you weave it into sales presentations!

### A work of art: Fact and fiction combined

When you create hybrid ad copy using both arguments and storytelling, you tap into both the rational and emotional sides of your customers with relative ease. Let me show you what I mean by creating a hybrid of the two approaches I showed you earlier for the Handling Angry Customers training program. I lead with the story version for the simple reason that people often react initially on an emotional basis and then engage their rational minds. So an opening appeal to emotion is a great initial attention getter. And a strong finish based on rational facts and arguments is a great way to cement those initial emotional responses by adding rational conviction to them. When I combine the two approaches into one (tightening them up a bit to avoid making the hybrid too lengthy), I get the following direct-mail or brochure copy:

*Dear Manager:*

*Rick, the purchasing manager for SysTech, is a man of action who hates to waste even a minute of his busy day. It is not like him to do nothing. But he has actually been doing nothing at all for four and a half minutes now, and it is definitely beginning to wear on him.*

[Show picture of a man in shirt sleeves and a tie, phone to ear, looking at his watch in exasperation.]

*Rick is on hold. On hold with your company, to be specific. He was put on hold when he called to complain about a problem with his last order — by an employee who didn't know how to handle the call.*

[Show picture of frazzled employee, phone in one hand, making a palms-up gesture as if to say, "I have no idea how to handle this."]

*If this were a real-life situation, you can imagine that your employee would be quite busy. Perhaps busy trying to track down the paperwork and figure out how to solve Rick's problem. Finally, after searching fruitlessly for the appropriate paperwork and getting a wide variety of unhelpful advice from her associates, your employee comes back on the line. Five minutes and sixteen seconds have passed since she put Rick on hold, and you don't want to know what Rick says in reply when her first words to him are, "I'm sorry, sir, but I can't find any record of your order. Are you sure you really sent it in?"*

### Everything depends on the employee's response

*Accidents happen, as the old saying goes. But whether you recover from them gracefully or lose a customer for life depends on how you handle those accidents. If the employee in the preceding story had only received Handling Angry Customers (H.A.C.) training, she would have known that putting Rick on hold violates the Adding-Insult-to-Injury principle, which says that you must handle all unhappy customers with a high degree of consideration and support. And never, ever, put them on hold or question their word when they are upset!*

### A major source of hidden losses

*Every manager knows that it costs ten times as much to win a new customer as it does to do business with an existing customer. Yet companies routinely lose good customers like Rick over slip-ups that anger those good customers and open the door for defection.*

### Did you know?

*A large majority of unhappy customers give very clear signs that they are unhappy. Yet, according to our research, the vast majority of employees fail to pick up on those signs or respond appropriately to them.*

*What can you do to keep your customers from leaving you? What is the secret of high customer loyalty?*

### People

*It comes down to people in 99.9 percent of the cases, according to our research. We studied the companies with the most loyal customers in a dozen different industries and, in every case, these winning companies had more sensitive, better-trained employees. Employees who know what to do when customers are upset or angry. Employees who know how to convert each problem into an opportunity to build loyalty instead of losing business.*

*That's why we designed Handling Angry Customers (H.A.C.), the radical new customer-service training that has a measurable impact on your customer retention rates — or you get your money back!*

*[Set this quote as a sidebar in contrasting type.]*

*"My employees are performing 100 percent better since their H.A.C. training, and I'm getting a lot of compliments from my customers. They really notice the difference."*

*— Charlotte McGwire, President, Global Food Supply, Inc.*

*You can take the first no-obligation step toward higher customer loyalty today by calling us or returning the enclosed postcard to get your Course Overview booklet and video today. And if you respond before the end of the month, you qualify for our introductory promotion, which locks in a 15 percent discount for any training events scheduled within the next six months. So please take a decisive step toward educating your employees by contacting us to preview or schedule the Handling Angry Customers training today.*

*Sincerely,*

*Millicent Marketer*

*V.P., Training Programs*

### About the hybrid letter strategy

Before I go into the details of the hybrid story-and-argument strategy, I want to point out a few things that I did in this example to develop it a little further than the earlier ones:

- ✔ **Visuals:** I came up with some concepts for visuals, which I can use if the medium permits. A couple of simple black-and-white photos may work well in a two-page letter. If I adapt this copy to a brochure format, I'd probably opt for nicer full-color photos, budget permitting.

- ✔ **Headings:** I dropped in a few headers to break up the text, which makes it more readable. The headers entice the eye, drawing the reader into each section. They also tend to reinforce the points by hitting the reader over the head with them.

- ✔ **Text boxes:** I added two text boxes that readers can read independently of the main copy. The text boxes reinforce the copy and give readers with short attention spans something to jump to. Note that the first box offers another factual appeal. The second box is an emotional appeal based on a story. Specifically, it quotes a customer who's had a good experience with the product. Such testimonials are often very powerful and tend to be under-used in marketing communications.

✔ **Bold and italic text:** I added some bold and italics to the text to emphasize key points that I was afraid might get lost in the length of this piece. Be careful with any such embellishments, however. If you get too carried away, you may make the copy look silly and reduce its credibility.

✔ **Call-to-action paragraph:** I finished this letter with a final paragraph containing a *call to action* — details of what the reader can do next along with some incentive to do it now.

Developing a letter like this one to a high level takes quite a bit of care, but the effort is worth it when you get increased responses.

Combining an opening story with hard-hitting, fact-based arguments and ending with a simple call to action should generate a nice response rate. Why? Because this marketing communication pushes two powerful buttons: It appeals to emotion, and it appeals to logic. Which means it stands a good chance of creating immediate involvement with any reader who has reason to worry about how well his employees handle customer problems and complaints.

Think of getting attention as having full reader involvement — which means the reader is involved both emotionally and rationally. The preceding sample letter attempts to get attention and turn it into action by combining an emotional appeal (based on a story) with a rational appeal (based on factual argument).

## What makes hybrid ads so effective?

I've demonstrated an obvious bias for hybrid ads, letters, sales presentations, and other communications that combine the best of fact-based argument with the best of narrative. Why is this strategy my favorite? Because it has two things going for it:

✔ **Creating a hybrid letter is usually the third step in a creative process.** Generally, people tend to create ads or ad concepts in the order I list them in the previous section — that is, first, they create the rational argument based on facts; second, they create the dramatic persuasion based on storytelling; and third, they develop the hybrid that includes some of both tactics. Why do you have an advantage using the form that you created last? Because by doing so, you spend more time and invest more effort in your ad. You really had to work hard to develop two completely different approaches and then find a good way to combine them. So the hybrid form represents more creative energy and a higher level of involvement on the marketer's part. And, in general, when you put more of yourself into an ad, you get more out of it.

✔ **Hybrid ads take advantage of the fact that we humans have both a rational and an emotional side.** In fact, many scientists believe that arguments literally appeal to a different side of the brain than stories do. By combining appeals to both our rational and emotional sides, hybrid ads tend to cast the broadest net. And when both the rational and emotional appeals work well, these ads build the highest involvement on the parts of their readers, listeners, or viewers.

# Getting Serious about Testing Your Copy

In the previous section, I show you how I combined a rational appeal with a story to make a direct-mail piece that has high impact. Good strategy, but will it work? Of course, you never really know how it'll work until you try it. But you have no reason to market blindly. You can use a lot of easy ways to test what you've written and see how it performs. In this section, I show you a few of the best tests.

## Checking your writing against screening criteria

One way you can test your copy is to check your writing against your screening criteria. To do so, develop some statements based on the criteria (these become your screening criteria) and then evaluate the writing against these statements. Ask others to evaluate your copy in the same manner, too.

### Evaluating rational arguments and fact-based appeals

Ideally, your copy should be convincing and persuasive, and it shouldn't lead to counter-arguments. Your copy should also be believable.

Use the following statements as your criteria when evaluating writing with a rational appeal:

✔ I find this writing very convincing.

✔ I agree with the main points completely.

✔ I can't think of any reasons to avoid this product/service while reading/ listening to/viewing the copy.

✔ I don't feel like arguing with the writer/speaker.

✔ The writing makes sense to me.

✔ This ad is important.

Your goal is to create an ad that people don't feel like arguing with. Ads that generate the fewest counter-arguments are the most persuasive.

### Evaluating emotional appeals and stories or case histories

An ad's emotional appeal, story, or case history should be engaging and interesting. It should engage feelings to a significant degree, and it should be realistic and believable.

Use these factors as your criteria when evaluating writing that uses emotional appeals:

- ✔ I find the writing compelling.
- ✔ The writing holds my attention.
- ✔ I feel that the copy describes a situation that could easily apply to me/ my business.
- ✔ I like the ad.
- ✔ The ad is definitely true to life.
- ✔ I relate easily to the feelings of the people in this ad.

### Evaluating hybrid ads

Hybrid ads involve both rational arguments and stories, so you need to evaluate them using both sets of criteria (in other words, all 12 statements described in the preceding two sections). For ads that are purely fact-oriented or purely story-oriented, you can use just the six statements that apply to their specific form. Or, go ahead and evaluate each communication using all the statements, because you can't always be sure that you know what the ad's appeal really is. Figure 13-1 shows a form you can use to evaluate marketing communications based on the need for both rational and emotional appeals. You can also find this form on the CD (filename CD1301).

On the form, notice that I alternate the items measuring the effectiveness of your argument with the ones measuring the effectiveness of your story. The story-oriented items have odd numbers, starting with item number one. The argument-oriented items have even numbers, starting with item number two. So an ad that's effective as a story will score high on the odd-numbered items, for example. And a hybrid letter, such as the one I show you under "A work of art: Fact and fiction combined," will score fairly high on all items and receive a high overall score.

You can use this form to check your own work and refine your drafts as you work on customer letters or any other marketing communications. Or you can take your research to a higher level by soliciting customer input.

## Evaluation Form 1 (Argument/Story Effectiveness)

Please circle the number that best represents your feelings toward the marketing communication you have been asked to evaluate. Thank you for your help.

Scale: 1 = not at all to 5 = definitely

Item A

| #1. | 1 2 3 4 5 | I found it compelling. |
|---|---|---|
| #2. | 1 2 3 4 5 | I found it very convincing. |
| #3. | 1 2 3 4 5 | It held my attention. |
| #4. | 1 2 3 4 5 | I agreed with the main points completely. |
| #5. | 1 2 3 4 5 | I felt that it described a situation that could easily apply to me/my business. |
| #6. | 1 2 3 4 5 | I could think of no reasons to avoid this product/service. |
| #7. | 1 2 3 4 5 | I liked the ad/marketing communication. |
| #8. | 1 2 3 4 5 | I did not feel like arguing with the writer/speaker. |
| #9. | 1 2 3 4 5 | It was definitely true to life. |
| #10. | 1 2 3 4 5 | It made good sense to me. |
| #11. | 1 2 3 4 5 | I could relate easily to the feelings in it. |
| #12. | 1 2 3 4 5 | It is important. |

**Figure 13-1:**
Evaluation
Form 1
(Argument/
Story
Effective-
ness).

## *Getting other people's opinions*

You can use the statements in Figure 13-1 to evaluate a marketing communication before you even try it out in the media or mail it. If you run your ad by a half-dozen or more people who are similar to your customers (or are your customers), you can find out what they think of it and, often, you can find ways to improve the ad before you spend money and take the risk of using the ad.

I recommend talking to some of your friends in the industry and to some of your most friendly customers, as well as to some people you don't know quite so well, to sign them up for ad-evaluation duty. You can point out that the procedure is quick and painless, and they must simply look at drafts of marketing communications and then fill in a quick one-page-or-less question- naire by circling some numbers. So their duty is easy, and they get to have a peek into your marketing operations and may get some good ideas of their own. Or, you can sweeten the pot by offering participants a discount to make their participation more worthwhile.

Having a panel of even a few people who you can run your communications by before you finalize them is a really wonderful thing. In addition to asking your panel to respond to some specific questions, such as the ones I give you in Figure 13-1, you should also spend a few minutes debriefing them in person or by phone to find out what they really think about your marketing piece. Try asking them to identify several things they like and dislike about the piece as an easy way to get them talking.

And while you're having people read and evaluate your marketing commu- nication, you can also ask them to make sure that it's simple, error-free, and clear (some of the common problems that I always find myself correcting when I do communications audits).

If you really don't have the time to put together an informal audience panel to test your ad, at least test it yourself and get others within the organization to test it. Any evaluation is better than none!

## Creating options and picking a winner

Another way to use research is to develop and evaluate three or more communication pieces. I know designing three ads, letters, brochures, or whatever is more work, but if you mock up three different designs and then compare them using evaluation questions (like the ones I gave you in the earlier section "Checking your writing against screening criteria"), you're more likely to end up picking a winner. Many ad agencies develop at least three different ads, and sometimes, as many as a dozen. Then everyone argues over which approach is best. If deciding which approach is the best is difficult, then you may have the luxury of multiple good options. But in my experience, one option often rises to the top, and it's rarely the first concept you developed. So creating more choices and testing your options before you make a decision really does pay off!

# *Evaluating for High Involvement*

Does your marketing communication get high involvement from your audience? In other words, do your readers notice it and become interested in it — that's *high involvement* — or do they just blow it off without paying much mind?

Because most people ignore most marketing communications, involvement is an important first step toward winning the customer. You need to win his attention and interest, and you need to get him involved in your effort to communicate.

In this section, don't worry about the content of your material or whether you convince people; just focus on how you build high involvement. High involvement is often essential, especially if you're designing an ad for a crowded place (like a magazine full of ads), where your biggest challenge is just winning some attention. A TV spot, a magazine or newspaper ad, a banner ad for the Web, (yet another) mailing, or an outdoor poster must grab attention and build involvement in a hurry, or customers pass it right by.

So how do you create high involvement for an ad? Here's a hypothetical example:

> A picture of a laughing baby will probably create emotional involvement, especially in parents of young children.

> A table that shows that babies whose parents feed them organic baby food will have fewer health problems later in life than those whose parents feed them conventional baby food will get rational involvement.

> Combine the picture of a laughing baby with the data from our imagined study showing that organic baby food is healthier, and you have the potential to capture full involvement because the ad appeals to both the rational and emotional sides of the parents you want to reach.

A number of large ad agencies actually measure rational and emotional involvement with questionnaires as a way of evaluating ads. Then they plot the results on a graph like the one shown in Figure 13-2. (See file CD1302.) Ads that plot high and to the right win the most involvement on both dimensions. And these ads tend to be more effective, all else being equal, especially in situations where catching your target audience's attention is hard to do.

So here's another way to evaluate your own marketing communications or to have a panel or group of people representing your audience evaluate them: Simply ask people to rate each ad, letter, Web page, or whatever the communication is by filling in the Evaluation Form 2 (Emotional/Rational Involvement), shown in Figure 13-3. This form is available on your CD, in case you want to print some copies; the filename is CD1303.

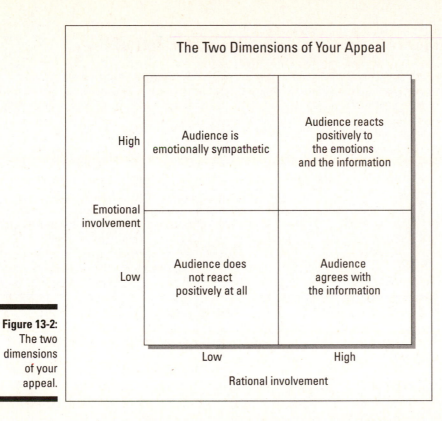

The Two Dimensions of Your Appeal

Emotional involvement

High — Audience is emotionally sympathetic

High — Audience reacts positively to the emotions and the information

Low — Audience does not react positively at all

Low — Audience agrees with the information

Low      High

Rational involvement

**Figure 13-2:**
The two dimensions of your appeal.

If you're testing multiple ads or other marketing communications, simply ask your panel to evaluate each one using the scale in CD1303. In this CD file, you find a form with room to evaluate up to ten options at a time, lettered from Item A to Item J. Label each ad or other communication clearly with one of these letters to make sure that you can accurately decode the data you collect.

Even if you have only one or two communications to evaluate, consider including others that you collected from the marketplace — especially ones that you think are effective because of their track records. Looking at the range of responses that customers give to a variety of options is always interesting, and doing so gives you insight into how to interpret their responses. For example, if people rate your new brochure design at 3.9 on average, and the average for competitors' brochures is only 3.1, then you probably have a winner, even though your absolute score isn't at the top of the 1 through 5 range.

To maximize involvement, look for designs that score reasonably high on both the odd- and even-numbered items in Figure 13-3 and CD1303. But if you designed your communication to have either a highly emotional or a highly rational appeal, don't expect to score high overall. Instead, look for top marks on the items that measure the dimension of involvement that you're shooting for. (Odd-numbered items measure rational appeal.)

Evaluation Form 2 (Emotional/Rational Involvement)

Please circle the number that best represents your feelings toward the marketing communication you have been asked to evaluate. Thank you for your help.

Scale: 1 = not at all to 5 = definitely

Item A

| #1. | 1 2 3 4 5 | I found myself caught up emotionally in it. |
| #2. | 1 2 3 4 5 | I was interested in the information it contained. |
| #3. | 1 2 3 4 5 | I got a definite sense of the feelings it is trying to communicate. |
| #4. | 1 2 3 4 5 | I could follow the logic of the argument easily. |
| #5. | 1 2 3 4 5 | It has a definite emotional appeal. |
| #6. | 1 2 3 4 5 | I thought it was well researched. |
| #7. | 1 2 3 4 5 | It captures my own feelings quite well. |
| #8. | 1 2 3 4 5 | It is a good source of useful ideas. |

**Figure 13-3:** Evaluation Form 2 (Emotional/ Rational Involvement).

# Interpreting Your Ad Research to Select or Refine a Design

In this section, I examine the data from three different ad designs, each one a draft of a possible direct-response ad designed to run in the Sunday magazines of various newspapers. I'm just going to describe these ads, not show them, because I want to focus on how you interpret research about people's reactions to them.

✔ The first design uses an eye-catching photo and a brief story as its focus.

✔ The second design presents several little-known facts and builds an argument for the product based on them.

✔ The third design is a hybrid of the first two, combining a smaller photo and brief quote from a customer with a short discussion of relevant facts.

Here's how a panel of 15 prospective customers evaluated each ad on the customer involvement scales (see the previous section for more details on this scale) and also on the emotional/rational appeals scales (see the earlier section "Checking your writing against screening criteria" on story-based versus argument-based appeals). I simplified the results by coding them as L = low, M = medium, and H = high.

| Ads | Average Scores | | | |
| | Appeal | | Involvement | |
| | Story | Argument | Emotional | Rational |
|---|---|---|---|---|
| 1. Photo/story | H | L | H | L |
| 2. Facts/argument | L | M | L | M |
| 3. Hybrid of 1 & 2 | M | M | M | M |

You can see that the panel's reactions to the ads are nicely summarized in a table like this. At a glance, you get a feel for the strengths and weaknesses of each of the options. The first one had high appeal as a story and also achieved high emotional involvement. It bombed on the other scales, though, reflecting its lack of hard information. The second ad got medium scores for the appeal of its argument and for its ability to involve people rationally, but it bombed on the other scales because it lacked emotional impact. And the third ad, the hybrid ad, received medium scores across the board.

So which ad is better? A conservative marketer probably would pick the third ad because it seems to have something for everyone. I usually favor hybrids with a combination of stories and arguments and the ability to create both rational and emotional involvement. My choice based on this data, however, is definitely the first ad. I like to see exceptionally high scores on anything, even if they require a sacrifice on other dimensions. Grabbing attention with an ad is hard, so one that packs an emotional punch is obviously a good choice.

If you're still worried about ad number one's low scores on the argument and rational involvement scales, well, feel free to fiddle with it and do some more testing. Perhaps you can make it just a bit bigger and work a line or two of copy in at the bottom with some compelling facts. Even an asterisk with a footnote citing some facts or statistics may raise those low scores to the medium range without diluting the ad's emotional impact and bringing down its other scores. So you can fiddle with it and try to formulate a better hybrid ad, but I wouldn't fiddle too much. An emotionally powerful ad is a rare commodity, and you may mess it up if you add too much to it. A good rule for marketing communications is that less is more.

# Designing for Stopping Power

Another important consideration for any marketing communication is how well it screams for attention. Not all marketing communications need to shout out to their audience, but many benefit from the ability to grab attention. *Stopping power* is the ability of a marketing communication to attract immediate notice. To command attention.

What does your logo look like? Do people stop and give it a long look because they find it interesting? Do they want to open an envelope because the logo on the outside is striking and catches their eye? Well, maybe not — most logos lack stopping power. I was impressed by a new logo Xerox Corporation unveiled in 2008 because it truly had strong stopping power. According to the company's press release in January 2008, the logo "is a lowercase treatment of the Xerox name — in a vibrant red — alongside a sphere-shaped symbol sketched with lines that link to form an illustrative 'X'." The press release included a JPEG of the logo design which I've put in CD1304 for your reference.

What gives this logo stopping power? The "vibrant" red certainly helps, but Zerox's new logo is strong even in black and white. It uses chunky, strong letters and an appealing three-dimensional-looking circle with an X on it that really does draw the eye.

This chapter is, of course, on copywriting, so how can we translate the concept of stopping power to writing? You can, and should, showcase your copy visually, with appealing layouts, bold headlines and subheads, and so on. (I give lots of advice about layout in both Chapters 7 and 9.) And a strong illustration also helps. But you also need some words that leap up and grab attention, so as to stop people from whatever else they're doing and make them start reading.

A strong caption, headline, first line, or last-line special offer may be where you put your stopping power. Make sure that it's in at least one of those places. The need for words that jump up and stop people in their tracks is behind the use of the clever and catchy headlines you see in magazine ads. For example, instead of saying, "Home remodeling services that meet your needs," which isn't exciting enough to make me want to read an ad or brochure, you could have a headline that reads, "Home is where the heart can afford to live well."

What does that mean? Got me. I'll have to make up something in the first paragraph that ties the phrase into my ad for home remodeling services. But I like the headline. It's catchy. It makes you wonder what comes next. So if I were writing a print ad, brochure, or Web homepage for a construction company that specializes in home remodeling, I might start with this headline and weave some copy to go along with it. For example, my first paragraph could say:

**Home is where the heart can afford to live well**

Too often, people live in their dream homes only when they are sleeping. Our hundreds of happy clients can tell you that they live that dream every day in homes that reflect their special tastes and desires. With free consultation by our architects and hundreds of design concepts in our VR remodeling software, you can fall in love with your new home before we drive a single nail. And there are no hidden costs — we'll show you exactly how you can make your dream affordable.

After this eye-catching headline and interest-building first paragraph, I would simply provide clear, factual information about the company and its services. The main copy of this ad needs to support the exciting opening claim with solid foundations. Then, depending on what you're using the copy for, you could add some kind of call to action at the end, such as, "Call or e-mail today for a free home-redesign kit or to schedule a no-obligation, free visit from one of our redesign professionals."

Stopping power's great virtue is that it gets you in. And when you're in, when you've captured the attention of a prospect, then the rest of your design can go to work.

Putting a sexy photo on the outside of a direct-mail envelope probably won't increase the response rate, and it may irritate some of your prospects. Stopping power isn't really that simple.

To really generate stopping power, you need to give any marketing communication six different qualities. Here are some qualities an ad can use in order to generate serious stopping power:

- ✔ Drama
- ✔ Audience participation
- ✔ Emotion
- ✔ Curiosity
- ✔ Surprise
- ✔ Beauty

## Does sexy sell?

Many marketers assume that a sure way to give any marketing communication stopping power is to put something sexy into it. If you show some attractive people in suggestive positions or even just put the word "sex" in the headline, people will take a quick look to see what's going on. But generally sex has nothing much to do with what you're communicating, so that sort of stopping power doesn't work well. People just move on again after they realize you've tried to trick them into paying attention.

You may surprise readers by talking about your product in an unconventional way. When I write a headline about home remodeling services that says "Home is where the heart can afford to live well," I make people curious and even a bit surprised by my unusual phrasing. This encourages them to want to read, stimulating participation on their part as they try to figure out what the headline means. This headline has stopping power.

Do your marketing communications have stopping power? Maybe, but probably not. Most communications don't. In fact, if you think about this concept, it's impossible for most communications to have high stopping power. Stopping power requires qualities that make the communication stand out from the crowd. So, an ad with stopping power is always going to be a rare trait.

Beauty also has stopping power — a lot of stopping power. When a product design is beautiful (occasionally, this is the case with a new car, for example), the thing to do is just show the product in the ads. Its beauty will make people stop and look. If you don't have an inherently beautiful product or if you have a service that people can't easily see or you can't easily photograph, then consider finding a beautiful image to represent your product (see Chapter 5 for details).

## Measuring stopping power

As in the previous sections, where I use evaluation forms to rate communications on their appeal and involvement, you can use a simple evaluation form to measure a communication's stopping power. What you can measure, you can manage, so when you start evaluating your communications with the stopping power form, you may find yourself working more stopping power into your marketing. You can give more stopping power to any ad, letter, telemarketing script, sales presentation, Web page, fax, business card, advertisement, or other communication. And stopping power always helps get attention and gives your communication the opportunity to do its job.

## After you've gotten their attention

It's great to have a catchy headline or other device to stop people and make them pay attention for long enough to start reading. However, the writing itself must be appealing to start with, or the powerful headline won't help much. Your writing needs to be clear and strong. To achieve clarity and strength, rewrite and edit with these two related goals in mind.

Yes, that's what I said: *Rewrite and edit!* As an author, I've always remembered what one of my mentors told me years ago: The art of good writing is rewriting. This can be taken as bad or good news. Are you an optimist? Then think of the good news: You just need to draft a few paragraphs quickly, and you're well on your way! Rewrite them rigorously a few times, and you probably will have some pretty good writing. (If you're a pessimist, you may feel discouraged by the thought that you'll have to spend hours reworking a single page — but hey, that's the secret to good writing! Just budget enough time and make a really big pot of coffee.)

As you write and rewrite with the goals of clear and strong language in mind, it may help to ask yourself this question: "What's most important to my reader?" For example, if you're selling home remodeling services, you might answer that question by deciding that they care about good work, completed on budget and within schedule. If your Yellow Pages ad is full of words that don't emphasize these most important qualities of your service, then rewrite until the important points burst off the page and into the reader's mind.

# Applying Great Writing to Your Web Site

Open any of your own Web pages and take a hard, objective look at them. Are they visually appealing, drawing your eye in so that you want to read what's on-screen? If not, add a unifying design element, like a central photo or a bold headline. Or, reduce the clutter and make it clean and easy for readers to approach.

Next, read the first text that catches your eye. Is the text clear? Interesting? Brief? Does it make you want to read more? Probably not. Most of the writing on the Web is just terrible. Really awful. Unclear, too complicated, and full of errors of usage and grammar. I've never met a Web site I didn't want to edit. Here's a quick checklist of things to work on if you want to try to improve the clarity and appeal of your Web site's text:

✔ **Can you reduce the number of words?** On the Web, shorter is usually better. You can tighten your text by eliminating unnecessary words and by choosing words that express your meaning more succinctly.

✔ **Can you make everything crystal clear?** It's amazing how hard it is to understand all the writing on the average Web site. That's because company insiders (like you) who write the text have a hard time imagining how ignorant someone like me can be when visiting the site for the first time. I just went to www.3m.com to see what this major company was up to, and I encountered the cryptic message "Aldara cream now indicated for AK" on its home page. I hate to be ignorant, but what's Aldara cream? Does 3M make it? Does "now indicated" mean it has some sort of regulatory approval for use? And what's AK? Part of what makes this message confusing is that it's next to messages about carpet cleaners and toilet bowl scrubbers — not the most logical place to boast about a new medication, if that's what the cream is. Next time you look at your own site, imagine how it may read to someone like me who has fresh eyes and little or no knowledge of your business.

✔ **What's the point?** Every Web page, like any form of writing, needs to have a clear point. The headline and topic sentence should express one clear, simple claim to fame. What is it? I rarely can tell because Web pages tend to be divided into lots of little sections and zones, and each one competes for attention with all the others. Make sure that you have an overarching message. Your home page ought to devote at least one-third of its area to conveying a message about what makes your company or service special and brilliant. And you need to mention this message in variations as reminders on most of the other pages on your site, too. *Focus* is the key ingredient in great Web writing!

✔ **Can you reduce errors?** Oh, sure, your site doesn't have any typos, inaccuracies, nonfunctional links, or other errors . . . but do me a favor, and just check it carefully one more time anyway. Thanks!

Don't take time and space to try to wow your viewer with elaborate high-tech bells and whistles. Stopping power is unimportant on Web sites because viewers don't wander by on the sidewalk. They choose to click through to your Web address, so you already have their interest. Keep the writing clear, clean, and focused so as not to lose their interest.

Avoid these common pitfalls, and your Web writing will be as tight, appealing, and effective as the rest of your marketing communications. And remember to make sure that you have factual arguments that persuade logically and/or good feelings and interesting stories that appeal emotionally in everything you write for marketing. Stories can work well on Web pages, just as they can work well in sales materials, direct-mail letters, or personal sales presentations. Call them cases, keep them short, and try to work three to six of them into your Web site. If you can obtain permission, include a quote or testimonial from a happy customer with one or more of these case histories. There's nothing like a good story to create high involvement and make your point persuasively.

# A Final Check: Auditing Your Marketing Communications

One of the services my firm offers to clients is a complete audit of all their written sales and marketing communications. When we do these audits, we always find that we can improve these communications by

- **Making the writing briefer:** If you can shorten the number and complexity of words, you make the communication easier and quicker for customers and prospects to read. Those changes mean more people will read and understand your message. And that's a good thing. A very good thing.

- **Correcting errors:** You may think accuracy isn't an issue, but I'm often surprised at the number of errors that I find in marketing communications. Trust me, somewhere in your printed materials or on your Web site or in an ad, your products or services are misrepresented. Wrong names, inaccurate technical details, incorrect addresses or product codes, and old prices may be creating confusion and losing the company sales.

- **Identifying omissions:** In every company I audited, I found many places where the information was insufficient for customers or prospects to take the next step toward purchase. Sometimes in our evaluations, we add something as simple as a contact address or phone number; other times, we need to provide instructions for how to select the right product or option. But the most common of all is that we have to explain what the company is and does.

  For example, I have a nice golf umbrella from a company that I'm helping with its marketing communications. The umbrella has stripes in the company colors and has the company name on it. But unfortunately, most people don't know the name, so when they see the umbrella, they have no idea what the company is or what it does. This umbrella is a simple little giveaway promotion, but it won't do any good until the company adds a tag line explaining what it is, plus some contact information so that prospective customers can find it by phone or on the Web.

- **Achieving consistency:** Each individual marketing message is a part of your overall message, and you need to view each one that way. In my audits, I often find that pointing out major and minor inconsistencies in how the client communicates is necessary; then I ask the client to come up with suggestions for standardization. When a client communicates a consistent message, each individual communication helps create and maintain a strong, professional image in the marketplace, instead of creating a weak, inconsistent, or confusing one.

> ✔ **Improving persuasiveness:** I'm amazed at how boring most marketing communications are. I like seeing writing jump off the page or the computer screen and seize the reader by her eyeballs. When I audit clients' communications, I often flag dull or unpersuasive communications and work on giving them more power to grab attention and shape attitudes and actions. Marketing communications should be active, not passive!

I'm sharing these common corrections to marketing communications with you so that you can try to fix the problems yourself. Perform your own audit of every piece of written (or scripted) marketing communications your organization does, looking for ways to make it the best it can be.

# Create an Ad on Steroids

The headline can work magic, especially when combined with a good visual. Let me illustrate my point by designing my own ad that captures the idea that headlines and images can combine to have considerable marketing power. You can look over my shoulder as I work and see how I do.

The easiest and best way to write a strong headline is to start with an analogy or metaphor that captures the core concept. In this case, the concept is that a good headline can tie into the photo and be powerful. Imagine that I'm working up an ad for my own firm's design services and I want to explain that I write powerful ads with strong headlines. Here's a way to express that idea with an analogy: *"A headline with a good photograph is like a traditional picture and caption on steroids."*

This is not the headline. Not yet. It takes several steps to create a strong headline. Next step: I ask myself if I like it. Am I on to something? If I say yes, then I will continue to work on it. Simplify and clarify it. For example, I might decide that it's clearer and better this way: **"Should *Your* Ad Be on Steroids?"**

Good! I've got a strong headline concept that seems to capture the point I want to make in an exciting and intriguing way. But how to illustrate it? Hmmm. I'm thinking. . . . Got it! How about a photo of a baseball player swinging a bat that has my headline written *on* it? Right there on the face of the bat: "Should Your Ad Be on Steroids?" Beneath the ad, we could have a paragraph of copy such as, *"Why not? It's perfectly legal in the great sport of marketing. The more power you can give your ad, the better! And when the power comes from words — plain, simple, old-fashioned words — nobody gets hurt. But you might hit a home run."* My ad could go on to describe the powerful copywriting and creative services of my marketing firm.

Hmmm. Maybe I'll run an ad just like this one and see whether my firm's phone rings off the hook. But back to writing great ads for *your* firm. You can use the same technique in any consumer or business-to-business ad. Here's a real-life example of a powerful headline. The Container Store (which sells organizers for closet storage) ran a full-page magazine ad in home magazines that was largely a photograph of a very well-organized closet with nice clothing and shoes on racks and hangers. Beneath the photograph, a headline captured the message by saying, "**What the Best-Dressed Closets are Wearing**."

If you were writing a normal caption for that photograph, you'd say something obvious and ordinary, such as, *"A well-organized closet using products from The Container Store."* However, that would not make for an exciting ad because it's too obvious and ordinary to catch the eye or hold the imagination — hence the need to bump up the power of the writing with an analogy or idea that puts that caption on steroids. Normally, it's people we describe as "best dressed," but why not a closet? The closet is an extension of the person. You would not expect a best-dressed person to have a disorganized, ugly closet, right? Nice clothes need to be treated well. The closet in the photograph looks like a display of nice clothes, not just a place to put them. The ad's clever headline hints that you may feel better about yourself and your clothes if you organize your closet better. This is a big idea to capture in a simple headline. It's an excellent example of good headline writing.

Here's another example, this one from business-to-business marketing. Harvard Business School Publishing ran full-page ads in business magazines, such as *Training,* in which it used a large area of bright red ink with huge white block letters declaring, "**TURN TRIAL BY FIRE INTO TRIAL BY WARM EMBERS**." This clever, catchy headline makes you want to see what the ad is about. The copy read, "You can't eliminate the pressures that new managers face. But you can certainly ease the transition." The ad went on to plug an online training program called Stepping Up to Management.

Your challenge as a copywriter is to push through the early ideas and drafts of your ad and refuse to stop until you have a concept that supports a powerful headline. A headline that pumps the power of steroids into your ad. Most ads don't have this kind of power. I had to leaf through many magazines before coming up with those two real-world examples. And most ads don't get high readership and response. Hmmm. Wonder why? Maybe somebody decided to punt instead of swinging for the fence. When you design or commission your next print ad, Web ad, poster, billboard, or brochure, take the extra time to pump up an ordinary photo caption and make it into a caption on steroids. All great headlines are just that — captions on steroids. Don't stop until you've got an ad that swings for the fences.

# Obtaining and Using Customer Testimonials

You can increase the persuasiveness of your marketing writing by adding a quote from a happy customer. For example, a restaurant ad that says, "Our food is the best in the city" is less persuasive than an ad for the same restaurant that quotes a food critic who says the same thing. If you happen to have gotten good publicity, check with the publication (or other media) to make sure that it doesn't mind your quoting its story and then include a short, accurate excerpt in your own marketing materials.

What if the media hasn't published glowing reviews that you can quote? You can still obtain testimonials, which are positive quotes from customers or other credible sources. However, you'll have to ask for them and then edit them into something short and clear enough to put quotes around and add to your brochure, sales letter, Web site, or other marketing communication. (In the case of radio, TV, and streaming video for the Web, you'll also have to record the testimonial.) And most important, you have to obtain written permission form the source (or, if the source is under age, a parent) to use the testimonial in your marketing.

## Asking for testimonials

It's a good idea to ask early for testimonials. If you have a technology product, get a demo out as soon as possible. If you're manufacturing a new product, get the prototype in someone's hands as soon as it's ready. Coming out of the gate with testimonials is an excellent way to start. However, if you are writing an ad or brochure for an existing business, product, or service, you can still obtain testimonials. It doesn't have to be something new — just something customers like enough to put their name behind it.

If you're wondering who is fair game for a testimonial, keep in mind that you can ask anyone who has a legitimate, authoritative opinion about your product, service, or business. Here are some of the more common prospects to consider when seeking a testimonial, case history, or other useable contribution:

- Your customers
- Friends in management positions in businesses or in other positions of recognized authority, such as accountants, doctors, or politicians
- Experts, such as well-known authors, professors, musicians, or journalists
- Anyone who runs a consulting, real-estate, or insurance firm; they're always looking for exposure, and the public often sees them as experts

✔ Anyone you can get to sample or review your offerings (such as in a test market, in-store sampling, or introductory promotional offer)

✔ People who are sufficiently well known and routinely get such requests and have an established system for handling them

✔ Editors of newsletters, magazines, or e-newsletters about your industry

You have or can make plenty of opportunities to talk to people in most of these categories. So asking them for their opinion on a specific question concerning your business can be perfectly natural. Take advantage of these opportunities to pop the question and see what raw testimonials you can harvest just by shaking your tree a little.

Other people whom you'd like to ask may not be within your circle of regular contacts. Don't despair. If they're well known, they're no doubt used to such requests. They may have a publicist, secretary, or assistant who handles requests for testimonials or other public appearances routinely. Just call or ask around until you find out what the proper approach is and then send a professional written request. With celebrity endorsers, you may want to suggest some simple phrases or quotes that they can consider using if they don't have the desire to write their own from scratch. Also, be sure to describe the sort of use you think you'll put their quote to, with specific references to how neatly and professionally you'll present it and how many people you expect to see and read (or hear) it. That way, the big fish can decide more easily whether this is a good exposure opportunity for her.

Whenever you ask for a testimonial, enclose a short, simple release form that says something like, "I freely give _____ permission to use the following quote from me in their marketing communications and to cite me by name as the source of this quote." Check with a lawyer from your state for more specific advice about how to craft the best release statement.

 Don't be too pushy when asking people for quotes. Some people just don't feel comfortable lending their names. Often, lower-level employees in a company don't have the authority to lend their names and titles to others without clearance from their bosses, which isn't that easy to secure. Other people are simply not into the idea of participating in your project and don't have any interest in seeing their names in your marketing materials. That's fine. Don't bug these noncontributors.

 Stay far away from people who raise the question of payment. Anyone who says, "Sure, I'd be willing to give you a quote. How much are you offering?" isn't thinking about the opportunity in a helpful way. They don't see it as a simple favor that may come around to help them some day in the future. They're trying to milk the situation for a few quick bucks. People who think that way are likely to come up with other ways to bother you for money in the future. And besides, you won't really get an objective testimonial if you pay for it. So when you bump into someone who wants to profit from your request for a quote, just thank them kindly and back out as gracefully and quickly as you can.

## Asking for specific testimonials

Your request for a testimonial should be specific. Specificity makes your request easier to answer and less easy to object to. Specific requests include

- The person's opinion of your product or service
- A description of how she used your product or service and what happened as a result
- The person's view of where the industry, product category, technology, economy, or whatever is going
- Information about which of your products or services she uses
- How often she uses your product or service or how much of it she uses
- Why she uses your product or service
- What she thinks the best things about your product or service are
- Who she would recommend your product or service to
- What she would recommend your product or service for

And the less well you know someone, the more specific your request should be. You can always ask a close friend for a reference, and they'll generally say, "Sure, just tell me what you want me to say." But people you know more casually aren't likely to be as easy to work with. To them, a general request for a favor like that may seem inappropriate or difficult. So be more specific as you work outward from your immediate circle of friends and associates.

## Processing the testimonial

When someone gives you a quote, what you usually get is their unedited writing. To process a raw testimonial, first you need to isolate and refine the language. Here's an example of a sentence from a customer that needs some editing:

> *"Basically, I'd say ABC's services would be useful for any company within this geographic area, as long as they have computers that need maintenance. I think your service is great!"*

This recommendation is a good start, but it isn't quite as short or punchy as it needs to be. You can tighten the text a bit by cutting superfluous words (like *basically*) and by substituting briefer words or phrases for lengthy or poorly chosen ones. Just don't make the recommendation say anything that it didn't originally. For example, you can't add "I love this company" if that thought wasn't there to start with. But you can edit the text into the following form without violating the spirit of the original quote:

> *"ABC's services are great! They're useful to any company in the area with computers that need maintenance."*

I moved up the bit with stopping power and changed "would be" to "are" because present tense is always stronger for testimonials. And now that I isolated and cleaned up that offhand sentence from the middle of a customer's unedited quote, the quote is beginning to show some real promise as a testimonial. It could be used in a brochure, for example, or added to the home page of a Web site.

## Using customer videos and photos

Candid customer comments or reactions on video or audiotape have many of the same virtues and uses as written testimonials. You can use them to create effective radio or television ads, and you can use them in a promotional video you distribute to prospects if you do business-to-business marketing. Some private schools and colleges now hand out videos to prospective students, and these videos are a great medium for some candid reactions as well as for testimonials from students and alums.

I also encourage you to consider using customer footage on your Web site. The technology exists to put short (keep it short, please!) clips of video or audio recordings on sites and to make them available at the click of a button. People love watching TV, and they'll gladly sit and watch short videos on your Web site. Videos pull people into a site, increase the amount of time that they spend there, and also increase the credibility of your marketing claims.

Photos of customers combined with their quotes or comments are also powerful marketing tools. You can include them on a Web page, in a catalog, in print ads, and even on a product's packaging. Just remember to get written permission from anyone you show in a photo or video. Make up a release form in advance that explains what you intend to do with their photograph or recording and that makes it clear that they're allowing you to use the product for that purpose. Again, if someone objects, stop using the image or recording of them. But usually people are happy to be included.

## *Explaining who the testimonial is from*

Include as much information as possible regarding the person that is endorsing your product of service. Many people are afraid to ask permission to put it all out there, so they will list Alex H., instead of a full name. This acknowledgment gives the perception that the recommendation may be fake.

The best way to have full, clear, and accurate information about the source of a testimonial is to ask the source to fill in a short form about herself along with the permission form. Ask for name, position or title, and employer (if relevant) *as the source wishes this information to appear in your marketing materials.* Include that phrase on the form to make sure that the source has given you permission not only for the quote but also for their identifying information.

## *On the CD*

Check out the following files on the CD-ROM:

- ✔ Evaluation Form 1 (CD1301)
- ✔ Two Dimensions of Your Appeal (CD1302)
- ✔ Evaluation Form 2 (CD1303)
- ✔ Press release about new Xerox logo (CD1304)

# Part V
# Sales and Service Success

The 5th Wave                    By Rich Tennant

BUNDY
POWER TOOLS
"STRONG AS A
TURTLE"
BUNDY

"The ox put us over budget."

## In this part . . .

It all comes down to sales in the end. Are they up or down? Did you land the new account or not? Did the customer reorder or switch to a competitor? Did the leads from the trade show convert to sales or just end up wasting your time? The answers to these vital questions are often written in the details of how you select, approach, and interact with your prospects. Even the best marketing programs too often founder on the shoals of sales errors and mistakes.

In this part, I share techniques and processes for managing customer interactions and for closing important sales. I also show you how managing your attitudes can, and does, drive sales success — or lack thereof.

# Chapter 14

# Mastering the Sales Process

This chapter focuses on ways of making a sale in person. Retail sales clerks interact with customers to help them find what they want and feel good about making a purchase. Construction contractors discuss a project with the prospective customer and then prepare and present a proposal they hope will win them the job. Business-to-business marketers contact prospects in person, by e-mail, and by telephone to generate business. Even businesses that don't seem to use personal selling often do have occasional need for the skill. For example, the owner of a Web-based business may need to make a sales pitch to a bank loan officer or investor in order to fund an expansion plan.

Personal selling is an incredibly important part of marketing. This chapter looks at how the sales process works and how to maximize its effectiveness in your business.

## Walking through the Sales Process

Every expert has a different model of the sales process. Some models are simple. Many are highly elaborate. And, to be honest, few of them really give you much help in improving your sales success because they're rarely realistic or prescriptive. I favor a model that reflects the reality that you need to do some work to figure out what the prospect needs, and then you present your offerings to meet that need. I also favor a model that suggests what to do and how and when to do it to optimize your sales efficiency. Sometimes, for example, you may have to abandon a sales call and go on another — something few sales models or trainings are willing to promote.

The following is the sales process model I generally prefer when I train sales-people or work on the sales and marketing process for my clients:

- **Step 1: Contact.** This first step involves identifying prospects through lead-generation systems, cold calls, referrals, and any other methods you can think of to recruit potential buyers. As the name of this step implies, the point is to create the context for prolonged contact with prospects so that you can attempt to make the sale. Speak (by phone or in person) or write (via e-mail or letter) to prospects to ask for a chance to see them. Set up appointments or find a way to drop by and catch them at an available moment. Plan and make that vital contact that opens the door to the sales process.

- **Step 2: Need discovery.** This step focuses on gaining a sufficient under-standing of the prospect and his situation to be able to propose a pur-chase that makes sense for him. Use brief interactions or the beginning of a longer sales meeting to ask confirming and exploring questions in order to discover more about the prospect's requirements. The knowl-edge and insight you gain in this phase helps you present a proposal that's customized to his needs.

- **Step 3: Proposal(s).** In this step, present your offerings to your prospect — show what you have to sell. But because you've done some discovery in the previous step, you adapt your presentation to the needs and wants of the prospect. You may describe certain services or products and not others. You may emphasize price to one prospect, quality to another, and speed to a third. And where possible, show specifically how your products and/or services can help the prospect overcome constraints and achieve his goals.

- **Step 4: Attempted closes.** In this step, you ask the prospect for busi-ness. You initiate the process of making an actual sale and see how he reacts. If the prospect is reluctant, you can cycle back to Step 3 or even to Step 2, based on your judgment of the situation. Then, make another attempt to close the deal later on.

In general, I suggest trying at least three times to close before you conclude that the prospect is truly unwilling to make a purchase at the moment. After that, you need to do a reality check to make sure that you have an appropriate prospect. If attempts to close go poorly, you may decide that this is the wrong prospect for you. Maybe he just isn't ready to buy yet, or maybe he wants to but can't afford to. If you discover a problem that prevents the sale from going through, back off gracefully and quickly look for another prospect. No use wasting time on improbabilities when the world is full of new possibilities waiting for you to discover.

✔ **Step 5: Follow up.** In this step, you contact the prospect after the sales meeting to thank him for his time (and for the order, if you closed), to reinforce any key points, and to prepare the prospect for the next contact. If your attempts to close failed, explore the reasons why and seek a future opportunity to recontact him and initiate another sales effort. If the close succeeded, confirm the purchase and prepare the prospect for the next step.

✔ **Step 6: Service.** In this step, you build upon the initial sale. You seek future sales, and you continue to explore needs and propose solutions in an ongoing effort to form a consultative selling partnership with the prospect. Excellent customer service and follow-through on all promises are vital now. You may need to monitor the service and keep up good relations for a long time after the initial sales meeting ends.

Figure 14-1 illustrates this sales process, showing several options for moving through it depending on how the prospect reacts. The sales process may not flow smoothly from step to step. Sometimes, you need to revisit earlier steps. Other times, you need to abandon all hope and write off the prospect, moving on to another prospect and sales attempt, at least for the time being. (Lost causes sap your time and enthusiasm, so please avoid them!)

The sales process flowchart in Figure 14-1 contains considerable insight about when and how to make the sale. I use it in my training business to improve the performance of salespeople in a wide variety of businesses and industries, so it makes a good framework for the next few sections of this chapter.

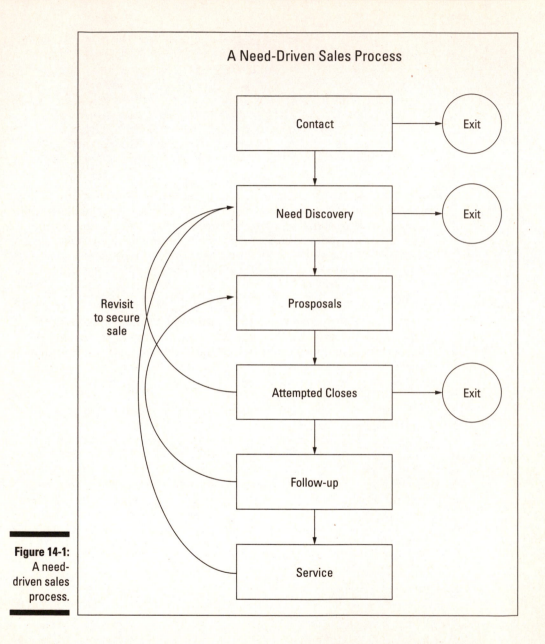

A Need-Driven Sales Process

Contact → Exit

Need Discovery → Exit

Prosposals

Attempted Closes → Exit

Follow-up

Service

Revisit to secure sale

**Figure 14-1:** A need-driven sales process.

# Getting the Most Out of Your Contacts

You need to identify and then establish contact with any prospect before you can hope to make a sale to her. In this section, I present a few of the strategies you can use to reach out and identify prospects and cue them up for a sales contact. I also present ideas on how to make the most of your call centers. Finally, I explain the importance of need-discovery techniques in building a successful relationship with your contact.

# Gaining contacts

Here are some of the ways of generating *leads* (names and contact information of likely prospects):

- Attend or display at a trade show, convention, or other event that attracts prospects. Make sure that you find ways to interact with prospects and collect information about them for later follow-ups. Although many trade shows have had reduced numbers in the past several years, the numbers are picking up again. And one thing is for sure: If you don't attend, you're surely invisible to potential clients.

- Buy mailing lists from list compilers, brokers, membership organizations, or subscription-based publications. Send letters, postcards, fliers, or other mail solicitations inviting prospects to return something by mail, visit your Web site, or call if they're interested in more information. Use telephone sales or personal sales calls to follow up with the ones who respond.

- Buy e-mail or fax lists (until these options are regulated out of existence) and use them just as you would a mailing list.

- Network with friends and customers to find new prospects.

- Speak at industry or community events to let people know the work you do and to share your expertise. Collect leads after the event.

- Run a small display ad in an appropriate magazine or newspaper and include your telephone number, Web site, and/or address. Use the ad to generate inquiries from interested prospects.

- Develop a telephone sales script and have an employee, temp worker, or telemarketing firm (for larger lists) make calls to generate leads or to try closing some sales for you.

- Write and post a weekly blog full of tips and ideas that prospective customers will appreciate. Include ways for readers to get in touch with you if they're interested in more information.

- Include a Join Our Mailing List or Sign Up for Our Newsletter button on your Web page to attract interested prospects. When they fill out a form with their contact information, send them your newsletter and other mailings, and also put them on your call list for a future contact.

- Send an e-mail newsletter to interested prospects, sharing useful information and positioning yourself or your business as a source of expertise. In the newsletter, include marketing messages designed to bring prospects your way, either by phone or through a supporting Web site.

## Utilizing your call center

Many businesses list a toll-free number and Web address in directories, marketing materials, and ads and then wait for calls or Web orders. When calls come in, they're typically from prospects expecting to talk to someone who may be able to help them make a purchase. So the salesperson answering the phone is in an enviable position: She simply needs to help callers figure out what they need and then write up the orders. But is it that simple?

If you have nonsalespeople answering the phones and taking orders, you're missing a great chance to do some selling. Anyone who responds to a marketing communication and makes the effort to call you is a serious prospect and deserves serious sales attention. Whoever handles that call needs to be knowledgeable and skilled in soft-sell sales methods because, in addition to simply writing up the prospect's order, the salesperson can conceivably pursue a number of other marketing objectives, such as

- Gather useful information about the caller for your database (and for use in future marketing initiatives aimed at the caller)

- Cross-sell other products/services to the caller

- Help the caller make a tough decision

- Diagnose the caller's situation and suggest solutions (involving your products/services if possible, of course!)

- Project a positive, helpful, interested image for your business that will bring the prospect back again and stimulate positive word of mouth

- Handle any complaints or concerns with sensitivity, recovering the caller and preventing him from hanging up with a negative feeling toward your business

- Gather useful suggestions and ideas from the caller for use in refining the marketing program, product offerings, or other elements of your business process

You shouldn't ignore these valuable objectives. However, many businesses put people to work at their reception phone or call center without giving them enough training and support to pursue such objectives. In fact, few operators or telephone salespeople are ever given a list to think about. They don't even know they should aim for these objectives, let alone know how to achieve them!

## Exploring need-discovery techniques

The better you understand customers' needs and how they prefer fulfilling those needs, the better you can position yourself and your products or services to get a good sale. Large-company marketing programs use extensive marketing research to explore customer needs. In smaller organizations, individual one-on-one discussions with customers and occasional do-it-yourself surveys can work just as well. In all organizations in which individuals interact face to face with prospects and customers, you can gather a great deal of information using need-discovery techniques.

*Need-discovery techniques* were developed for use in consultative selling, where the salesperson acts as a problem solver for the customer and tries to become part of the customer's business team. Like a business consultant, the salesperson uses a combination of research and exploratory questions to diagnose the client's situation. (See "Asking exploring questions," later in this section, for more on questioning.) This need-discovery process puts the salesperson in a position to generate and propose helpful solutions to the customer's problems. Often, those solutions involve the products and services of the salesperson's business.

Over time, the customer comes to trust and rely on the consultative salesperson. The customer shares more details so that the salesperson can discover more needs and offer more solutions. The result of this process is a collaborative business partnership that is beneficial to both parties. Because collaboration provides many intangible benefits, consultative selling often shifts the focus away from price.

Customers value businesses that emphasize consultative selling for their superior service, flexibility, and willingness to help the customer succeed. The customer who enjoys such benefits isn't as quick to give the business to some new competitor just because the competitor offers a minor price reduction or other incentive.

The following sections look closely at some simple but powerful conversational techniques that help you uncover customer needs and concerns.

### Planning your questions

Start by reviewing what you know about your prospects. What are their needs? What are their constraints? What sorts of changes or trends in the news may be affecting them? If you're planning to call on a business, seek out information about the business on the Web and in the local newspapers. In addition, review the business's marketing communications and talk to others who work for or do business with the prospect.

From these inquiries, you should find yourself asking questions and generating hypotheses about the prospect. You should be able to come up with some theories about the prospect's needs. If you have trouble clarifying your thoughts about the prospect, fill in the form shown in Figure 14-2 (a template of this form is on the CD with the filename CD1401, so you can print a stack of them and keep them in your customer files).

You may need ten minutes to fill in this form. If you're eager to see as many prospects as possible, you may be tempted to skip it. Why plan when you can just give a canned presentation and trust to luck? Because the planning phase greatly increases the chances of building a consultative relationship and securing a sale. Most salespeople find that ten minutes of planning is well invested and worthwhile.

## Prospect Analysis Sheet

| | |
|---|---|
| **Prospect name** | |
| | |
| Does prospect make purchase decision? (If not, who does?) | |
| Who else is involved in the decision? | |
| Past purchase history | |
| Known brand preferences | |
| **Suspected priorities** | |
| Any budget constraints? | |
| Any time constraints? | |
| Other constraints of relevance? | |
| **What is their most important challenge or goal right now?** | |

**Figure 14-2:**
Prospect
Analysis
Sheet.

Next, you need to preplan some questions for the prospect. Doing so takes another five minutes. Again, you may be tempted to skip this step, but the sales call will go much better if you prepare. To preplan your questions, review your Prospect Analysis Sheet and simply generate confirming or exploring questions.

## Asking confirming questions

A *confirming question* is one that checks facts or checks your understanding or interpretation of the situation. You're wise to use confirming questions to check your assumptions and to update your Prospect Profile. You may be amazed how much of the information you think you know about prospects turns out not to be so!

Here are some examples of confirming questions:

- *I recall that you said you need to make a purchase decision by _____. Is that still the case?*
- *Is it true that Bob wants to stick with black-and-white labels for now?*
- *Are you definitely committed to buying only organic produce?*
- *Is this a good time to go into the details of what you need?*
- *Am I right that your top priority is service, followed by price?*

## Asking exploring questions

*Exploring questions* probe to find out more about your prospect's situation. Use exploring questions to fill in missing facts, seek reasons for preferences or unusual requests, and seek to reveal more about the prospect's preferences and needs. When you ask exploring questions, you often discover something surprising and helpful about the prospect.

Here are examples of typical exploring questions:

- *Why is it so important for your organization to get same-day deliveries?*
- *Are you the one who's in charge of the final purchase decision?*
- *Does the color have to match your office color scheme?*
- *Do you have any other problems that we may be able to help you with?*
- *Why do you do it that way?*
- *Why haven't you updated this equipment in recent years?*
- *What goals do you hope to accomplish this season?*
- *Are you experiencing any service problems or frustrations right now?*
- *Are you looking for ways to cut costs?*
- *Are you looking for better quality?*

Figure 14-3 shows a form you can use to preplan your questions.

Now that you've done all this planning, you're bound to have some good insights and questions as you approach the prospect. Basically, the idea is to use your insights from the need-discovery stage to make your presentation interactive and consultative instead of just forcing your information down the prospect's throat. (CD1402 has a printable version of the question preplanning form.)

---

## Question Preplanning Form

Prospect: _____

| Confirming Questions: | Exploring Questions: |
|---|---|
| 1. | 1. |
| 2. | 2. |
| 3. | 3. |
| 4. | 4. |
| 5. | 5. |
| | |
| | |

Other comments or notes:

---

**Figure 14-3:**
Question
preplanning
form.

# *Making the Presentation*

The next goal of the sales process is to present your offer. Otherwise, you wouldn't have gone to the trouble of finding a prospect and setting up an opportunity for contact. You probably already know what you want to say then. Or do you?

Before you present your products or services to the prospect, ask yourself what you found out about the prospect during the need-discovery process. Then focus on how you can help meet your prospect's needs. The idea is to adapt your presentation to fit the specific needs and wants of each prospect. Be flexible. Emphasize different ideas. Offer different approaches or select different items to present.

When you make your sales presentation (whether verbally or in writing), make sure to recap your understanding of the prospect's situation and needs. As you do, ask whether your understanding is correct. It's important to let the person know that you're trying to appreciate and address his specific needs.

If you've used the sales process and asked enough questions to understand the prospect's position, taking a flexible approach to presenting your offerings should feel natural. All you need to do is translate your extensive knowledge of the product or service into a clear, compelling presentation. You did say you were an expert in the ins and outs of your product, didn't you? If not, you'd better work on it.

Don't forget: *In the end, everything and anything you do or show is part of your presentation.* You need to have impeccable manners, clean and attractive clothing, a nice smile, and a firm handshake. You also need to have good, attractive reference materials about the product at your fingertips. The chapters on writing and designing good marketing materials come to bear here in the presentation phase of the sales process. Sometimes (like when you send a sales letter) you or another salesperson won't be in front of the prospect, so all the work presenting your offering and asking for business is left up to your marketing materials. Please make sure that you present yourself and your marketing materials in a highly effective manner.

# Asking for the Business

You contacted the prospect, explored her needs, and presented your offerings as the most natural and appropriate solution. You think she likes you and your product or service, and you believe the timing is right. Now what?

You have to ask her to do business with you. You have to try closing the sale. Sure, some customers may volunteer their orders and make the sale easy for you. In retail stores, especially, you can easily fall into a passive role and wait for people to step up with a desired purchase. But this technique is always a mistake. You need to manage the close, whether subtly or overtly. And in my mind, nothing's as challenging and interesting in sales as the close. (That's why I cover closing in more detail in Chapter 15.)

Think about what you'll say to ask for the business. The best salespeople know the art of closing by finding a polite way to ask the prospect for the sale. Here are a few ways to ask for the business (see Chapter 15 for more options):

- *If I have answered all your questions, may I put together an agreement?*

- *Based on everything we've discussed, are you ready to go forward in our partnership?*

- *I'll call you in the morning between 9:00 a.m. and 9:15 a.m. to answer any remaining questions that you may think about tonight, and then I'll send over an agreement so we can go forward. Does that time work for you?*

In the right context, an assertive effort to close can get the prospect past the natural indecisiveness many people feel before making a purchase. Practice closes and make a note of any that seem to work well for you and your customers.

If your assertive efforts to close the sale are a failure, don't give up on the prospect. Ask yourself whether the timing may have been wrong. People buy some things quite often, but buy many other things infrequently. People buy food every day, toothpaste every month, new laptops every year or two, and new cars every few years. Businesses also buy big-ticket items infrequently. If you're trying to get someone to switch to a new brand or service, and they only buy every now and then to start with, it may be a long time until they're truly ready to make a switch. Don't throw the contact information away. Set it aside and try again later.

# On the CD

Check out the following items on the CD-ROM:

- Prospect Analysis Sheet (CD1401)
- Question Preplanning Form (CD1402)

# Chapter 15

# Closing the Sale

**Y**ou have your foot in the door. The prospect agreed to meet with you. You presented your products or services. You answered their questions. The prospect seems interested, and you think you have something he needs. Now what? How do you turn that interest into immediate action? Can you actually secure an order before you leave?

To find out, you have to ask for the business by trying to close the deal. In fact, in many cases, you may have to try to close it more than once. Some salespeople say you can't accept a "No" until you've tried to close the deal at least three times. Others say you never accept a "No" when you sense an opportunity for a "Yes." I think the truth lies somewhere in between. I also think that if you make a careful study of closing techniques, you'll have to accept far fewer rejections because *how* you ask for the business often determines whether you get the business and how much business you get. In this chapter, I discuss some strategies for closing the deal.

## Relying on Practice, Not Talent, to Close the Sale

I want to address what I consider to be the biggest myth in marketing, which is the belief that top-performing salespeople are born, not made. Because people assume that peak sales results are reserved for the naturally talented, marketers excuse themselves when they don't close a sale, and they also hesitate to go out and pound the proverbial pavement.

The truth (according to numerous studies of sales force recruiting and performance) is that training and motivation are more important than talent. For example, here is a quote from a research paper published in the *Journal of Marketing:* "Whom one recruits is not as important as what one does with the recruits after they have been hired." (*Journal of Marketing*, Jan. 1989, p. 16). Big companies get good results when they train and support their sales forces. If you train and support yourself, you, too, can be a high-performing salesperson. And learning and practicing closing techniques is, in my opinion, the most important thing you can do to boost your sales performance.

# Realizing That Closes Aren't Only for Salespeople

Few people realize that the challenges of personal selling and marketing are very much the same. Marketing simply sells from a distance. Its ultimate goal is to make the sale, just as in personal selling, so every marketing program needs to have some good closes built into it, whether salespeople deliver them or not.

Sometimes, at the point of purchase, your marketing program "asks for the business" by presenting a tempting product with a price tag, warranty information, usage instructions, shipping options, or other indications that you expect the prospect to purchase it. And sometimes, the marketing materials themselves must incorporate the close. Many calls, letters, faxes, and e-mails to prospects are simply long-distance sales calls. And less personal forms of marketing communication, such as a direct-mail piece or catalog, also need to incorporate multiple efforts to close the deal.

Because every marketing program needs to include multiple efforts to close, you can often improve the effectiveness of marketing materials by using classic sales closing techniques in the materials rather than in a personal presentation. For example, in a direct-mail letter or mailed catalog, you can incorporate a number of trial closes that say something like

*You'll find that our order form is detachable in case you want to check off possible purchases on it as you read the catalog.*

*If you're serious about solving your problems, you'll no doubt be making regular use of our service, which means you'll want to have our contact information handy. So why not get a head start by popping out the perforated Rolodex card on the bottom of this page and filing it under "O" for our name right now?*

REMEMBER

By presenting hypothetical situations relating to future use of your product or service, such *trial closes* help move the reader toward a real close and a big fat order for your business. You can incorporate trial closes into any and all marketing materials with a little imagination and some basic knowledge of the salesperson's catalog of closing techniques. (See the next section for more information.)

# Mastering Closing Techniques

I've collected a variety of closing techniques from super salespeople who I've met and interviewed over the years and from the sales training programs of a variety of companies. Based on these various sources and the sales trainings that my firm teaches in its workshops, I've compiled a master list of superior closes that you can try out in your own sales and marketing efforts. In this section, I discuss each of the items on this list.

## The direct close

The *direct close* simply involves asking prospects to place an order or to sign a contract now. You generally want to ask for the business in a specific manner by saying what you'd like them to do, how much you'd like them to buy, or when you'd like them to start accepting deliveries. The direct close is the most basic technique, so you may as well start with it. If you're lucky, it works, and you don't have to try anything harder.

The idea behind the direct close is to propose a business relationship and see what the prospect says. He may just say, "Fine, let's get started. Can you draw up a contract?" or "Do you need a purchase order from me?"

More often, he begins to negotiate the specifics of doing business, which is also a positive result because it means you're probably going to close the deal after a little haggling. For example, the prospect may say, "Not so fast. I'd like to hire you, but we'll need to find a way to do this project for less money than what you suggested, and I need to have some guarantees of performance." Great! The direct-close approach has opened the door to a serious business discussion. If you negotiate in good faith, you should be able to walk away with a deal.

When you're selling products, the direct close should generally include the suggestion that the prospect purchases whatever amount of product is usual or appropriate. You can't expect a store buyer to commit to six months' inventory of your product. Asking her to put in a two-week supply may be just about right, if that's conventional in the category or industry in question.

If you're designing a brochure, catalog, or ad, make sure that you incorporate direct-close requests. For example, include an order form or a message such as, "To place your order, call. . . ." On your Web site, ask for business by including a "Proceed to Checkout" prompt or having a section or tab labeled "To Place an Order" or "To Request a Quote."

Here are some examples of direct-close scripts:

✔ *Shall I write up an order for XYZ product now?*

✔ *Would an order for x amount be appropriate right now?*

✔ *It sounds like it might make sense for us to try working together. Would you be willing to sign a contract for — let's say x units — if I get one prepared for you and fax it over later today?*

✔ *I sent you a detailed proposal for the consulting work we discussed. Did you receive it? Okay, good. I'm calling to see whether you have any questions about it and if you want to move ahead with the project.*

✔ *Based on what you've told me, it sounds like you really could use the XYZ product right now. I can start processing your order tomorrow, if you want to give me a purchase order number for it before I go.*

Sometimes the direct-close technique just doesn't work. The prospect ducks the question, refusing to give you an immediate yes or no. Often, people avoid responding to a direct close by raising questions or objections that require your detailed response. Respond to their questions fully. Don't be put off by their unwillingness to close a deal. They aren't going to say yes until they're ready. Customers don't care if you're ready. Bide your time, keep the conversation going, if possible, and try another type of close in a few minutes or the next time they give you a chance to talk to them.

## The trial close

The *trial close* is a good technique to use casually throughout a sales presentation or discussion as a way of seeing how ready to buy the prospect is. It does *not* directly ask for business, but it does test the waters by asking the prospect hypothetical questions.

To come up with appropriate hypothetical questions, ask yourself what the prospect would know or do if he were really going to order from you. Then ask him questions about those topics. If the prospect's answers are specific and thoughtful, the prospect is thinking the same way you are and may be ready for you to escalate to a real close by using the direct-close technique (discussed in the previous section).

For example, imagine you're selling leases on office equipment, and you've just given an impressive presentation of a new copier that includes some desktop-publishing features. To test the waters with a trial close, you may ask hypothetical questions such as, "If you lease this machine, would you get rid of one or more of your older machines?" or "Do you think this machine would permit you to do some things in-house that you currently have to pay to have done by graphic artists or printers?"

If the prospect answers these questions with ease, you know that she's thinking in a detailed manner about what leasing your equipment would be like. Your trial close tells you the time is right to work toward a real closing effort. You may go on to say something like, "Well, it sounds like you've thought this through pretty carefully already. Are you ready to sign a contract right now?"

Here are some sample trial close scripts:

- ✔ *If you start carrying our brand, will you drop another brand to make room for it?*

- ✔ *If you decide to use our delivery service, what sort of volume would we need to be able to handle for you on a weekly basis?*

- ✔ *If you decide to switch to us, when do you think would be a good time to make the transition?*

- ✔ *Do you have a date in mind for when this consulting project would start?*

- ✔ *Do you have a specific project in mind so we can develop a proposal for you?*

- ✔ *How much have you budgeted for this purchase, and what kind of payment schedule are you thinking of?*

You can also use trial closes in sales letters, Web sites, brochures, or other arms-length marketing communications. Incorporate questions such as, "Are you in need of specific supplies right now?" When prospects read these questions, some may be spurred to action. And a Shopping Cart area in which Web site visitors can inventory a list of possible purchases is also a great way to offer hypothetical purchase options.

Your attempt at a trial close may not generate the response you hoped for. If that happens, no harm's been done. The prospect who answers a trial-close question with an "I don't know" or "I haven't really had time to think about it" isn't ready for a close yet. Go back to probing for insights into his needs and wants and to communicating information about your offerings. Then try another trial close later on. Sometimes you have to try three or four times before you get a positive response. Using trial closes often is okay, as long as you read the body language and verbal responses of your prospect and avoid irritating him.

# The wrap-up close

The *wrap-up close,* also called the *summary close* or the *scripted close* by some salespeople, signals to the prospect that the time has come to make a decision. This technique works especially well if you've given some kind of presentation or reviewed information about your offering and their needs and wants.

You perform the wrap-up close by summarizing the main points of the meeting or presentation. Try to recap not only the main points you made, but also the points that the prospect made. In many cases, you can ask the prospect to clarify any information you didn't understand or to ask you any final questions. When you sense that the wrap-up is close to completion, you can naturally move on to the question of whether and how much the prospect wants to buy. Your closing technique at the end of the wrap-up should generally involve a direct close.

Here are some sample wrap-up close scripts:

 ✔ *If I may just take a minute to summarize the main concerns I think you've raised, . . . .*

 ✔ *To wrap up my presentation, I'd like to reiterate our commitment to meeting or exceeding all your specifications. Specifically, we can . . . and . . . and. . . .*

 ✔ *I appreciate all the time you've made for me today, but I'm sure you have other appointments, too. Would this be a good time to wrap up our discussion and see where we stand?*

 ✔ *I think I'm beginning to get a clear picture of what you're looking for. As I understand it, you need. . . . Does that sound about right?*

In a wrap-up close, use language signaling that you've reached a natural ending point and that you're ready to move on to the next stage. Also, use body language to signal that you're attempting to wrap up the proceedings. For example, if you're sitting, sit up straight, put your hands on your knees, and look the prospect in the eye. These body movements traditionally signal an intention to depart, so they help set the stage for a wrap-up.

If you're standing during the presentation, move away from the podium or screen (if there is one), and toward the prospects. Face the decision-maker (the prospect with the most seniority or power) directly as you deliver your wrap-up close. Then pause and let him have an opportunity to reply with a question or with a decision to order.

If you're communicating in a brochure or letter, use a heading, such as "In Conclusion" or "Now It's Your Turn," to signal the start of a wrap-up close. On a Web site, use a summary of the order or a check-the-numbers form that allows the prospect to see what an order would cost — with an option of converting the data into a real order.

## The process close

If you use a *process close,* also called an *action close,* a *contract close,* or an *order-form close,* you simply start a closing process and see how far into it the prospect will go. I recommend this technique when it seems reasonably certain that the prospect intends to order. For example, the process close usually works when writing a reorder. The process close is also appropriate when a new prospect asks for an appointment or otherwise indicates interest in making a purchase.

To make a process close work, you need to have a multistep purchase process in which the prospect is likely to go along with the first few steps. For example, you may start prospects off by completing a spec sheet with them. Or you may enter them into your database of national accounts so that they qualify for a discount. After you get them to take an initial step, move on to the next step of the close. That step may be to write down detailed information about their order or project and then read it back to them as if you were checking a formal order.

Here are some sample process close scripts:

- ✔ *Okay, let's get started on this order form. Do you use the same billing and shipping addresses?*

- ✔ *To qualify for credit terms, we need to make sure that your company is in our customer database. Can I go through what we've got in the computer right now and make sure that it's complete?*

- ✔ *Assuming you do end up making this purchase, we'll need to have a completed order form. I can get that process started now. What kind of quantities are you thinking about?*

- ✔ *The next step is usually for us to prepare a detailed proposal. To do that, I need to clarify a few points. Can we go over those now so I can send you a proposal in the next day or two?*

In some businesses, the deal closes when money changes hands. In others, the deal closes when prospects sign a contract or initial an order form. Whatever that last step is for you, your process close should move you and the buyer inexorably nearer to it. And the nearer you get, the more committed the buyer must be to stick with your process. The process usually ends with a direct request to "sign the order form," "provide your credit-card number," or otherwise complete the process and formalize the sale.

In addition to securing business quite quickly, the process close also weeds out prospects who are just shopping around and aren't ready to close the deal. These prospects will get more and more resistant and uncomfortable as you try to move them through the process. They may bail out by saying something like, "I'm just not ready to sign anything right now" or "I don't think we need to go into all this right now." If they don't appear ready to close, keep them alive as prospects, continue trying to find out more about their needs and wants, tell them more about your offerings, and then try a different close next time.

## The analytical close

The *analytical close* is a guided decision-making process in which you help the prospect compare options and weigh alternatives. You can frame the analysis however you think best fits the situation. Sometimes the key question in the prospect's mind is whether or not to buy. Other times, the question is which of the competing alternatives should the prospect try. More rarely, the prospect may be wrestling over which of your offerings to purchase or how much to buy. The analytical close helps the prospect think through his decision, because until he assesses the decision from all angles, he won't be ready to close.

*Consultative selling* is a popular buzz-word, and it is, in fact, a useful technique — but only when the purchase process is difficult. The essence of consultative selling is to ask lots of questions that allow you to develop a specific understanding of the prospect's unique or individual needs and then propose a customized solution. If the prospect faces complex and/or technical decisions (as is the case for someone purchasing a home remodel or a business information system), then consultative selling is helpful. The analytical close is a consultative selling technique. Whenever you think the prospect seems unclear or confused about what to buy, switch to a consultative approach and help them analyze their options.

The analytical close works well for fairly complicated purchase decisions, especially when the prospects are careful, thoughtful, and highly involved in the purchase decision. Use the analytical close when selling an expensive new car to someone who's shopping around to compare models. Use it when someone's deciding what sort of new camera to buy or which insurance policy makes the most sense. Also, use it in many business-to-business sales situations, because when people make purchases on behalf of their businesses, they generally take a fairly analytical approach.

Here are some sample analytical close scripts:

- ✔ *It sounds like you're having a little bit of trouble thinking this decision through in all its complexity. Why don't we analyze your options and see what really makes the most sense?*

- ✔ *We've explored quite a few different issues as we discussed the idea of a possible purchase. In fact, I'm feeling a little confused by all the details. Would you mind if I did a simple pro/con analysis of the decision you're facing right now so that I can see the issues more clearly?*

> ✔ *I gather you're seriously considering several alternatives right now. I'd like to help you analyze each of these alternatives, because it will help me see whether my offering makes sense. And it should help you make a better decision, too. Do you mind if we spend a few minutes thinking each of these options through to see how they'd affect you in the long run?*

### Presenting the pros and cons

Perhaps the easiest way to conduct an analytical close is to help someone think through the options and reach a comfortable decision by presenting the pros and cons of each alternative. You can present verbally or on paper, depending on the physical environment and the prospect's openness to various alternatives.

To present the pros and cons of making a purchase right now, you can divide a sheet of paper or flip chart into two columns (or use the two-column layout option in a PowerPoint slide). Label the left column "Pros" and the right column "Cons." But don't feel like you have to complete the table in that order. You don't want to end your analysis with the cons of the purchase. So start by skipping over the Pros column and asking the prospect to help you identify cons — anything that he may think is negative about the purchase. For example, you may suggest that the purchase will, of course, cost some money. Then go on to the Pros side, listing as many good qualities about the purchase as you can. Frame the qualities in terms of their effect on the buyer. Keep the list personal and specific. You'll find that the Pros column naturally grows considerably longer than the Cons column because you can more easily list benefits of a purchase than negative consequences.

When you finish the analysis, you can ask the prospect how it balances out in his mind. Say something like, "So, what do you think? Do the benefits outweigh the costs in your eyes?" Hopefully, your offer is good enough and is targeted to someone who really would benefit from it so that the analysis clearly favors a decision to purchase. But if not, don't give up. Just keep the lines of communication open and try another close later on.

### Offering multiple scenarios

Another way to approach the analytical close is to offer multiple scenarios and work out in detail how each impacts the prospect. One scenario may be for the prospect to do nothing right now. Another may be for him to purchase from some alternative vendor that the prospect is obviously considering. And, of course, you have to include at least one alternative in which the prospect buys from you. Then you try to engage him as you analyze each of his alternatives. Your goal is to show the prospect what happens over time and how each scenario affects him. Hopefully, the prospect finds the scenario you construct around the purchase of your product or service most appealing, and your analysis helps him make the decision to buy.

## Weeding out the unwilling

In most businesses where I've worked with salespeople, I've found that they spend a lot of their time (15 to 50 percent, depending on the industry) talking with prospects who seem interested but who drag their heels and then don't make a purchase. Shopping is a lot easier than buying, so I'm not surprised that a lot of apparently interested prospects end up dropping out before the purchase stage of the sales process. But they sure do waste your time! What can you do to reclaim some of this wasted time?

Don't be afraid to ask for the business. Try to close as soon as possible. If the prospect balks, work with her a little more and then try again. After a few tries, you'll have a better idea of how serious she is. If she's just shopping around, she'll pull back as soon as you begin talking about closing a deal, and she'll continue backing off when you probe for objections and try to close again. Your testing of her indicates that she just isn't ready to buy right now. You can ask her whether she's ready. If she's not, thank her for her interest, explain that you're ready to talk later if she decides she wants to buy, and then get the heck out of there. A new prospect awaits, so don't waste time on one who won't close.

If walking away from a potential sale sounds counterintuitive to you, think about it this way: While you're trying to convince someone to buy who doesn't really want to, can't afford it, or is just fishing for free information, your competitor is probably with a customer who needs what you have and is ready to buy.

Printed marketing materials also lend themselves to analytical closes. Use tables, charts, diagrams, or statistics to prove the value of your offering.

## *The sales promotion close*

The *sales promotion close* uses an incentive to encourage prospects to take immediate action. The incentive may be a special discount offer that expires soon, an offer to bundle additional products or services into the sale, or any promotion you can dream up, as long as it's likely to interest the prospect and not wipe out your entire profit margin.

Giving new customers a gift is often a great device for securing an immediate close. *Sports Illustrated* has used this technique for many years. It buys large numbers of inexpensive but reasonably nice gifts — a bag with its logo, a portable radio, and so on — and offers to send you a gift for free if you subscribe by a certain deadline.

Gifts can work especially well for business-to-business sales, where the margins are often large enough that you can afford something nice. But remember not to make the gift overly expensive; otherwise, you're entering the realm of bribery. A good rule is that you don't want to offer buyers any gift so lavish that they'd be embarrassed to openly display it in their office or home. And remember that some companies and most government entities restrict employees from accepting any personal gift (to avoid the risk of bribery), so your offer has to be for the benefit of the company, not the individual employee.

If you're uncomfortable with personal gifts when selling to businesses, consider making a modest donation in the individual's name to a charity of his choice. You can call it your "Sales for Society Program" or whatever you like. The prospect may find it quite exciting to select a charity and fill out a donor form. (Have some nice cards made up for this purpose.) This novel inducement feels good, not only because it does some good for society, but also because it helps you accomplish your goal of getting the prospect in the right frame of mind to close the deal now rather than next week.

I used to prefer direct closes because I believe my firm's products and services are good and "speak for themselves." But in the last few years, I've come around to favoring sales promotion closes, and our response rates on mailings, sales calls, and our Web sites have gone up. When my firm sends out a catalog or letter, it often includes a special deal, such as a deep discount or a free sample, if the prospect places an order within the month. And our Web site often features a giveaway, such as a free copy of a book, as an incentive to place an order right away. I like the sales promotion close because it encourages prospects to get serious about their purchase decisions, instead of procrastinating. Many people mean to make a purchase selection but are too busy or lazy to decide right away. A good sales promotion close can get these prospects to take action.

## The relationship-building close

The idea behind this strategy is to focus on building a natural relationship with the prospective buyer and let the closes happen in their own good time. It's sort of the Zen approach to closing: Don't worry about the closing, and it will take care of itself!

To put this strategy into action, take note of the prospect's needs, concerns, and interests. Send the prospect an e-mail with a useful link, give her a referral to someone who can help her, or drop off an informative book or a useful tool. In a low-key way, show her that you've been paying attention and are a helpful resource. This way, she's likely to turn to you (instead of your competitors) when she's ready to make a purchase.

Also, make sure that you keep your promises. If you said you'd send the prospect some information, do it right away; don't keep her waiting. If she asks you to call her later in the week, put it on your calendar and make sure that you do! You may not realize it, but the prospect judges your character from how well you follow through on your commitments. Show that you're reliable, and you may find that the prospect initiates a sales close for you!

# Something Stinks! Passing the Prospect's Smell Test

No matter what you sell, and no matter when, where, or how customers buy your product, you risk losing customers at the last moment unless everything you do seems professional and appropriate. All customers use what I call the *smell test* when they buy — although they often use it quite unconsciously.

When did a person, product, or business last flunk your smell test? Here's a recent example from my own shopping experience: I was all set to hire a company I'd done business with before to do a major upgrading on the heating and air-conditioning systems in a building I'd bought and was planning to move my office into. But when the company sent a junior person to give me a quote and he didn't seem to know enough to answer my questions, I got nervous and delayed the project so that I could get competing quotes from other vendors. In the end, I hired another firm that sent a senior person and prepared a more professional quote.

I bet you can think of plenty of similar experiences. Do you want to buy a product from the grocery store if the package looks dirty or dented? Do you want to do business at a bank where the tellers are sloppily dressed and seem disorganized or confused? Of course not!

At the last moment before purchase, even a small problem can spook your buyers and cause them to hesitate and look for alternatives. So make sure that your presentation is professional — all the way through the close. Don't let any minor problems derail a good sale. Dress well. Spell-check your proposals, e-mails, and letters. Spell the prospect's name and company correctly. (Yes, misspellings are one of the most common errors salespeople make, and they can lose you the sale.) And in personal selling, avoid body odor, colognes or perfumes, and bad breath; it's amazing how sensitive some people are to these smells, so avoid flunking their literal smell tests, too. Professionalism is ten times as important at the close as at any other time during a sale, so give the close ten times as much care and attention.

# Chapter 16

# The Sales Success Workshop

**W**hat are the secrets of superior performance in selling? Several simple things can do a lot to boost your sales effectiveness:

✔ Quality leads

✔ A good impression

✔ A flexible sales strategy

✔ A positive attitude toward success and failure

## Improving the Flow of High-Quality Leads

Most salespeople and marketers are held back by a lack of high-quality leads. If you don't have enough good leads, you're forced to work extra hard to try to close a high percentage of the leads you do have — and that's not a healthy pressure to impose on your sales efforts.

Who is *your* best lead? When you ask yourself this question, you're on the road to figuring out what sort of leads you want most, which in turn should help you generate more of those high-quality leads. When many people ask themselves what kind of leads they want most, the answer usually sounds something like

*I want leads who are actively considering a purchase and who want to talk to me to find out more about my offerings.*

Leads who are ready to explore purchase options and want your information are ideal. It's a matter of getting the timing right. At the right moment in their purchase-and-use cycle, they *want* to hear your information. They may even approach you, instead of your having to go find them. And that's much more efficient and easier for you! So how do you generate these ideal leads?

## Beefing up your marketing program

To generate great leads, make sure that you have an active, multifaceted marketing program working to bring you good leads. Here are some ways to bring in good leads, which you should consider doing if you don't already:

- ✔ **Obtain and publicize a toll-free telephone number with someone polite, friendly, knowledgeable, and always available to answer it.** If the person answering the phone doesn't know the answer, have a system for getting a response back to the customer within 24 hours. More leads come in over toll-free phone lines than from any other source, according to most studies. Lately, Web sites have begun to be as important as telephone leads, but the telephone is always an important source of leads. Don't over look it.

- ✔ **Make your Web site work for you.** For most businesses, the Web is the second-biggest source of leads after the phone. Give your site lots of appeal and rich information for comparison shoppers to use. Make sure that your Web site includes multiple ways to contact you — from e-mail and phone calls to chat-room options and e-commerce purchasing capabilities, if appropriate for your business.

- ✔ **Advertise in magazines and use their reader-service card options (postcards included in many magazines for requesting more information from advertisers).** This technique works particularly well for business-to-business marketers. It's also great for home products and services, which can be advertised in home decorating and remodeling magazines.

- ✔ **Advertise an offer for a free catalog.** You can choose to advertise in print, on the Web, or in postcards or letters sent to mailing lists. If you want to increase the response rate a bit, add a one-time discount or deal that readers can redeem if they order from the catalog. Or just mail out your catalog or a brochure version of it (a smaller catalog of highlights is good for testing new lists inexpensively). To get the timing right, send your catalog at least once a quarter. Last quarter's disinterested consumer may be eager to buy by now!

- ✔ **Offer free, trial-size samples (or the service equivalent) in ads, e-mails, or letters.** Often, people come forward and identify themselves as good leads when you give them a chance to try something for free. Car dealerships utilize this technique by offering test drives — a great way to attract interested leads.

At my corporate training business, we use this technique by sending letters to our past customers, offering them a free copy of our newest publication. Those who take us up on the offer often turn into regular buyers within the next six months.

In many businesses, a toll-free telephone number is the best way to bring in leads. Even in the modern Internet era, more prospects prefer talking to someone by phone than contacting someone in any other way. So make sure that you publicize your phone number widely by including it in and on every communication you send — from ads to bills. And please make sure that you have well-trained, polite people (not machines!) ready to answer those calls. Give them a good form or a computerized database to record information about each caller and train them in how to use it.

I know that most businesses have switched to interactive computer-answering systems, but I believe that these lose some of your leads and that a human being is still the best way to go. I recently called my local Taylor Rental, and even though I hadn't been in the store for a couple of years, the employee who took my call quickly sourced my records using my phone number and was ready to do business without my having to spell my name five times for him. The telephone should be a cornerstone of your sales and marketing program!

## Getting creative when you still need more leads

If you aren't getting enough high-quality leads, the following fixes often help:

- Offer free samples or consultations in exchange for contact information at your industry's regional or national trade shows and on your Web site.

- Put a special offer on your Web site, such as a free month of service or a free special product, for the customer who purchases or makes an appointment with a salesperson within the month.

- Mail, call, or e-mail the people on your customer list from the past three years to ask whether they need anything else and to let them know about all the products you sell. (They may not realize that you can provide additional products and services beyond what they already purchased.)

- Run a direct-response ad in an appropriate magazine or newspaper (see Part II for ad design tips).

- Buy a list of 1,000 names of people who fit the profile of your better customers (for example, people who own homes with gardens in high-income counties or managers of businesses with 50 or more employees). Send an introductory letter inviting them to find out more about your products or services by setting up an appointment, visiting your Web site, or calling for more information. Follow the mailing with a telephone call to see whether you can set up an appointment.

✔ Send out a press release and generate positive publicity about an interesting product or service you offer. Sometimes media coverage produces a flood of leads (see Chapter 10).

Computer programmers invented the saying, "Garbage in, garbage out," but they could have been talking about sales. Make sure that your leads are high quality. If you don't have enough leads to chuck the poor ones and solely focus on eager-to-buy prospects, then work on your lead-generation methods until you do. Everything else in the field of marketing can and should work to support sales by producing a rich flow of leads!

My final tip for lead generation is to set leads aside if the prospect really doesn't seem interested. But don't throw away the lead. Cue it up for next month. Often the timing is off and if you try again later, you'll get a better response.

According to MarketingSherpa (www.marketingsherpa.com), a typical sales lead database can be broken down as

✔ 7 percent: Sales ready; buy within 90 days

✔ 9 percent: Duds; competitors, perpetual tire kickers

✔ 84 percent: Mid to long-range prospects

If you're focused on sales, you'll most likely go after those 7 percent ready to buy now and neglect the 84 percent of longer term prospects. However, the statistics show that 80 percent of them will buy your product or service — either from you or someone else — within 24 months. Don't neglect the bulk of the people on your list who are not actively shopping right now. Continue to contact them by e-mail, mail, phone, or in person and also make sure that they're exposed to any publicity and advertising you're doing. For example, if an article appears about your product or firm, send a photocopy by mail or a PDF by e-mail to your entire list. When you remember to communicate with your entire list, you invest in the next 7 percent of ready-to-buy customers. This cream-of-the-crop group turns over every month, so you have to be forward-looking in order to have active buyers in the future.

# Using Sales Collateral to Help Win 'Em Over

One secret of superior selling performance is to make a good impression. You can impress your customers by using *sales collateral* — an umbrella term that covers anything designed and supplied to help salespeople achieve success. I'm using a broad definition because I want you to turn your marketing imagination loose and see whether you can come up with better sales collateral.

## Sticking with good collateral

Make a dream list of everything you may need throughout the sales process. Good support ensures success! Here are some ideas to get you started:

- **Impressive stationery and fax forms:** Order your company's paper in multiple sizes for advance letters and other correspondence.

- **Matching business cards, preferably with information about the company/product and all the correct contact options:** Consider special paper, unusual designs, or even oversized or fold-out cards. If they're noticeably special and interesting, they'll generate calls.

- **Clear, appealing specification sheets:** Your spec sheets need to describe the facts of each and every product or service accurately so that all your prospects' possible factual questions are answered.

- **Samples, demos, and/or catalogs:** These marketing materials make showing and telling your prospects about your products and services much easier.

- **Cases, stories, testimonials, and other evidence from happy customers:** Only a few percent of salespeople have any collateral of this type. Yet, it's the most powerful form of sales collateral!

- **Attractive, valuable, premium items:** Such premium items include a pen, mug, cap, or box of candies, marked subtly with your company's name and contact information. Prospects appreciate these leave-behinds when they're good quality. These tokens remind prospects that your company exists and that you value their business. Your leave-behinds don't need to be expensive, but prospects should see them as valuable enough to keep.

## Avoiding bad collateral

Don't use collateral that hurts sales. Any materials, such as brochures or product literature, that don't look professional and appealing will hurt sales. The sales collateral is a vital part of the "packaging" of the salesperson. If the sales collateral looks bad, the salesperson and product looks bad, too. The effects of poor collateral on the prospect are subtle and often unconscious, but they're *extremely* powerful. So make sure that everything your salespeople carry and/or distribute is polished and impressive. Sales collateral is a very good place to spend your design and printing budget.

---

# Perception is reality

What's the difference between a nice premium item and a cheap one? A box of truffles in gold foil, stamped with your company name and "We appreciate your business," is nice. A plastic mug stamped with your company logo, filled with hard candies, and wrapped in cellophane and a ribbon is tacky. The items probably cost about the same, but customers perceive them quite differently. It makes sense to match the promotion gift to what you do; if your company fixes computers, offer a mouse pad or laser mouse with your name and emergency number. If you're a dentist, offer a toothbrush with your name and phone number on it. But whatever you choose, make sure that customers think it's valuable, not tacky.

---

In choosing your sales collateral, avoid

- **Plastic:** Cheap plastic folders, clear plastic page protectors, or big, ugly plastic sample cases all say "tacky" and "cheap" to prospects. Use high-quality papers and favor cloth or leather cases and bindings, if at all possible.

- **Amateur designs and layouts:** Sure, anyone can design sales and marketing materials in this era of desktop publishing, but most people shouldn't. Amateurs often create poor-looking, confusing layouts. Their work just doesn't have that special look that characterizes fine design — and the better prospects notice. If you have a talent for designing marketing communications, go ahead and do your own, but plan to give the project the time and care needed to produce excellent materials (see Parts II and III for help with your designs).

- **Errors:** An amazing number of factual and spelling errors exist in sales collateral. Salespeople perpetually have to make corrections or explain errors in front of prospects, which is like saying, "We can't even type a spec sheet accurately, but I'm sure we can muddle through your order somehow." Right.

- **Omissions:** Most salespeople go on calls without all the collateral materials and information they need to do a great job. They don't have a good brochure. Their business cards don't have the current address or the company's fax number and Web site. The price list is out of date. Their order form is a cheap pad bought at the local stationery store. Make sure that you or whoever is doing the selling is well equipped.

# Overcoming Sales Setbacks

Consider this startling statistic: The best way to predict how much a sales-person will sell is to measure her — no, not I.Q., not product knowledge, not connections or experience, but yes — her *level of optimism*. Psychology has shown that how you manage your own attitude really does have a powerful effect on how you sell. It's not a myth; the link between attitude to performance is real and powerful, especially in sales, where the high amount of negative feedback can cause attitudes to easily deteriorate.

Sometimes people refuse your sales pitch. Sometimes they aren't ready, don't like the product, or just aren't in a good mood. In sales and marketing, rejections and failures always exist, and it can be hard to persist. How well do you handle rejection and failure?

A good sales or marketing program is more efficient and suffers fewer wasted calls than a poor program. Although you can improve your success rates and reduce your rejection rates significantly, you can *never* achieve perfection. Marketing is not a precise science. In fact, finding yourself dealing with prospects that always say "yes" is a sign that you need to push your program a bit. Try asking more people or raising your prices. Unless some people say "no," you're not really stretching yourself. So, failures are a natural and important part of healthy sales and marketing.

## The bounce-back factor

How successful you are has a great deal to do with how well you handle failures:

- If you bounce back from each rejection with an optimistic outlook, failure can't hold you back. You keep trying instead of giving up. In fact, you may even try harder.

- If you gain insight from each rejection, you can reduce the failure rate in the future and improve your odds of success over time.

Both points are closely related. Your ability to bounce back — to stay positive and motivated — has everything to do with how you explain each failure to yourself. If you maintain a positive attitude, attributing failures to appropriate, accurate causes that you can exercise some control over, then you will be resilient. Failures won't upset you or slow you down. In fact, they'll give you renewed energy because you discover something from each failure that should help you with the next try. So, listen to how you talk to yourself when you're trying to make a sale or grow a business. Normally, people don't attend carefully to their internal explanations, but to achieve higher-than-average success, you need to begin to manage normally unconscious or automatic self-talk.

To be a successful marketer or salesperson — or to be successful at achieving your goals in general — you need to take credit for success and avoid blaming yourself for failure (Martin Seligman's books on learned optimism explain the extensive research behind this conclusion if you want to learn more.)

### Generalizing success

Attribute successes to aspects of your own personality, talents, and behavior. Giving yourself at least a share of the credit for each success builds the essential positive attitude needed to maintain motivation and build momentum. People who explain away their successes as simply good luck are encouraging a feeling of helplessness.

Generalizing from a success is helpful, too. Avoid narrow, meaningless ways of giving yourself credit. Don't say something demeaning to yourself like, "Oh, I guess I was responsible for closing that sale, but it was only because I happened to know that prospect personally." It's more productive to explain such a success as follows: "I closed that sale easily with an old acquaintance, which proves that I am able to present this product effectively. I should be able to close sales with other people, too." Generalizing from one accomplishment that you have an ability to achieve others is important as you build the attitudes needed to pursue success.

### Getting specific about failure

Attributing failures to factors outside your own personality and abilities is very important. Many people question themselves when they receive a rejection or "no" answer. Instead, you should consider many other external factors that are within your control and are easy to adjust. These factors include the wrong list of prospects, the wrong closing technique, the wrong timing, the wrong way of presenting the product, or even the wrong product. When you look at specific, controllable factors, you can take a philosophical attitude toward failure.

Notice that when you blame specific, controllable factors for your failures, you avoid generalizations. You can easily make sweeping generalizations when you encounter a sales rejection or marketing failure. Big mistake. Big, big mistake. When you allow yourself to generalize about failures, you come to see them as unavoidable. The cards appear to be stacked against you, which discourages you from playing in the future. I've heard many managers and marketers say things like

*We don't advertise. We tried it once or twice, and it just doesn't work for our business.*

*We can't do direct mail. Our products don't have high enough prices to work, given the typical low response rates for mailings.*

*Web sites are fine for communicating information about our business, but it doesn't work to try to close actual sales on the Web. We take a low-key approach to our site. It's really just an online brochure.*

*I can't sell. I'm just no good at it. Believe me, I've tried! That's why I sub all our sales out to independent sales reps.*

I recorded these actual direct quotes from otherwise intelligent, clear-thinking people I know in the business world. Each quote reflects a belief that prevents the speaker from ever trying something again. And each quote is a broad, absolute conclusion based on a very narrow set of unsuccessful experiences. For example, the person who said, "We can't do direct mail," works for a business that can certainly profit from direct mail. I know that several of the company's direct competitors use mailings quite effectively. But the man's defeatist attitude, based on a few early failures, prevents his business from profiting in this arena. And the person who told me that the Web can't sell her services is creating a self-fulfilling prophecy by failing to develop a Web site good enough to support e-commerce.

So you can see that allowing yourself to make broad, pessimistic generalizations from failures is very dangerous. It narrows your view of the future and shortens your strategic horizons. It turns off your marketing imagination and drains you of motivation and self-confidence. How you think about and explain those failures has everything to do with whether you bounce back from them, wiser and more motivated than before, or whether you curl up in a ball and refuse to try again.

## Retrained for success

Only the few people who instinctively take to sales or who have a natural flair for entrepreneurship truly have healthy, positive explanatory styles. That's bad news because my hunch is that you, like me, were not born with the positive attitude toward success and failure that you need to be a sales and marketing high achiever.

Now for the good news: You can easily change your style and adopt more positive approaches to success and failure. When you retrain those old, unhelpful mental habits, you find yourself coping with failures far more productively and positively. And you find that your new, healthier attitudes naturally lead to greater success in sales and marketing, as well as in life in general.

# Top salespeople manage themselves well

If you know someone who's a master marketer or salesperson, I recommend taking him out for a cup of coffee and quizzing him on his approach. Often, you'll be surprised by what he tells you. Allow me to tell you about a certain acquaintance of mine.

John is affiliated with a big life insurance underwriter but is basically an entrepreneur and must take full responsibility for earning his own commission. As you may know, many people try their hand at this work, but only very few manage to turn it into a lucrative and successful career. John is very disciplined about his work and has managed to write an amazing number of insurance policies over the years, including several for my family and me.

Once, when he was visiting my office, I happened to look over his shoulder at his appointment book, and some funny little tick marks at the bottom of each day caught my eye. Obviously, John was keeping count of something on a daily basis. I asked him about the ticks, and he laughed and said, "Oh, those are just my tallies. I use a code so people won't bug me about it, but really, all I do is keep count of the number of prospects I phone each morning and the number of sales calls I actually go on in the course of the day. See, yesterday, for example, I made 12 prospecting calls, and I went on 5 sales visits."

I asked him why he kept those tallies, and he explained that he had found that the easiest way to get more business was simply to go on more sales calls, and the easiest way to do that was to make more phone calls each morning. The more people he called, the more meetings he was able to set up. So, by tracking the number of prospecting calls, he reminded himself of his goal of calling a certain number each

week. And by tracking the number of meetings, he could see the positive results of his efforts.

Then he laughed and explained that he had a story behind his system. Back in his early business days, he and another salesman had been complaining and saying that they wished they could double their income by making twice as many sales. John pointed out that all they needed to do was make twice as many sales calls, but sitting at the phone trying to set up appointments wasn't much fun, which is why they'd usually quit phoning and go out and start selling as soon as they had a few calls lined up. So John challenged his friend: They both agreed to keep an accurate tally of how many prospecting calls they made by phone each day. And they each agreed to pay the other man $500 at the end of the month if he didn't make twice as many calls as usual. John met his friend at the end of the month, and they both opened their books and counted up their phone calls. John had made his quota of calls, but his friend was just a tad under. So, the friend wrote a check for $500 on the spot.

You may think the story ends there, but not so. Even though he was $500 poorer, John's friend said he wanted to try the challenge again next month. Apparently, he had made enough extra calls that his income almost doubled, and the $500 loss was trivial compared to his gain. After several months of making twice as many calls and reaching their goals, the practice became a habit for both men. In fact, they never quit using this technique because they were both so pleased to find that they were bringing in twice as much revenue as before. And although John doesn't need the kicker of a contest any longer to make those calls, he still keeps up with his simple information system. It serves to remind him of his goal, and with it, he always makes his targets.

ON THE CD

So how do you train yourself to ensure that you have the most helpful attitudes toward success and failure? Glad you asked:

- First, you need to develop a profile of your own attitudes by using the Attitudes of Success Profile I include on the CD (file CD1601).

- Second, you simply need to follow the instructions for interpreting your profile. Where your profile deviates from the profile associated with the highest levels of success in sales and marketing, you find pointers to simple, easy exercises and tips to help you shift your attitudes.

# Taking a Flexible Approach

In Chapter 1, I talk about finding your *marketing zone,* defined as the set of formulas that work well for your business. There is, of course, a *sales zone,* too — it's the specific approach to selecting leads and making sales pitches that produces a profitable result and helps your business grow. If you're frustrated by sales and find it difficult, then you're not yet in your sales zone and need to keep experimenting. Try new approaches. Question all your assumptions. Anyone who is not getting complete sales success needs to try new approaches.

One way to be flexible in your sales strategy is to experiment with different closes until you find one or two that seem to work reliably for most of your customers. Chapter 15 offers a selection of closes you can experiment with.

Another way to be flexible is to use a consultative approach. Instead of telling prospects about your product or service, ask them about their needs. Once you have asked several questions, then you can begin to offer information. The consultative approach is solution-oriented, meaning that you don't tell them what you have to sell; you tell them how you can solve their problem or meet their objectives.

A third way to be flexible is to learn from failure. I recommend taking the time at least once a week to go over each lost sale and look for patterns. Some prospects just weren't right for a sale, so don't worry about those. However, if you think you lost potential sales, examine these failures closely. Ask yourself what you could have done differently. Then try a different approach next time you encounter a similar situation.

In general, salespeople (and, in fact, all marketers) do best when they're open to new ideas and willing to adjust their approach flexibly.

# Adjusting Your Interpersonal Style

You can't eliminate the occasional crazy customers determined to make not only their own lives miserable, but also yours as well. These few worst cases should be cut from your customer list as soon as possible. But, with the right treatment on your part, the remaining 90 percent of so-called difficult customers can become some of your best and most loyal customers. Usually, the hard-to-deal-with customers are simply people whose interpersonal style is different from yours. When you adjust your style so that they feel more comfortable with you, these hard-to-handle customers often become your best.

What makes customers difficult? Sometimes a critical incident upsets or angers a customer or prospect, and you need to deal with that incident carefully and completely. Most problems, however, arise because of communication issues. So, the best overall strategy for dealing with difficult customers is to focus on how to better communicate with them. In this section, I show you how to figure out which communication style works better than the one you're currently using.

Good salespeople know that they do best when they communicate in the style the customer prefers. They adapt their communication techniques because different customers have different interpersonal styles. *Flexing your style* means changing to the most comfortable style for the other person or, in other words, doing it their way.

## Accommodating the introverted customer

In order to flex your style, you must make small changes in your behavior. The sorts of changes you need to make depend on the style differences between you and your customer. If you're dealing with a very private, introverted person and you have an extroverted, social style, she may be put off by your more outgoing style. To make her feel comfortable, you need to

- ✓ Cut back your sales presentation so as to talk much less than you usually do.

- ✓ Give your customer plenty of personal space; don't crowd her!

- ✓ Don't ask too many personal questions.

- ✓ Speak quietly.

- ✓ Ask for her permission to talk with her about her purchase decision instead of assuming that she wants to talk about it.

✔ Schedule meetings and telephone conversations at her convenience, giving her control over when she talks with you.

✔ Use arm's-length channels of communication. Write her notes and send e-mails and faxes. Prepare a written report to present your suggested solution to her problem rather than presenting it in person.

If you know that a particular customer values her privacy, you can make sure that she's comfortable around you by adjusting to her needs. Give her more personal space, be careful not to overstay your welcome, and make a point of listening more and leaving gaps in the conversation to let her think about what you've said.

Many salespeople and marketers are social by nature and tend to use an extroverted style, which puts off introverted customers. By flexing your own style, you — the public, extroverted salesperson — cool down your style significantly. The personal, introverted customer will feel more comfortable and at ease in future interactions. The customer is less likely to form a negative opinion of you and, in fact, probably will grow to like you. You seem more respectful and polite, and you appear to be a better listener who's more interested in and aware of her preferences and feelings.

## Accommodating the logical customer

Some marketers are very creative. I am, myself. When I talk to a client about a marketing plan, a new brochure design, or any other project, I tend to get excited and offer lots of creative ideas. This approach confuses some people. A logical person likes to hear one clear plan, with a series of well-defined steps. I do best with logical customers when I do my creative thinking on my own time and then present them with three choices and keep my mouth shut while they decide which they like best. To help them decide, I may also prepare a table listing the pros and cons of each of their options. If I get more ideas in the meeting, I write them down and think about them later, on my own time. I know I have to curb my enthusiasm for creativity when presenting a proposal to a logical customer, so as not to confuse and upset them.

If you tend to be creative, you may also need to be careful to package your ideas and work into clear, logical presentations and sequential plans. Your customer may be a logical person. Clues to a logical, sequential temperament include

✔ Neat desk

✔ Punctuality

✔ Tendency to stay on one topic during conversation

✔ Use of datebooks, file cabinets, and other organizing tools

If you're a piler rather than a filer or a multitasker (meaning you tend to skip from topic to topic as you make creative associations), then your natural style is going to drive logical, organized customers nuts. Remember to flex to their style when interacting with them. Organize in advance, stick to the agenda, and avoid appearing disorganized.

## Accommodating the creative, free-wheeling customer

Sometimes the sales or marketing person is the organized, logical one, and the customer is more free and easy. When your customer is less organized than you, seems forgetful, and changes his mind about what he wants at the last minute, you may find yourself uncomfortable with the lack of structure. If so, you need to recognize that your customer's style is more free-wheeling than yours, and that your need for structure may not suit your customer. If you have a customer who doesn't like to be structured, back off. Let the customer change the topic or jump from one possible purchase to another. Have faith that in his own creative way, this customer will still manage to make a purchase decision, even if it's not the one he said he was considering when you first talked about it.

However, sometimes when dealing with very disorganized customers or clients, you do have to provide the structure. If they keep switching from one idea to another but never actually finalize a purchase, you may need to try a wrap-up close, in which you summarize what you think their needs are and suggest a solution. If they reject this effort to narrow them down to one solution, try giving them a choice of three options. Free-wheeling customers like to have options, so it may be easier for them if you give them three ways to close the sale and let them choose which one they like. Oh, but a word of warning! Your free-wheeling, creative customer may choose none of the options. Be prepared to respond to their desire to customize a solution that is a combination of two or three of the options you presented to them.

## On the CD

Check out the following item included on the CD-ROM:

- ✔ Attitudes of Success Profile (CD1601)

# Part VI
# The Part of Tens

The 5th Wave      By Rich Tennant

## In this part . . .

I give you more than 30 quick tips and suggestions for boosting your sales and making your marketing more effective and profitable. This part offers ideas that can save you money, maximize your marketing impact, boost results from your Web site, and stimulate new and creative ways of landing new business. And if these ideas aren't enough, feel free to steal as many more ideas as you want from the Web site that supports this book, `www.insightsformarketing.com`. I'll keep updating this site with more ways for you to make your marketing pay off in profitable sales growth!

# Chapter 17

# Ten Great Marketing Strategies

............................................................................

*In This Chapter*

▶ Boosting your visibility and appeal

▶ Considering an assortment of interesting tips and ideas

▶ Strengthening your relationships with good customers

............................................................................

*I*n this chapter, I summarize a range of strategies that have worked to boost sales and build businesses for other marketers. See whether one of them is a good fit for your marketing program right now.

## Go for Market Share Now — and Worry About Raising Profits Next Year

It is a well-established fact that the businesses with the most market share do best — they make more profits and have an easier time growing their sales, too. That's why Dell slashed prices as it introduced significantly improved servers and computers in 2008, at a time when its market share had been eaten into by Hewlett-Packard and other competitors. Dell's marketing strategy was to increase share now, so as to ensure better profits later.

Ask yourself whether you're already the clear leader in your market, whether that market is local or a narrow niche compared to Dell's global arena. Either way, the relationship between market share and profits is likely to apply. If you aren't the clear leader, can you grow your market share significantly while operating at least at break-even? If so, it may be worth sucking up the losses for a year or two in order to reposition yourself for longer term profitability and market dominance. But be careful to protect your pricing while growing your share. Don't slash your prices. Instead, invest in marketing that burnishes your image, reaches out to new customers, and strengthens your sales process.

## Sponsor a Community Event

PeoplesBank is a New England regional bank that's making a push to open branches in new communities. In my town, the folks at PeoplesBank are promoting their new branch by sponsoring a summer art festival run by the local Chamber of Commerce. The festival, which takes place twice a month from June through September, showcases 30 to 40 artists in outdoor tents scattered up and down the main street of town. The tents are attractive, high-roofed blue structures, and the name PeoplesBank and its logo are emblazoned on one side of each tent.

Suffice it to say that PeoplesBank is the single-most visible brand name in the entire town when the show is going on. And because the show draws visitors from throughout the bank's regional market, PeoplesBank gets a lot of bang for its marketing buck. But please take time to find the right event, not just any old event. You want to sponsor an event that is good for your image and that attracts large numbers of your prospective customers.

## Find the Right Trade Show

Molly Cantor is a successful potter who runs her own studio where she produces an assortment of attractive handmade mugs, plates, bowls, teapots, and so on. Unlike many small-scale studios, Molly's studio distributes products all over the United States. Stores in many states buy her work, and she's usually booked with orders as much as one year in advance.

How does Molly manage to be so effectively "on the map" as a supplier to upscale gift stores? She simply attends one trade show each year where she rents a booth, shows her work, and collects orders. The show attracts buyers from gift stores and galleries far and wide, and they place their orders at the show and then reorder by phone during the year if the products sell well.

Picking the right trade show — and focusing all your resources on getting there and presenting you and your products well — is often the best way to build a wholesale business. If you aren't already familiar with the trade show, attend it as an individual guest the first time around and make sure it is attracting lots of your prospective customers. Also, check out the marketing support the trade show gives its exhibitors. Some shows are great about support, sending lots of promotional materials prior to the show. Others are more oriented toward a conference or other associated event and don't seem to be as focused on helping you market your wares. Favor the shows that really "get it" and are on the same marketing page you are.

# Update the Benefits You Emphasize in Your Marketing Communications

Customer needs change. What are your customers' biggest priorities today?

A simple example is provided by automobiles. When the price of gas spikes, mileage rises to the top of the list of priorities. When gas is cheap and the economy is booming, fashion and status are dominant. But when customers have babies, safety and carrying capacity may come to the fore. Seasonally, priorities can change, too. A cold winter with lots of snow pushes handling and winter road performance to the top of the list, along with remote starting and the quality of the heating and defrosting systems.

You get the idea: Customer priorities aren't stable. If you keep your ear to the ground and adjust your marketing message accordingly, you'll be more in step with current concerns and priorities than most marketers are.

# Reward Large Purchasers

One Christmas shopping season, retailer Toys "R" Us gave away a free Tickle Me Elmo doll to any customer who made a purchase of more than $100, which is significantly more than the average purchase at the store. This promotion inspired me to begin offering free products to customers of my firm's Web site when they placed an order above a certain size — a strategy that we still use today because it's so effective in boosting the number and size of our orders.

Too often marketers offer deals that aren't linked to the size of purchase. Thus, businesses tend to reward many small customers. But in most businesses, the fewer, big customers are the most valuable. Why not target your promotions to them? Here's one way to go about it:

1. **Calculate your average purchase size.**

2. **Multiply it by 1.5.**

3. **Offer an incentive (discount, free product, special gift, reward, or extra service) to anyone who buys more than that amount.**

   The incentive can also be a 10 to 15 percent discount on a future purchase.

# Tell Your Customers How You're Saving Energy and Materials

A so-called *green marketing strategy* is simply an effort to reduce waste by using recycled materials, reducing energy usage, and doing other things that benefit both your bottom line and the environment. Most businesses are doing some of these things already, but fail to tell their customers about their green initiatives. I recommend telling them more, and using the simple and non-intimidating term Green Initiatives to describe these activities.

Put a bulleted list of your green endeavors in your catalog or Web site and on your packaging or envelopes. If you have even three items for the list, go ahead and post it. Over time, you'll probably get good feedback and start adding more initiatives.

# Allow Customers to Access You Easily

At Motorola, key customers receive telephone numbers that link them to top executives at any hour of the day. The idea is to make sure that customers can get in touch immediately, whenever they feel the urge. No leaving phone messages. No busy signals or voice mail. No waiting — ever!

Inspired by this example, I started giving my personal cellphone number to my best customers. They don't use it very often, but when they do, it's because they have an important question. And I'm always glad I'm available to take their calls.

# Introduce Products or Services at a High Price and Then Cut Price with Volume

This strategy is a favorite at high-tech companies. Toshiba's HD DVD players were very costly when they first appeared on the market, but at date of publication, the company had just announced a new strategy to price their line starting at $149.99.

Often when you introduce something new, you're unsure of how big the market will be or of what the ultimate price should be. You may not even be sure yet of your own costs. It is therefore a safer bet to introduce a new product at a fairly high price, see what happens, and then adjust downward as needed. If you find you've got a bestseller (as Apple did when it introduced the iPhone), you can cut price aggressively. If not, your margin is protected at lower volume by the high introductory price.

# Let Prospects Test You Out

Do you think that your product is superior? Let prospects find out by offering them a free trial. Apple used this technique successfully with its "test drive a Macintosh" promotion, and it's a traditional practice among high-end rug dealers. They know that if prospects put a beautiful Oriental rug in their living room for just a few days, the odds of their buying it increase dramatically.

# Get Everyone Talking about You

With a little creativity, any business or salesperson can take advantage of the outrageousness strategy. One children's bookstore called Wild Rumpus (Minneapolis, Minnesota) lets roosters and cats roam freely through the aisles. Birds, lizards, and tarantulas peer out of cages, and a family of rats lives beneath a glass floor. A special children's entrance features a 4-foot-high purple doorway. Anyone who visits this store tells everyone else to go there, too.

In another example, a building-materials distributor made sales visits with his favorite prop — a cinder block sitting on an elaborate velvet cushion. He entered the prospect's office bearing his cinder block like the crown jewels of England. Placing the jewel gingerly on the desk, he'd launch into his sales pitch before the prospect had fully recovered from amazement.

# Introduce a New Attraction Every Three Months

I got this idea from the Georgia Aquarium in Atlanta, which is why I use the term "attraction." You're not going to display a new shark tank or other such attraction, of course, but you can and should have some new service, product, event, or story to create interest and build traffic, too.

The Atlanta Aquarium adopted its new-attraction strategy in the face of a decline in attendance during 2008 (when many tourist attractions felt the pinch of the spike in travel costs). The aquarium's plan to introduce a new attraction every 90 days is based on some solid thinking about how hard it is to come up with new news — I doubt they, or you, could do it every month!

Also, the Atlanta Aquarium recognized that it takes a couple months to wage a good PR and marketing campaign, even in a local market. So 90 days is about the minimum for this strategy. However, news ages fast, so if you keep the attraction much more than 90 days, the media and public will no longer think the attraction is a novelty. The 90-day cycle maximizes the chances of getting good editorial coverage, which, of course, is free marketing. I like free marketing. How about you? (See Chapter 10 for details of how to publicize your new attraction.)

# Chapter 18

# Ten Ways to Make Marketing Pay

· · · · · · · · · · · · · · · · · · · · · · · · · · · · · · · · · · · · · · · · · ·

*In This Chapter*

▶ Cutting your marketing costs

▶ Attracting more customers

· · · · · · · · · · · · · · · · · · · · · · · · · · · · · · · · · · · · · · · · · · ·

Marketing needs to be bottom-line oriented. It's not a black hole that you toss money into after you pay for the payroll and healthcare; it's a vital part of a growing, successful business, and you must approach it professionally at all times. This chapter offers tips to help you make marketing a productive and financially sound part of your business.

## Print It Yourself

Traditionally, marketers have been heavy users of printing and copying services, and the printing bills tend to get out of control in a hurry. Today you can purchase color laser printers that handle tabloid sheets of paper (up to 11 x 17 inches) and even print long banners.

For example, my office uses an Oki C9300 to crank out color catalog pages, covers for pamphlets and booklets, color fliers and product sheets, color covers for binders, and many other marketing materials. The cost per sheet ranges between 1 and 10¢, depending on the size and amount of color. With this printer, my company can produce a high-quality color catalog and mail it to 1,000 people without using any printing services. The savings is substantial — we estimated that we paid back the printer's $2,500 purchase cost in the first month!

If you do short runs of marketing materials, consider printing them yourself. But remember that quality matters and make sure that you use appealing, professional graphic design and a good quality paper. A little extra care in the design of your piece doesn't add costs but does increase effectiveness.

# Do More PR

If anything you do or say might be newsworthy, make sure that you tell the media about it early and often. You need to send a press release at least every season, if not every month. Publicity is free advertising, and it ought to be a bigger part of your marketing than it probably is.

# Use More Distributors

I haven't seen any business that can't sell through other businesses in one way or another. Creatively using distributors (call them sales partners, if you like) is a great way to expand your marketing footprint on someone else's nickel.

For example, in my business, someone has the responsibility of seeking and courting distributors, and the goal is to try to add a new one each month. Our sales through distributors have grown from zero a few years ago to about 20 percent of our total sales now. That's a lot of business we wouldn't have found on our own.

# Give More Product Away

It's a paradox: The more you give away, the more you make, and the more economical your marketing program is. This paradox is true because, in general, the best advertisement for a product is the product itself (and I'm using the word "product" broadly here, to include services or whatever it is you may want to sell).

So please, find more ways to give prospects an opportunity to sample your wares or experience your service. Doing so cuts out a lot of expensive marketing by giving your prospects the real thing instead of having to spend your time and money trying to tell them about it. Some of the best consulting jobs I've ever done in marketing involved simply figuring out how to get the client's free samples, test drives, or other giveaways to good prospects so that the product could sell itself. Nothing is more powerful in all of marketing.

# Edit

As a writer and a marketer, I often notice that marketing materials, Web sites, and so on are out of control. Sometimes my company helps a client save money and produce better results by simply cutting down and cleaning up all its written materials.

I guarantee that you can punch up the impact and cut costs if you edit all your materials with the goal of cutting the total number of marketing pages in half. Give it a try.

# Eat Out More

In many businesses, there is the formal marketing program, and then there is the real program — where the good customers actually come from. More often than not, customers really come from word of mouth — from the personal contacts and networks of key people in the business.

If this generalization is true for your business, then consider cutting the formal marketing stuff (ads, catalogs, and so on) back by 15 percent and putting that money into networking instead. Go to more events and conferences. Take more customers and industry experts out for lunch. If your personal contacts can produce good leads, then you ought to be eating out every day. Become the best entertainer in your industry!

# Slash Unproductive Programs

Every business has a few marketing activities or expenses that don't pull their weight. Usually they exist because they're traditional, and nobody thinks to question having them. Well, I think it's time to sacrifice these sacred cows. If you never seem to get any sales from those expensive ads in your industry's premiere trade magazine, try cutting them out of the budget and see whether anything bad happens.

# Invest More in Your Stars

The 80:20 rule usually applies to marketing: 80 percent of the results come from 20 percent of the marketing activities. So figure out what your best marketing activities are and shift funding toward them. For example, in many businesses today, the return on investment for Web-based marketing is considerably higher than for print advertising, yet print still gets a bigger share of the budget.

Increasing your return on investment from marketing is easy — you simply shift your spending into the highest return activities that you have. Focusing on the one to several most effective marketing activities is the essence of my advice in Chapter 1 about finding your marketing zone. Keep experimenting until you have a pyramid-shaped program with most of your marketing budget going to effective primary and secondary marketing methods.

# Stage Events

Events like industry breakfasts and how-to seminars for customers and prospects are a powerful way to make a connection and establish your identity as a leading expert in your field. But events take planning and organization, so many marketers are intimidated by them and never use them.

Your business should stage at least one high-profile event each quarter. They're surprisingly economical ways to build visibility and attract or retain top customers. (See *Marketing For Dummies,* written by Yours Truly and published by Wiley, for how-to information.)

Oh, but keep those events modest in scope, making sure to invite only those prospects who fit your profile for good customers. You don't want to waste time and money entertaining people who won't ever make a big purchase.

# Control Product Costs

The cost of purchasing or producing your product is a hidden driver of your marketing and sales efficiency. Given a big enough margin, you can afford to market anything. Too often, however, I find that my clients are trying to make their marketing program sell something on a razor-thin margin. With a tight profit margin, nothing is left to spend on sales and marketing. This common problem may be misdiagnosed. It gives the illusion that the marketing program is to blame when profits are poor.

Rather than blaming the marketing, try cutting costs and improving the margin on the product. A good general rule in many businesses is that you want at least a five-fold difference between basic production or purchase cost and the list price that you sell the product at. Spend time and imagination seeking ways to reduce your product costs so that you can market with a big margin. Then you can afford to do good marketing and build a following for the product.

# Chapter 19

# Ten Ways to Market on the Web

**In This Chapter**

▶ Determining your Web site's purpose

▶ Taking advantage of Web marketing

*T*he Internet is obviously a hot marketing medium and it's here to stay, so most businesses are now experimenting with it — and with good reason! This chapter details winning ideas for marketing on the Web.

## Experiment with Virtual Brochures and Catalogs

Whether you decide to go whole hog and launch an e-commerce business or you just dabble in Web marketing, you need to be aware of its many valuable contributions to marketing. Here are a few options that are working well for many businesses:

✔ Create interactive, interesting, and/or informational *virtual brochures* on Web sites for customers and prospects. Sites often generate good leads.

✔ Go fishing for prospects by sending e-mails or buying banner ads.

✔ Build relationships with prospects by creating e-mail newsletters.

✔ Create a *virtual store* or *virtual catalog* where people can go to examine your wares and place orders.

✔ Create a site that fulfills the service needs of your customers — for example, by giving them up-to-date information about their orders.

# Have a Well-Defined Objective

No matter how you choose to use your Web site, you must have a clear marketing objective. When you have a marketing objective, you can see what each Web-marketing option is supposed to do for you and why it may appeal to prospects. The basic rule to marketing on the Internet is *Always design your Web marketing with a specific, well-defined marketing objective in mind.*

You'll never make money by picking up a hammer and banging things with it, nor will you help your business by spending time or money "creating a presence" on the Web. Know what you're accomplishing. Know why the Web is a good way to accomplish it. Then, and only then, are you ready to discover how to take advantage of this complex tool's many possibilities.

 One of the best objectives is to use the Web to generate leads. Another good objective is to try switching your customers from person-to-person to Web-based ordering. Whatever your objective, be clear about it and design your Web site to achieve it.

# Use a Power Name

After you figure out what you want your Web site to accomplish, you can pick and register a name for it. (If you have a Web site that doesn't get enough traffic, consider improving the domain name.) Check with your Internet Service Provider (ISP) or any number of registration services that advertise on the Web to find out how to register the name of your choice. (I generally use Register.com.) And don't be disappointed if the first name you try is already taken. Just try a variant of it.

The best names meet three simple criteria:

- ✔ They're relevant to the site's purpose.
- ✔ They're easy to remember and spell.
- ✔ They're unique, meaning that they're not easily confused with competitors.

So, for example, `www.airtravel.com` is a great name for a site that brokers airplane tickets and vacations involving an airplane flight. It's relevant. It's easy. Nobody is likely to spell it wrong. People tend to remember it because it's obvious and intuitive. Names like that have real marketing power, and you should keep thinking until you have a power name for your Web business, too. (In fact, I see that a business is using that name to broker Caribbean vacations. More power to them!)

# Be outrageous

An interesting alternative to a power name is to choose an outrageous name that sticks in everyone's minds.

Bookseller Amazon.com is a good example of the effectiveness of this strategy. The name sounds like the company has something to do with travel in Brazil or the preservation of rain forests. But that's not really a problem for Amazon.com because it got so much press coverage that it taught everyone to associate its name with its products. Maybe you should use this strategy, too. For example, if you market quality cuts of beef on the Web, you could see whether `http://karatechop.com` is available and create a high-powered site that uses lots of exciting martial arts images to promote your product.

# Be clear

When choosing a domain name, avoid words that can be spelled more than one way. Often people give out Web addresses verbally over the phone, in conversation, or on the radio in an interview or ad. You don't want to have to spell a name or explain that the user has to type an underline to separate two words.

For example, if you're a sail maker, you might choose the address `http://sail.com`. But this address is ambiguous because people may think that you're saying *sale* rather than *sail*. Better to lengthen it enough to make the name unambiguous. `http://Sailmakers.com` works better. If you're set on picking a name that may be misspelled or spelled in more than one way, buy the other domain as well and point it directly to your main site.

# Be polymorphic

If you're marketing in a non-English-speaking country, consider creating more than one domain name: one in the local language and one in English. English seems to be emerging as the dominant language of the Web, at least for businesses. And your ISP can easily route visitors from more than one address to the same site.

# Give Away Great Content

People don't surf the Internet to read sales pitches and lengthy brag-a-logues about how great a company is. The No. 1 reason people return to a site is content.

To attract and retain high-quality visitors, you need to create and post valuable content. That task is a challenge. Are you up to it? If not, consider hiring a writer to create some good content.

Also, see whether you can give away some technical information or advice that people will value. Your site needs to be a modern-day encyclopedia, a place where prospective customers go for help. The more information you give away, the more you'll sell.

Take a look at the site I created (with the able help of my associates Angela and Eric — thanks guys!) to support this book, www.insightsformarketing. com. It has dozens of pages of serious, hard-core information that we give away for free.

What information do you have that you can give away on your site? Most businesses have lots of raw content just gathering dust. Search your file cabinets and hard drives for how-to lists, old press releases, catalogs, brochures, and even old customer proposals or reports. You can create lots of useful pages by editing these source materials.

# Minimize Your Load Time

When people have to wait for a table, their interest in a restaurant declines. The same is true for a Web site. No matter how much cool information you give away or how many great products you sell at incredible prices, your site may not be appealing unless people can get to it in a hurry.

What's a hurry? One way to think about it is to compare your site's load time to the load times of some of the most popular e-commerce sites:

| *Site* | *Average Load Time (Seconds)* |
| --- | --- |
| http://Amazon.com | 2.6 |
| http://bn.com | 4.7 |
| http://Cdnow.com | 5.1 |
| http://jcpenney.com | 2.8 |

I wonder whether it's a coincidence that `Amazon.com` does a lot more business than competitor `bn.com` (the Barnes and Noble Web site) and that it happens to have a 45 percent shorter load time, too?

Anyway, you get the idea. If your load time isn't virtually instantaneous, you're going to lose a lot of potential visitors. Those big, expensive sites are investing a lot in fast load times, and they're setting the pace for anyone who wants to market on the Web. Also, recognize that there is a tradeoff between fancy content and load time. Keep in mind that Flash files and large graphics and files will slow down load time. A good way to avoid this problem is to keep large graphic and video files off the home page and allow visitors to elect to open them after they page has loaded.

## Create a Sense of Community

Encourage interaction among visitors, for example, through the use of bulletin boards, discussion forums, and chat rooms. (The latter only works well if you have high traffic.) When people make meaningful connections on your site, traffic grows, and you generate more interest, leads, and sales. And the sense of community you build helps ensure that visitors will keep coming back.

## Hold Contests

Stimulate interest through the use of contests for visitors. Pick something that's participatory (visitors submit something of their own) and give prizes or announce winners fairly frequently — for example, every Friday. Post submissions, if possible, to encourage people to spend time examining them. (For example, a florist may invite people to submit photos of floral arrangements and pick the best arrangement every two weeks.)

You may have to do some publicity to let people know about your contest, but the ongoing results can be well worth the time!

## Add a News Feature

Provide new content regularly. You can do so in a What's New section or page or in a regularly updated News and Views section, guest column, or Headline News section summarizing the news in your industry.

In essence, this technique is what people now like to call *blogging*, but really, it's just putting an interesting column that you update as often as possible — daily is best, if you have the time.

# Take Advantage of Links

Use links to create lots of easy paths back to your site. Often people don't return to a Web site because they simply don't recall it. But if they run into a link and remember that your site was great, then they'll probably come back.

How do you create links? The general strategy is to ask other people with Web sites to add your URL to their page. Usually they'll want a reciprocal agreement, which is fine. Also, try adding a Link to Us page on your site with linking images that other site managers can copy and use on their sites.

# Bid on Key Terms

It's really helpful to play in the great game of search terms. Google and Yahoo! both offer easy-to-use, effective paid listings to go along with their search engines. I like the way you can adjust your selection of terms, message, and bid amount as often as you want. This way, you can control your Web ad spending and keep experimenting until you find a combination that generates lots of business.

If you're not already using one or both of these services, go online right now and explore the options. Set up an account. Start learning how to place your link where people will see it when they're searching for your product or service.

All good Web marketing plans use this method — and savvy marketers check their search-term ad performance and adjust it weekly or daily.

*Hint:* Avoid terms that have millions of hits a day. Narrow your field by bidding on more specific terms or combinations of terms. This technique will reduce your cost and improve effectiveness.

# Appendix

# About the CD

*W*elcome to your CD. It contains supporting files that can help you apply the ideas and techniques from this book. This appendix goes through some simple tips and guidelines for using your CD and previews the contents. The files on your CD should be easy and simple to use, but if anything goes wrong, and if you need any troubleshooting help, start here.

# System Requirements

Make sure that your computer meets the minimum system requirements shown in the following list. If your computer doesn't match up to most of these requirements, you may have problems using the software and files on the CD. For the latest and greatest information, please refer to the ReadMe file located at the root of the CD-ROM.

- ✔ A PC running Microsoft Windows
- ✔ A Macintosh running Apple OS X or later
- ✔ A CD-ROM drive

You don't need an Internet connection to use the files on this CD. (However, you may want to use the many links to useful Web sites referenced in your book, so an Internet connection will be helpful.)

If you need more information on the basics, check out these books published by Wiley Publishing, Inc.: *PCs For Dummies* by Dan Gookin; *Macs For Dummies* by Edward C. Baig; *iMacs For Dummies* by Mark L. Chambers; *Windows XP For Dummies* and *Windows Vista For Dummies,* both by Andy Rathbone.

# Using the CD

To install the items from the CD onto your hard drive, follow these steps:

1. **Insert the CD into your computer's CD-ROM drive.**

   The license agreement appears.

   *Note to Windows users:* The interface won't launch if you have autorun disabled. In that case, choose Start⇨Run. (For Windows Vista, choose Start⇨All Programs⇨Accessories⇨Run.) In the dialog box that appears, type **D:\Start.exe**. (Replace *D* with the proper letter if your CD drive uses a different letter. If you don't know the letter, see how your CD drive is listed under My Computer.) Click OK.

   *Note for Mac Users:* When the CD icon appears on your desktop, double-click the icon to open the CD and double-click the Start icon.

2. **Read through the license agreement and then click the Accept button if you want to use the CD.**

   The CD interface appears. The interface allows you to browse the contents and install the programs with just a click of a button (or two).

# What You'll Find on the CD

The following sections are arranged by category and provide a summary of the software and other goodies you'll find on the CD. If you need help with installing the items provided on the CD, refer to the installation instructions in the preceding section.

The CD's main purpose is to give you access to the special files I've created for you. You can use these Microsoft Word and Excel files as working templates. It's best to open these files in the program in which they were created. I also include graphic files in PDF and JPEG format that provide examples and resources for your marketing. You can open the PDFs in Adobe Reader (which is included on the CD), and you can open the JPEGS in whatever picture-handling utility you have on your computer, as well as by any graphic art program. However, in case you lack the needed programs, my publisher has arranged for some shareware options that may be helpful. The programs fall into one of the following categories:

✔ *Shareware programs* are fully functional, free, trial versions of copyrighted programs. If you like particular programs, register with their authors for a nominal fee and receive licenses, enhanced versions, and technical support.

✔ *Freeware programs* are free, copyrighted games, applications, and utilities. You can copy them to as many computers as you like — for free — but they offer no technical support.

✔ *GNU software* is governed by its own license, which is included inside the folder of the GNU software. There are no restrictions on distribution of GNU software. See the GNU license at the root of the CD for more details.

✔ *Trial, demo,* or *evaluation* versions of software are usually limited either by time or functionality (such as not letting you save a project after you create it).

## Software

You'll find the following software on your CD:

✔ **Excel Viewer:** Excel Viewer is a freeware program that allows you to view but not edit most Microsoft Excel spreadsheets. Certain features of Microsoft Excel documents may not work as expected from within Excel Viewer.

✔ **Adobe Reader:** Adobe Reader is a freeware program that allows you to view but not edit Adobe Portable Document Files (PDF).

✔ **OpenOffice.org:** OpenOffice.org is a free multiplatform office productivity suite. It's similar to Microsoft Office or Lotus SmartSuite, but OpenOffice.org is absolutely free. It includes word-processing, spreadsheet, presentation, and drawing applications that enable you to create professional documents, newsletters, reports, and presentations. It supports most file formats of other office software. You should be able to edit and view any files created with other office software.

## Chapter files

*For Windows and Mac.* All the examples provided in this book are located in the Author directory on the CD and work with Macintosh and Windows 98 and later computers. The structure of the examples directory is

```
Chapter 1
Chapter 2
```

and so on.

The chapter files on the CD all fall into one of the following categories:

✔ **Word documents:** You can work with these forms to fit your own marketing needs.

✔ **Excel spreadsheets:** Many of the book's worksheets are in this format. Simply fill in the blanks, and you're on your way.

✔ **PDF files:** These files illustrate various examples, such as a sample brochure or newsletter. You can't change these files, but you can print them out, if you like.

The following list summarizes all the chapter files on the CD:

| | |
|---|---|
| CD0101 | Five Minute Marketing Plan |
| CD0102 | Your Marketing Zone Program Worksheet |
| CD0103 | Your Marketing Zone Planning Diagram |
| CD0201 | Editable Marketing Audit |
| CD0202 | Marketing Audit |
| CD0203 | Audit Score Form |
| CD0204 | Marketing Agenda |
| CD0205 | Marketing Plan Template |
| CD0206 | Marketing Budget Worksheet |
| CD0207 | Sales Projection Worksheet |
| CD0301 | Tips for Boosting Sales |
| CD0302 | The Message Pyramid |
| CD0401 | Budgeting for Advertising: A Practical Approach |
| CD0402 | Annual Advertising Budget and Plan |
| CD0403 | Advertising Objectives Worksheet |
| CD0404 | Monthly & Annual Advertising Budget Templates |
| CD0501 | A library of photos for design use |
| CD0502 | An image ad template |
| CD0503 | Informative ad template |
| CD0504 | Informative ad template |
| CD0505 | Call-to-action ad template |
| CD0506 | Call-to-action ad template |
| CD0507 | Insurance company ad |
| CD0508 | Sherlock Holmes ad template |
| CD0509 | Postcard design sample |
| CD0510 | Postcard front and back templates |
| CD0601 | Sample business card designs |
| CD0602 | Sample logo design made entirely in Word |
| CD0603 | Business card sheet for printing with Avery stock |
| CD0604 | PDF version of business card sheet |
| CD0605 | Colorful business card made from a free HP template |
| CD0606 | Sample letterhead design with strong visual appeal |
| CD0607 | Editable Word version of sample letterhead design |

| | |
|---|---|
| CD0701 | Sample one-page B2B promotional flier |
| CD0702 | Sample brochure with unusual layout |
| CD0703 | Illustration of brochure from CDS0702 when folded |
| CD0704 | Product Offerings brochure template in Word |
| CD0705 | Brochure template with photographic design elements |
| CD0706 | Illustration of bitmapped versus vector line art options |
| CD0801 | Coupon Profitability Analysis example |
| CD0802 | Excel spreadsheet for doing your own Coupon Profitability Analysis |
| CD0901 | A sample of a well-designed newsletter |
| CD0902 | A newsletter marked to show how modular design was used |
| CD0903 | Seasonal newsletter Word template |
| CD0904 | Seasonal newsletter PDF file |
| CD0905 | What's New four-page Word newsletter template |
| CD0906 | What's New PDF file |
| CD0907 | Newsletter logo examples and notes |
| CD0908 | Tile & Flooring News nameplate |
| CD1001 | A well-done press release announcing a new product line |
| CD1002 | A screen shot of a PR Newswire release that includes streaming video |
| CD1003 | An example of an effective, brief electronic news release |
| CD1101 | Customer Debriefing Form Template |
| CD1102 | 7 x 7 Customer Satisfaction Survey |
| CD1103 | Customer Service Audit Template |
| CD1201 | Creative Roles Analysis |
| CD1301 | Evaluation Form 1 |
| CD1302 | Two Dimensions of Your Appeal |
| CD1303 | Evaluation Form 2 |
| CD1304 | Press release about new Xerox logo |
| CD1401 | Prospect Analysis Sheet |
| CD1402 | Question Preplanning Form |
| CD1601 | Attitudes of Success Profile |

# Troubleshooting

Your ability to open and use the files on the CD may be dependent on having fairly recent versions of Microsoft Office and/or Word and Excel, and as well as having (or downloading) the free Adobe Reader program from Adobe. Almost all computers have all these programs installed, along with some utility for viewing JPEGs. (Also, you can use Word to display and design with JPEGs by importing them using the Insert menu to insert a picture. Mac users can simply click and drag a JPEG into an open Word file.) To do more sophisticated graphic design, use a program such as Adobe's InDesign, which can handle JPEGs and allows you to add text and other design elements to them.) If you lack the needed programs, you may have difficulty viewing and using some of the files on the CD. The remedy for such problems is to either update your software or to borrow a computer that has the needed software.

# Customer Care

If you have trouble with the CD-ROM, please call Wiley Product Technical Support at 800-762-2974. Outside the United States, call 317-572-3994. You can also contact Wiley Product Technical Support at `http://support.wiley.com`. Wiley Publishing will provide technical support only for installation and other general quality control items. For technical support on the applications themselves, consult the program's vendor or author.

To place additional orders or to request information about other Wiley products, please call 877-762-2974.

# Index

### • O •

### • P •

## • Q •

## • R •